Tax List of York County Pennsylvania 1779

(Reprinted from Pennsylvania Archives)

F. Edward Wright

HERITAGE BOOKS
2008

HERITAGE BOOKS
AN IMPRINT OF HERITAGE BOOKS, INC.

Books, CDs, and more—Worldwide

For our listing of thousands of titles see our website at
www.HeritageBooks.com

Published 2008 by
HERITAGE BOOKS, INC.
Publishing Division
100 Railroad Ave. #104
Westminster, Maryland 21157

Copyright © 1989 Willow Bend Books

All rights reserved. No part of this book may be reproduced or transmitted in any form or by any means, electronic or mechanical, including photocopying, recording or by any information storage and retrieval system without written permission from the author, except for the inclusion of brief quotations in a review.

International Standard Book Numbers
Paperbound: 978-1-58549-132-2
Clothbound: 978-0-7884-7687-7

CONTENTS

Introduction	v
York	1
Manchester Township	8
Botts Town	13
Manhime [Manheim] Townhip	14
Newberry Township	19
Windsor Township	26
Tyrone Township	31
Hopewell Township	33
Fawn Township	37
Hellam Township	41
Dover Township	44
Mount Joy Township	48
Manallen Township	50
Paradise Township	54
Codorus Township	58
Mount Pleasant Township	62
Warrington Township	65
Shrewsbury Township	70
Heidelberg Township	74
Germany Township	78
Berwick Township	82
Strabann Township	86
Reading Township	89
Manahan Township	93
Huntington Township	97
Single Men Who Have Sworn	98
Young Men Who Have Not Sworn	98
Taxables Not Sworn	99
Hamilton's Bann Township	102
York Township	108
Chanceford Township	112
Cumberland Township	117
Index	125

INTRODUCTION

The following persons were taxed:
(1) Householders or landholders including land owners and tenants - no distinction was made between the two.
(2) Inmates, meaning residents in the household of another (not a renter) who worked for the landowner.
(3) Freemen, who were single men over the age of 21. They appear at the end of the listing of the township and were always assessed the same amount.
(4) Non-residents, unseated landowners (unoccupied land).

This listing was taken exactly as written in the published Third Series, Pennsylvania Archives (1897). The spelling of names has not been changed.

Abbreviations have the following meanings.

b. smith or b'smith - blacksmith
f. - ferry, forge or furnace
f.m. - fulling mill
g.m. - grist mill
h.m. - hemp mill
m. - miller
m.h. - malt house
o.m. - oil mill

p.m. - paper mill
s. - still
s.f. - steel forge
s.m. - saw mill
s.q. - stone quarry
t.k. - tavern keeper
w.s.q. - whetstone quarry
wid'o - widow

F. Edward Wright
Westminster, Maryland

YORK COUNTY RETURNS - 1779

	York Houses	Lots	Negroes	Tax
Albright, Philip	1	1/2	--	56.5.0
Alexander, William	--	--	1	41.5.0
Armor, Thomas, Sen'r	--	--	--	6.8.2
Armor, Thomas	--	--	--	30.0.0
Asby, William	1	1/2	--	4.1.3
Anthony, Nicholas	1	3	--	9.7.6
Adlum, Joseph, skin dresser	1	1	--	12.0.0
Billmeyer, Helena	1	1	--	--
Bailey, William, store	--	4	2	39.0.0
Bentz, Henry, butcher	--	--	--	12.0.0
Bentz, Philip	1	1/2	--	25.0.0
Bender, Henry, hosier	--	--	--	1.11.3
Bair, John, carpenter	1	1/2	1	12.0.0
Belshuber, Widow	1	1	--	--
Biers, John, store'r	--	--	--	18.0.0
Barnitz, Charles, brewer	2	2	--	80.0.0
Beltzhuber	1	1	--	1.5.0
Bringman, Frederick, cordwainer	1	1	--	1.5.0
Bringman, Frederick, Ju'r, tanner	--	--	--	15.0.0
Becker, William	1	1/2	--	--
Bick, John	1	1	--	10.0.0
Bennington, Ephraim, cordwainer	1	1/2	--	20.0.0
Billmeyer, Michael, turner	1	1	--	40.16.3
Billmeyer, Andrew, turner	--	--	--	30.0.0
Billmeyer, Jacob, surveyor	--	--	--	3.2.6
Brenneisen, Martin, taylor	1	1	--	10.0.0
Brobst, Jacob, roper	1	2	--	12.10.0
Borg, George, labourer	2	1 1/2	--	7.1.3
Berger, Peter, tobacconist	1	1/2	--	--
Bombach, George	1	1	--	3.0.0
Barnitz, Charles	--	--	--	30.0.0
Bentz, Wyrich	1	1	--	18.0.0
Bike, Abraham, saddle tree m'kr	1	1/2	--	6.17.6
Brand, Nicholas, barber	1	1	--	13.8.9
Bride, John, store	--	--	--	--
Bernhard, Nicholas,, labou'r	1	1	--	6.5.0
Bouser, Widow	1	1	--	2.5.0
Blymyer, Abraham, taylor	1	1	--	9.7.6
Bennet, Enoch, joiner	1	1	--	13.5.0
Brooks, John, commis'r	--	--	--	9.7.6
Bower, Daniel	1	1	--	2.10.0
Candler, David, store	--	--	--	24.0.0
Cronemiller, Widow	2	2	--	7.10.0
Collins, John, mason	1	1/2	--	23.7.6
Cole, Philip	1	1	--	20.12.6
Cornelius, James, taylor	1	1/2	--	9.7.6
Channel, Nathan, cardmaker	--	--	--	30.0.0
Chambers, Joseph	1	1	2	34.12.6
Dunn, Robert, innkeeper	1	2	1	51.17.6
Dinkel, Oster, sadler	2	1 1/2	--	118.18.0
Danner, Abraham), tobacconist	1	1/2	--	34.15.0
Doudle, Jacob	--	--	--	37.10.0
Doudle, Mary, widow, tanner	1	1	1	25.0.0

York	Houses	Lots	Negroes	Tax
Doudle, Michael, tanner	1	5	3	156.5.0
Danner, Martin, tobacconist	1	1/4	--	21.17.6
Dambach, Frederick, blacksmith	1	1/8	--	4.7.6
Dahlman, John, carpenter	1	1	--	12.10.0
Todd, William, inmate	--	--	--	3.2.6
Andrew, Reverend	1	1	--	3.0.0
Donaldson, Joseph	1	1	--	57.0.0
Eighinger, Jacob	1	1 1/2	--	40.0.0
Etting, Widow	--	1	--	--
Craft, Widow	2	1 1/2	--	--
Endler, Jacob, breeches maker	1	1/2	--	26.3.9
Endler, Philip, butcher	1	1/2	--	28.0.0
Ebert, Michael	1	1	--	9.7.6
Eichelberger, Widow	--	--	--	25.0.0
Epely, Christopher	1	1	--	5.0.0
Irion, Jacob, taylor	1	1/2	--	5.0.0
Ehrman, John, inn keeper	1	4	--	53.0.0
Eirich, Michael	1	1/2	--	1.11.3
Eichelberger, Jacob, Esq.	--	--	--	37.10.0
Etter, Lawrence, waggoner	1	1	--	7.10.0
Etter, George	1	1	--	5.12.6
Eichelberger, Martin	--	--	--	25.0.0
Fry, Martin, locksmith	1	1/2	--	--
Figely, Mathias, cordwainer	1	1/2	--	5.0.0
Fishel, John	1	1/2	--	3.0.0
Fisher, Samuel, blacksmith	1	--	--	3.2.6
Funk, Jacob, joiner	1	1 1/2	--	18.15.0
Flender, John, blacksmith	1	1	--	22.10.0
Fisher, John, clockmaker	1	2 3/4	--	18.15.0
Finzentz, Imfeld, weaver	1	1	--	7.0.0
Fritzley, George, baker	1	2	--	16.11.3
Fiernshield, William, barber	1	1/2	--	3.15.0
Fry, Godfrey	1	1	--	18.15.0
Fry, George, sadler	2	1/2	--	22.10.0
Fackler, Widow	1	--	--	--
Fackler, Jacob, hosier	--	--	--	--
Grier, David	1	1/2	2	93.15.0
Goll, Baltzer	1	1/2	--	40.17.6
Grafius, Abraham, tinman	--	--	--	20.0.0
Gossler, Philip, joiner	--	--	--	20.0.0
Graft, George, hatter	--	--	--	15.0.0
Grafius, Martin	1	1	--	4.1.3
Gerber, George, carpenter	1	1	--	9.7.6
Gump, George	1	1	--	10.0.0
Goodyear, George, cordwainer	1	1	--	10.6.3
Goho, John	--	--	--	3.2.6
Geyer, George	1	2	--	6.5.0
Gardner, Jacob, tanner	1	6	--	112.10.0
Gorgus, Benjamin, skin dresser	1	2	--	7.10.0
Groff, Jacob	1	1	--	12.10.0
Garretson, Joseph	--	--	--	6.0.0
Glesy, George, mason	--	--	--	6.15.0
Gardner, Adam, innkeeper	1	1/2	--	10.0.0
Grim, John	1	1	--	18.15.0
Gardman, Isaac, innkeeper	1	1	--	25.0.0

York	Houses	Lots	Negroes	Tax
Gardman, Isaac, Jun'r, weaver	1	1	--	9.7.6
Gerber, Michael	1	1	--	15.12.6
Graft, Widow	--	--	--	4.0.0
Hay, John, Esq'r., farmer	1	1 1/2	--	60.0.0
Hartley, Thomas, att'y	--	--	4	68.5.0
Henry, Robert, surgeon	--	--	1	36.17.0
Houseman Frederick, butcher	1	1 1/4	--	37.10.0
Herr, Eberhard, weaver	--	--	--	4.13.0
Hake, Conrad	1	1	--	6.5.0
Hetig, Ludwig, taylor	1	1/2	--	16.0.0
Hahn, Michael, store	1	1/2	--	90.0.0
Hess, John, wagoner	--	--	--	15.0.0
Heckentorn, John, farier	1	2	--	18.3.9
Heckentorn, Chris'n, weaver	--	--	--	9.0.0
Heneisy, Widow	1	1	--	--
Hollis, Richard, stamper	1	1/2	--	4.7.6
Herman, Christ'n, carpenter	1	1/2	--	15.13.6
Hughs, William, innkeeper	1	--	--	11.12.6
Heckert, Philip, gun smith	--	--	--	15.0.0
Holtzbaum, Widow	1	1 1/2	--	--
Hawk, Peter	1	1/2	--	8.8.9
Heckert, Jacob, wagoner	--	--	--	15.0.0
Hofman, Andrew, innkeeper	1	1/2	--	18.0.0
Holtzbaum's estate	1	1/2	--	--
Heckert, Widow	1	1	--	6.0.0
Hay, John & Moul, George	1	1	--	7.10.0
Irwin, George, store	2	1 1/2	3	180.0.0
Irons, Thomas, hatter	1	1-6	--	20.0.0
Yager, Simon, labourer	1	1/2	--	--
Jameson, David, surgeon	--	4	--	9.7.6
Ilgenfritz, Christian, cordwainer	1	1/2	--	12.10.0
Jones, John	1	1	--	15.14.6
Jones, Isaac	--	--	--	5.0.0
Shultz, John, hatter	1	1	--	18.0.0
Keppele, Henry, Jun'r	1	1/2	--	12.10.0
Keller, Michael, sadler	1	1/2	--	68.14.0
Krantz, Valentine, innkeeper & brewer	1	1 1/2	1	78.2.6
Kuntz, Francis, hatter	1	1/2	--	5.0.0
Keiffer, Widown	1	1	--	--
Cloyd, John, mason	--	--	--	4.7.6
Korpman--Schill, Jn'o, tenant	1	2	--	5.0.0
Kreber Adam, blacksmith	1	1 1/2	--	21.17.6
Kreber, Philip, waggoner	1	1	--	21.17.6
Kern, Jacob, taylor	2	1 1/2	--	22.10.0
Kunckel, John, cooper	1	1	--	13.18.9
Kauffelt, Jacob	1	1	--	25.0.0
Kraft, Ludwig, blue dyer	1	1	--	15.0.0
Kraft, Joseph, saddler	--	--	--	15.0.0
King, Philip Jacob	1	1	--	18.0.0
King, Henry, saddler	1	1/2	--	25.0.0
Kreber, Henry	1	2	--	10.10.0
Kurtz, Peter	--	--	--	15.0.0
Graybill, Michael	1	1	--	18.2.6
Kunckel, John, cooper	1	1	--	15.0.0

York	Houses	Lots	Negroes	Tax
Kuntz, Samuel, labourer	--	1/2	--	3.2.6
Kreenewalt, Henry, butcher	1	1 1/2	--	8.5.0
Kersey, William, cardmaker	1	2	--	31.5.0
Kreber, Martin, blacksmith	--	--	--	18.0.0
Langworthy, Mr.	--	--	--	45.0.0
Lenhard, Godfrey, clockmaker	1	--	--	27.0.0
Lauman, Widow	--	1	--	--
Latshar, John, clockmaker	--	--	--	12.10.0
Leisser, John, brewer	1	1	--	3.2.6
Leatherman, Conrad	1	2	--	112.10.0
Leatherman, Widow	1	1	--	18.15.0
Lauman, Christopher, turner	1	1	--	30.0.0
Lanius, William, taylor	1	1	--	10.7.6
Lefler, George Lewis, clerk	1	2	--	15.0.0
Love, William	1	1-6	--	18.15.0
Love, John, tanner	1	1	--	175.0.0
Leitner, Adam, gunsmith	1	1	--	28.2.6
Lottman, George, innkeeper	1	1	--	25.0.0
Leitner, Nathaniel, farmer	1	2	--	18.15.0
Leather, Jacob, gunsmith	--	--	--	7.10.0
Laumaster, Frederick, waggoner	1	1	--	18.15.0
Leedy, Samuel, shoemaker	1	2	--	20.0.0
Lindy, John, labourer	1	1	--	3.2.6
Long, William, taylor	1	1/2	--	9.7.6
McLaughlin, James, taylor	--	--	--	6.5.0
McCurly, Rob't, storekeeper	--	--	--	20.0.0
Ming, Ulrich, saddler	--	--	--	18.15.0
Miller, Jacob	1	1-3	--	15.12.6
Mehl, Frederick	--	--	--	18.0.0
Maulsby, David, carpenter	--	--	--	6.15.0
Myer, John, locksmith	1	1/4	--	12.10.0
McMunn, William, taylor	1	1	--	17.0.0
Meem, John, saddle treem'r	--	--	--	6.5.0
Miller, Francis Jacob, tanner	1	2	--	60.0.0
Morris, John, scribener	1	1 1/4	--	7.10.0
Miller, Casper, innkeeper	1	3 1/2	--	40.0.0
McConkey, Alexander	--	--	--	--
McCalmand, Jane	--	--	--	6.0.0
McCallister, John	1	1/4	--	69.7.6
Myer, Widow	1	1	--	3.0.0
McPherson, John	--	--	--	25.0.0
Miller, William, sugar baker	1	1/2	--	25.0.0
Myer, Joseph, tobacconist	1	1/2	--	3.0.0
Martin, William	--	--	--	--
McKitrick, Alexander	--	--	--	9.17.6
McBride, John	--	--	--	18.0.0
McMullen, John	1	1/2	--	8.2.6
Mock, George, weaver	1	1	--	8.2.0
Miller, Abraham	1	1/2	--	25.0.0
Miller, Henry, Com'isy Pr.	--	--	--	12.10.0
Moore, Widow	1	1/2	1	43.15.0
Michael, Jacob	1	1	--	6.15.0
McClean, Archibald, clerk	--	--	--	37.10.0
Maul, George, blacksmith	1	3/4	--	50.0.0
McCall, Robert, doctor's mate	--	--	--	6.5.0

4

York	Houses	Lots	Negroes	Tax
Mundorf, Peter, druggist	1	1	--	12.10.0
Nebinger, George, tobacconist	1	1/2	--	30.0.0
Nibble, John, taylor	--	--	--	5.0.0
Nebbinger, Widow	--	--	--	--
Nunnemaker, Abraham	1	1	--	6.5.0
Neyman, Jacob, cooper	1	1	--	12.10.0
Norris, William, saddle tree maker	1	1	--	6.6.0
Nunnemaker, Andrew, gunsmith	--	--	--	15.0.0
Owens, Thomas, taylor	--	--	--	9.7.6
Reed, Robert, coppersmith	--	--	--	10.0.0
Rothrock, Jacob, glazier	1	1/2	--	56.17.6
Rudisill, John, sadler	1	1/2	--	9.7.6
Rummel, Frederick, innkeeper	1	1	--	21.17.6
Rothrock, Joseph, silversmith	--	--	--	15.0.0
Rehm, Godfrey, potter	1	1	--	40.0.0
Robb, James, sadler	1	2 1/2	--	18.15.0
Rehm, Widow	--	--	--	--
Reel, Peter, saddletree maker	1	1/2	--	37.10.0
Reel, William, blue dyer	1	1	--	18.15.0
Rothrock, John, locksmith	1	1/2	--	20.0.0
Ritz, Anthony	1	2	--	12.10.0
Rudisiel, Widow	1	1	--	7.10.0
Rockwell, Joseph, cardmaker	--	--	--	20.0.0
Riess, John, innkeeper	--	--	--	6.5.0
Ryan, Thomas, labourer	--	--	--	6.5.0
Richmond, William, breeches maker	1	1	--	18.15.0
Riffet, Jonathan, clerk	--	--	--	10.0.0
Stoll, Widow	1	1	--	--
Sprenckel, Daniel, turner	1	1	--	9.7.6
Shuck, George, carpenter	1	1	--	12.10.0
Shrete, Martin, cordwainer	1	1	--	8.0.0
Stair, Mathias, potter	1	1	--	13.2.6
Swoope, Michael	1	1	2	110.0.0
Smith, Charles, doctor	1	1/4	--	16.5.0
Stake, George	1	1	1	118.15.0
Sinn, Christian, butcher	1	1/2	--	20.0.0
Sidler, Jacob, cardmaker	1	1/2	--	43.15.0
Spangler, Rudolph, shopkeeper	--	1	--	43.15.0
Smith, Joseph	2	2 1/2	--	60.0.0
Sensenich, Peter, doctor	1	1/2	--	40.0.0
Schmall, Laurence, locksmith	1	1	--	7.10.0
Stillinger, Richard	1	1/2	--	--
Stahl, Peter	--	--	--	--
Siegrist, Jacob	1	2	--	5.0.0
Sprogell, Widow	1	1	--	--
Schnierer, Jacob, blacksmith	1	2	--	25.0.0
Schrack, Henry	1	1	--	20.0.0
Snyder, Martin, poor, mason	--	--	--	5.0.0
Stehr, Christopher, potter	1	1	--	30.0.0
Stentz, Philip, shopkeeper	1	1/2	--	43.15.0
Shuck, Jacob, carpenter	1	1/2	--	30.0.0
Schreiber, Jacob, waggoner	1	1 1/2	--	22.10.0
Shitz, Peter	1	1/2	--	81.5.0
Stuck, Jacob, cooper	1	1	--	31.5.0
Spicker, Widow	--	--	--	--

York	Houses	Lots	Negroes	Tax
Schlemmer, Peter	1	1	--	15.0.0
Sefferentz, George	1	1/2	--	6.5.0
Schneider, Jacob, butcher	1	1	--	9.7.6
Schram, Jacob, weaver	1	1	--	12.7.6
Schanck Joseph	1	2	--	8.7.6
Schreck, John, hosier	--	--	--	1.17.6
Sihill, John, labourer	--	--	--	1.17.6
Schenck, Jacob, cordwainer	1	1	--	23.2.6
Schlosser, Ernst, hosier	1	1/2	--	20.0.0
Shaw, James, poor, waggoner	--	--	--	3.15.0
Shall, John	1	1	--	12.10.0
Sheffer, Jacob, cordwainer	1	1	--	12.10.0
Spangler, George Mich'l, cordwainer	1	1/2	--	18.15.0
Stousenberg, Conrad, weaver	1	1	--	6.5.0
Spangler, Balzer, innkeeper	1	1/2	3	86.11.3
Sultzberger	1	1/2	--	13.0.0
Streber, Peter, joiner	--	--	--	18.0.0
Small, Killian, joiner	1	1	--	28.2.6
Shettley, Frederick, turner	1	1/2	--	15.0.0
Stoll, George, cooper	--	--	--	15.0.0
Shultz, John, ex'r, hosier	--	--	--	43.15.0
Shiely, Christopher, butcher	1	1/4	--	12.10.0
Strohman, John, corwainer	--	--	--	15.17.6
Schmuck, John, cordwainer	1	1/2	--	6.5.0
Smith, John, labourer	1	1/2	--	6.5.0
Strebig, Jacob, cooper	1	1/2	--	6.5.0
Spangler, John	1	1/2	--	3.15.0
Sinn, Christian, butcher	--	--	--	18.0.0
Stake, Christian, silversmith	--	--	--	30.0.0
Scott, William	1	1	--	25.0.0
Shultz, John, hosier	--	--	--	5.0.0
Shwing, Michael, cordwainer	1	1	--	10.0.0
Smith, James, attorney	3	2 1/2	--	100.0.0
Test, George, sadler	1	1/2	1	40.12.6
Thomas, Francis, mason	--	--	--	--
Thomas, George, hosier	--	--	--	11.5.0
Updegraff, Joseph, sadler	--	--	--	5.0.0
Upp, Jacob, cordwainer	1	1	--	20.0.0
Uhler's estate	1	1/2	--	--
Updegraff, Samuel, breeches maker	1	1/2	--	130.0.0
Updegraff, Ambrose, hatter	1	2-5	--	50.0.0
Updegraff, Herman, tanner	1	1	--	87.10.0
Updegraff, Nathan, hatter	1	2-5	--	28.2.6
Updegraff, Jacob, lastmaker	1	1	--	25.0.0
Updegraff, Jacob, heelmaker	--	--	--	15.0.0
Updegraff, Joseph, hatter	--	--	--	187.10.0
Updegraff, Joseph, heelmaker	--	--	--	5.0.0
Weber, Philip, wheelwright	1	2	--	15.0.0
Wolf, Adam, hatter	1	1-6	--	15.2.6
Widener, Michael, blacksmith	1	1/2	--	25.0.0
Weller, George, reedmaker	1	1 1/2	--	35.0.0
Welsh, Michael, cordwainer	1	1/2	--	31.5.0
Wolf, Henry, Jun'r, tanner	--	1	--	18.15.0
Welsh, Henry, cordwainer	--	--	--	18.0.0

York	Houses	Lots	Negroes	Tax
Welsh, Michael, taylor	1	1/2	--	21.17.6
Welsh, Widow	1	1	--	--
Weisang, Ludwig, mason	1	1/2	--	5.12.6
Wolf, George, weaver	--	--	--	3.0.0
Welsh, Erasmus, butcher	--	--	--	5.12.6
Welsh, John, taylor	1	1	1	15.0.0
Wall, John, stiller	1	1	--	11.5.0
Wolf, Henry	1	3	--	81.5.0
Wolf, Peter, tobacconist	--	--	--	15.0.0
Welsh, John, tanner	1	2 1/2	--	115.2.0
Wolf, John, taylor	2	1	--	25.0.0
Worley, Francis, cutler	1	1/2	--	28.2.6
Welshn, Andrew, blacksmith	1	1/2	--	12.0.0
Walter, Henry	1	2	--	81.5.0
Willis, William	1	1/2	--	21.17.6
Worley, Nathan	--	--	--	6.5.0
Welsh, William, hatter	1	1	--	15.12.6
Wampler, Widow	1	1	--	--
Welshantz, Joseph, gunsmith	1	1	--	25.0.0
Welshantz, Jacob, gunsmith	--	--	--	9.7.6
Wampler, George, weaver	1	1	--	9.7.6
Wolf, John, sadler	1	1/2	--	25.0.0
Wagner, Philip, blacksmith	2	1 1/2	--	20.0.0
Weltzheimer, Philip, baker	1	2 1/2	--	28.2.6
Wagner, Frederick, cordwainer	--	--	--	5.0.0
Welshantz, Jacob, carpenter	1	1	--	12.10.0
Welshantz, David, nailsmith	1	1	--	10.0.0
Waltemyer, Ludwig, labourer	1	1	--	4.7.6
Wehr, George, labourer	1	1	--	5.0.0
Waltemyer, Philip, carpenter	1	1/2	--	10.0.0
Wehr, Frederick, baker	1	1/2	--	10.0.0
Youce, Frederick, blacksmith	1	1 1/2	--	25.0.0
Wagner, Jacob	--	1	--	7.10.0
Zimmer, Mathias, tinman	1	1/2	--	26.3.9
Zimmerman, Henry, painter	--	--	--	25.0.0
Ziegel, Widow	1	--	--	--
Ziegel, Godlieb	1	--	--	15.0.0
Todd, Joseph	--	--	--	7.10.0
Schwartz, Peter	--	--	--	15.0.0
Beltzner, John	--	--	--	15.0.0
Sinn, George	--	--	--	6.0.0
Kreber, John	--	--	--	20.0.0
Endler, Philip	--	--	--	--
Sheffer, Jacob	--	--	--	10.0.0
Brobst, John	--	--	--	10.0.0
Strohman, Jacob	--	--	--	12.0.0
---, Willard	--	--	--	18.0.0
Edwards, Jonathan	--	--	--	15.0.0
Ludwig, Charles, doctor	--	--	--	15.0.0
Edwards, Michael	--	--	--	3.0.0
Deitsh, Bartholomew, musician	--	--	--	20.0.0
Brooks, Charles	--	--	--	10.0.0

MANCHESTER TOWNSHIP

	Acres	Negroes	Horses	Cattle	Tax
Ament, Philip	--	--	--	--	6.9.0
Andrews, John, Rev'd	--	--	--	--	35.12.6
Bombach, George	--	--	--	--	6.10.0
Bixler, Joseph	126	--	3	7	97.0.0
Becher, Frederick	90	--	2	1	9.13.6
Bohn, Valentine	127	--	1	3	12.10.0
Brown, Jacob	--	--	1	1	6.9.0
Bixler, John	300	--	2	3	45.5.0
Bryerly, John	168	2	6	7	104.0.0
Barr, Henry	300	--	2	2	145.6.0
Britton, James	--	--	--	1	3.4.6
Bohn, Nicholas	150	--	2	2	19.0.0
Barns, William	--	--	--	2	--
Byer, John	150	--	2	2	13.18.6
Bruchard, Julius	200	--	3	4	32.6.0
Brenneman, Isaac	200	--	3	5	64.11.6
Becker, Conrad	229	--	3	5	40.7.0
Benedict, Philip	--	--	1	1	4.16.6
Bentz, Michael	74	--	2	2	15.18.0
Brenneman, Peter	--	--	1	3	64.11.0
Bushong, Jacob	--	--	3	4	--
Bott, Jonas	200	--	2	5	70.17.6
Bott, Reinhard	200	--	4	3	98.17.6
Bixler, Christian	--	--	--	--	154.8.0
Bailey, William	60	--	--	--	4.0.6
Cline, Conrad	150	--	2	3	19.0.0
Cerver, Casper	140	--	4	6	80.3.6
Davis, Thomas	--	--	--	--	3.4.6
Deshner, George	--	--	1	2	3.4.6
Dobbins, James	--	--	1	2	8.2.0
Doudle, Jacob, deceased	34	--	--	--	18.0.0
Doudle, Michael	14	--	--	--	9.14.0
Dinkle, Peter	6	--	--	--	4.17.0
Donaldson, Joseph	--	--	--	--	--
Emich, John, Senior	454	--	2	5	150.0.0
Eyster, Elias	300	--	4	6	88.16.0
Ebert, Martin	150	--	3	4	64.10.0
Ebert, Martin, Jun'r	140	--	3	5	--
Evy, John	--	--	--	4	--
Elenberger, Peter	150	--	2	3	40.7.0
Ettinger, Philip	100	--	2	2	29.0.0
Erisman, Jacob	130	--	3	2	19.8.6
Ensmenger, Conrad	40	--	2	2	8.0.0
Eisenhard, Conrad	160	--	2	4	32.5.6
Ebert, Michael, Sen'r	400	--	4	6	193.0.0
Eichelberger, Martin	400	2	4	6	170.18.0
Eyster, George	250	--	4	3	77.10.0
Emich, Valentine	--	--	2	3	8.12.6
Emich, John, Jun'r	--	--	2	3	8.12.6
Eichelberger, George, dec'd	--	--	--	--	4.10.6
Finfrock, Michael	--	--	3	3	12.18.6
Finfrock, Stephen	--	--	3	3	13.18.6
Fry, George	--	--	--	2	3.4.6
Fetter, John	--	--	--	1	3.4.6

Manchester Township	Acres	Negroes	Horses	Cattle	Tax
Forry's little place	--	--	--	--	8.7.6
Felger, Frederick	50	--	1	2	6.9.0
Fryer, George	--	--	--	1	3.4.6
Fackler, Godlieb	100	--	2	2	25.1.0
Gilbreath, Bertram	400	--	--	--	48.9.0
Good, Jacob	200	--	--	--	24.4.6
Gerhard, John	--	--	--	2	7.10.6
Greenewald, Stophel	100	--	2	3	16.0.0
Gross, Samuel	150	--	2	3	24.4.0
Giess, George	--	--	--	1	3.4.6
Groil, John	250	--	3	3	45.0.0
Gross, Dewald	--	--	--	1	3.4.6
Gottwalt, Jacob	37	--	2	3	17.10.0
Ginder, Michael	140	--	2	3	23.16.6
Graybill, John	100	--	--	2	30.16.6
Grass, Andrew	150	--	2	2	22.0.0
Greber, Philip	150	--	2	2	25.10.0
Groff, Henry	100	--	2	2	18.3.6
Groff, Jacob	--	--	2	2	77.13.6
Grim, Balzer	--	--	--	--	--
Guckes, John	33	--	3	2	120.0.0
Guckes, Harmanus	--	--	--	1	11.10.0
Grier, David	5 3/4	--	--	--	4.0.6
Greber, Henry	--	--	--	--	22.10.0
Gastner, Jacob	6	--	--	--	4.10.0
Hoke, John	217 1/2	--	1	3	98.17.6
Hutton, Joshua	--	--	--	--	19.7.6
Heckler, Jacob	--	--	2	2	9.13.6
Herbach, Yost	150	--	3	5	71.12.0
Hoffman, Philip	40	--	2	3	--
Hide, Christian	100	--	2	4	9.13.6
Hahn, Jacob	--	--	2	3	7.10.0
Holtzapfle, Adam	--	--	2	3	6.2.6
Hechler, George	185	--	2	3	24.4.6
Humrichhauser, John	100	--	3	3	25.16.0
Hake, Jacob	200	--	3	6	64.7.0
Hake, Andrew	100	--	2	2	19.0.0
Hershy, Andrew	250	--	3	5	36.19.0
Holtzapfl, Erasmus	120	--	2	3	25.0.0
Haynes, Nicholas	100	--	2	2	21.0.0
Herman, John	200	--	2	4	74.4.6
Herman, Emanuel	200	--	2	3	77.8.6
Holtzapfel, Bernard	150	--	2	--	22.12.0
Huft, Jacob	100	--	2	2	15.0.0
Horn, Frederick	--	--	--	1	3.4.6
Herman, Christian	84	--	--	--	19.0.0
Hoke, Peter	450	--	5	10	204.2.0
Hoke, Andrew	462	--	4	10	154.16.6
Heltzel, Philip	--	--	--	--	3.0.0
Huft, Widow	--	--	--	--	--
Hahn, Michael	20 3/4	--	--	--	4.15.0
Hetig, Ludwig	13	--	--	--	4.0.0
Herman, Jacob	--	--	--	--	4.5.6
Jacob, Jonathan	100	--	1	2	--
Jacob, George	--	--	--	--	--

9

Manchester Township	Acres	Negroes	Horses	Cattle	Tax
John, Jacob	--	--	--	--	--
Jones, Robert	211	1	2	4	66.15.0
Jones, Francis	--	--	4	1	22.12.6
Irwin, George	12 3/4	--	--	--	6.15.0
Klingman, Stophell	--	--	2	3	6.10.0
Kaufman, John	200	--	2	5	70.1.3
King, Godfrey	250	--	4	4	70.13.6
Koppenhaver, Simon	230	--	6	6	90.8.0
Klingman, George	--	--	--	1	3.4.6
King, Philip Jacob	256	--	3	4	132.7.6
Klingman, Jacob	--	--	1	4	26.7.6
Knab, Casper	193	--	4	8	84.14.6
Kohler, Balser	--	--	2	3	17.13.6
Kolman, Valentine	90	--	1	3	12.0.0
Kohler, Andrew	100	--	2	4	27.10.6
Kitch, John	--	--	--	--	3.4.6
Kraybill, Joseph	200	--	3	4	105.0.0
Keiffer, Henry	--	--	--	1	3.4.6
Kobb, Widow	--	--	--	1	--
Kabb, Martin	--	--	--	--	70.13.6
Krantz, George	218	1	3	5	77.3.6
Krantz, Valentine	15	--	--	--	10.0.0
Kauffman, John, Jun'r	--	--	--	--	4.10.6
Keller, Michael	8 1/2	--	--	--	4.0.0
Kern, Jacob	--	--	--	--	0.9.6
Keller, Jacob	--	--	--	--	19.7.6
Lau, Michael	200	--	5	6	96.0.0
Lichtenberger, Killian	74	--	1	3	8.1.6
Lichtenberger, Casper	20	--	--	2	6.9.0
Livingston, George	121	--	2	3	29.0.0
Livingston, Michael	--	--	--	1	6.9.0
Lichtenberger, George	--	--	--	1	6.9.0
Long, Widow	--	--	1	2	3.4.6
Long, Peter	--	--	2	4	61.0.0
Lenhard, Frederick	15	--	1	2	19.7.9
Lechron, Leonard	150	--	2	3	24.7.0
Leip, Christian	--	--	--	--	48.8.6
Life, Martin	--	--	--	3	7.10.0
Leitner, Naatz	120	--	--	--	32.0.0
Lau, Philip	200	--	4	6	70.13.0
Lefler, George Lewis	--	--	--	--	0.9.6
Mohr, Nicholas	143	--	3	4	16.2.6
Metzger, George	150	--	2	2	14.18.0
Melhorn, Michael	40	--	2	3	9.13.6
Miller, Philip	200	--	4	5	38.10.0
Miller, George	--	--	--	--	6.9.6
Miller, John	--	--	--	--	72.0.0
Miller, Samuel	--	--	--	--	27.0.0
Miller, Mathias	--	--	3	5	36.18.6
Menges, Peter	130	--	3	4	56.0.0
Nebenger, John	--	--	--	1	3.4.6
Ness, Henry	--	--	2	3	--
Ness, Jacob	125	--	2	3	17.15.0
Ort, Henry	150	--	4	5	32.0.0
Ottinger, Henry	--	--	3	2	41.18.6

Manchester Township	Acres	Negroes	Horses	Cattle	Tax
Ottinger, Jacob, Jun'r	--	--	4	4	31.7.0
Oderman, George	--	--	1	3	0.6.9
Ottinger, Jacob	150	--	3	3	38.14.0
Ottinger, Peter	--	--	--	1	3.4.6
Rice, Wm.	--	--	--	--	60.0.0
Raymer, Frederick	200	--	4	3	80.0.0
Ritter, Andrew	200	1	4	8	80.0.0
Rudisill, Balzer	135	--	2	4	30.11.6
Robert, John	--	--	--	--	--
Rudisill, Jacob	165	--	3	3	65.0.0
Roth, Anthony	116	--	3	5	64.11.6
Roth, Henry	--	--	--	1	6.9.0
Rosenbaum, John	--	--	4	3	48.9.0
Reiff, John	--	--	1	2	6.9.0
Ringer, George	130	--	3	4	22.0.0
Rudisill, Jonas	210	--	3	4	45.4.0
Roth, John	--	--	--	--	6.9.0
Reidinger, Stephen	140	--	2	2	38.15.0
Roming, Michael	150	--	2	2	38.15.0
Ruppert, Deetrich	150	--	2	2	22.12.0
Reisinger, John	--	--	--	--	6.9.0
Reel, Peter	6 1/2	--	--	--	4.0.6
Speck, Michael	--	--	--	1	6.9.0
Shaad, David	--	--	--	1	3.4.6
Sprenckel, George	200	--	3	4	52.19.6
Stoner, Isaac	388	--	3	6	90.8.6
Smith, James	--	--	2	2	3.4.6
Snyder, Conrad	--	--	--	--	11.0.0
Slegle, Stophel	11 1/2	--	--	1	25.16.6
Smith, Ja's, lawyer	--	--	--	--	37.10.0
Shultz, Peter	150	--	4	6	53.13.0
Shultz & Koppenhafer	--	--	--	--	--
Snyder, Peter	200	--	4	6	22.12.0
Snyder, Philip, Ju'r	--	--	--	--	3.4.6
Snyder, Conrad	--	--	--	1	3.4.6
Snyder, Jacob	--	--	1	2	44.3.0
Schenk, Adam	185	--	2	4	44.3.0
Spickert, Philip	150	--	2	3	29.1.0
Storm, Paul	50	--	2	1	8.0.6
Smith, Ja's, English	100	--	1	2	21.0.0
Smith, Ja's, German	66	--	--	4	21.0.0
Smith, Andrew, Sen'r	250	--	3	5	37.0.0
Smith, Andrew	--	--	2	2	12.0.0
Sherb, John	100	--	2	4	16.2.6
Schindel, Frederick	150	--	3	4	32.5.6
Scheffer, Peter	--	--	1	3	9.13.6
Schreiber, Michael	135	--	2	3	27.10.2
Schreiber, John	130	--	3	3	27.10.6
Schreiber, Peter	--	--	--	1	--
Schultz, Peter, jobber	--	--	--	2	3.16.0
Schram, Widow	200	--	2	--	25.0.0
Strack, Yost	--	--	--	1	3.16.0
Stoner, Frederick	--	--	--	1	3.4.6
Shultz, Henry	138	--	2	2	64.11.6
Smyser, Michael	238	1	3	6	100.2.0

Manchester Township

	Acres	Negroes	Horses	Cattle	Tax
Smyser, Jacob	190	--	4	5	75.44.6
Smyser, Mathias	190	--	3	4	77.0.0
Sprenckel, Peter	500	--	6	7	209.0.0
Shuck, Jacob	290	--	--	--	51.0.0
Stake, George	--	--	--	--	6.0.0
Treiber, Michael	100	--	2	2	16.2.6
Updegraff, Joseph	110	--	--	--	25.16.0
Updegraff, Sam'l	--	--	--	--	106.6.6
Willis, William	--	--	--	--	106.6.6
Wogan, Jacob	300	3	4	6	128.8.5
Worley, Jacob	--	--	--	--	49.18.6
Willis, John	--	--	1	1	4.4.6
Wagner, Philip	--	--	--	--	7.10.0
Wolf, George	190 1/2	--	3	4	64.11.6
Welch, George	100	--	3	3	38.14.0
Wilt, Adam	--	--	--	2	3.4.6
Welty, Jacob	100	--	2	1	9.13.0
Wahl, Yost	200	--	2	5	32.7.6
Wilt, Valentine	150	--	3	3	22.12.6
Wilt, Nicholas	--	--	1	--	--
Witerrecht, George	--	--	2	2	14.18.6
Wintermyer, Philip	150	--	3	3	32.5.0
Witerrecht, Michal	150	--	1	2	22.12.6
Witerrecht, Peter	--	--	1	2	6.9.0
Weigel, Loenard	50	--	2	2	15.13.6
Worley, James	100	--	4	4	78.4.6
Worley, Daniel	140	--	2	3	74.1.0
Worley, Francis, Jun'r	--	--	1	1	4.16.6
Wagner, Jacob	156	--	2	2	71.1.0
Weigel, Sabastian	139	--	2	3	25.16.0
Wittmeyer, Simon	140	--	2	3	32.5.6
Wolf, Philip	300	--	2	4	28.7.6
Wolf, Peter	250	--	6	6	124.6.0
Wolf, Adam	--	--	1	3	6.9.0
Worley, Francis	69	--	--	--	22.12.6
Worley, Nathan	100	--	--	--	48.0.0
Weigel, Martin	--	--	--	--	64.11.6
Wolf, Henry	224	--	--	--	59.11.6
Welsh, Michal	2 1/2	--	--	--	1.5.0
Zimerman, Bernard	--	--	3	3	--
Zeigler, Killian	--	--	3	5	12.18.0
Ziegler, Philip	328	--	1	8	105.0.0
Ziegler, Philip, Jun'r	--	--	1	--	12.18.0
Ziegler, Jacob	--	--	--	2	6.9.0
Welsh, Michael	2 1/2	--	--	--	1.10.0
Wall, Wm., Cap't.	--	--	--	--	4.16.0
Barr, Wm.,	--	--	--	--	4.16.6
Becker, William	--	--	--	--	4.5.6
Eichelberger, Frederick	--	--	--	--	--

BOTTS TOWN

	Acres	Negroes	Horses	Cattle	Tax
Haller, John	--	--	--	1	12.18.0
Bower, Martin	--	--	--	1	--
Lind, Peter	5	--	--	1	25.16.6
Roush, Anthony	--	--	--	--	3.4.6
Richard, Godlieb	--	--	4	1	14.15.0
Derr, Gabriel	--	--	--	1	14.15.0
Bott, Jacob	10	--	--	--	25.10.0
Shryack, John	--	--	--	1	--
Ament, Dice	--	--	--	--	6.9.0
Emlet, Michael	--	--	--	--	6.9.0
Weyer, Andrew	--	--	--	1	6.9.0
Hoffman, Philip	--	--	1	2	9.13.0
Rothrock, Philip	--	--	--	--	7.10.0
Rothrock, George	--	--	--	--	3.4.6
Eberhard, Henry	--	--	--	--	--
Hammer, Peter	--	--	1	1	4.16.0
Wetshofer, Henry	--	--	--	1	3.14.0
Lewis, Robert	--	--	--	1	11.3.6
Crouse, Michael	--	--	--	--	7.0.0
Brown, Alexander	--	--	--	1	6.3.0
Rowan, William	--	--	1	2	9.13.0
Snider, Andrew	--	--	--	1	--
Myer, John	--	--	--	--	--
Kurtz, John	--	--	--	1	11.3.6
Oldham, Thomas	--	--	--	2	14.8.6
Rudy, Jacob	--	--	--	--	6.9.0
Weigel, Peter	--	--	1	1	--
Risinger, Nicholas	--	--	--	1	--
Raymer, Frederick	--	--	--	--	7.10.0
Stake, Christian	--	--	--	--	--
Weyant, Peter	--	--	--	--	19.7.6
Detter, Mathias	5	--	--	1	25.16.6
Eichelberger, Frederick	300	--	--	2	89.14.6
Dunn, Thomas	--	--	1	2	12.18.0
Kimmel	--	--	--	--	6.9.0
Weigel, Leonard	--	--	--	--	12.13.6

Single Men

	Amount of Tax		Amount of Tax
Weaver, Jacob	15.0.0	Jacob, John	12.10.0
Knab, Jacob	12.10.0	Bruckhard, David	15.0.0
Reist, Christian	25.0.0	Bruckhard, Abram	12.0.0
Lichtenberger, Geo'r Adam	12.10.0	Kohler, Valentine	12.10.0
Knab, Casper	12.10.0	Kohler, Joseph	12.10.0
Goul, William	15.10.0	Ettinger, Michael	12.10.0
Jones, John, fuller	20.10.0	Ringer, Michael	12.10.0
Bott, George	12.10.0	Erisman, Frederick	12.10.0
Ebert, Philip	12.10.0	Jacob, Jonathan	16.0.0
Koppenhaver, Simon	12.10.0	Gottwalt, Jacob	12.10.0
Menges, George	12.10.0	Bohn, Jacob	12.10.0
Schram, John	12.10.0	Kuhn, Peter	12.10.0

Botts Town	Single Men

Ziegler, Andrew	12.10.0	Becker, Adam	12.10.0
Sprenckel, Peter	12.10.0	Lechron, Leonard	8.0.0
Sprenckel, Michael	12.10.0	Miller, Adam	12.0.0
Klingman, Frederick	12.10.0	Bixler, Jacob	12.10.0
Kleckler, John	7.10.0	Klein, Michael	10.0.0
Jacob, George	15.0.0		

MANHIME TOWNSHIP

	Acres	Negroes	Horses	Cattle	Tax
Albright, Bernard	100	--	1	1	12.0.0
Apfel, George	50	--	1	2	14.0.0
Becker, Christian	--	--	1	1	6.0.0
Bucher, Nicholas, Jun'r	--	--	--	1	12.0.0
Bittinger, Nicholas	50	--	--	--	10.0.0
Bouser, Daniel	200	--	3	6	35.0.0
Bruckhard, Martin	100	--	2	6	23.0.0
Bruckhard, Adam	100	--	2	4	41.0.0
Bachman, Widow	--	--	--	--	6.0.0
Behler, Jacob	150	--	3	4	32.0.0
Bachman, Christian	100	--	1	1	6.0.0
Bachman, Christopher	50	--	1	1	6.0.0
Bricker, Nicholas	200	--	4	5	35.0.0
Bollinger, Joseph	100	--	2	3	10.0.0
Bircker, Andrew	100	--	--	2	8.0.0
Bower, Jacob	--	--	1	2	5.0.0
Bose, John	150	--	--	--	10.10.0
Baum, Peter	123	--	2	5	25.10.0
Baum, Peter, Jun'r	--	--	--	1	4.0.0
Bauman, Jacob	145	--	2	4	18.0.0
Bauman, Jacob, Jun'r	--	--	--	1	3.0.0
Bauman, Henry	100	--	3	5	60.0.0
Barr, Michael	100	--	2	4	25.0.0
Barr, Jacob	150	--	2	4	50.0.0
Brauser, John	--	--	1	1	--
Bushy, Henry	150	--	1	3	36.0.0
Bucher, Nicholas	150	--	2	5	90.0.0
Bauman, John	--	--	--	--	5.0.0
Bollinger, Jacob	--	--	--	--	120.0.0
Bollinger, Jacob, Jun'r	360	--	4	5	--
Burkhard, Jacob	300	--	4	3	100.0.0
Beyer, John	285	--	3	4	110.0.0
Blocker, Mathias	59	--	2	3	5.10.0
Battenfelt, Philip	200	--	2	4	18.0.0
Bixler, John	100	--	2	3	71.0.0
Bechtel, Christian	300	--	4	6	160.0.0
Bauman, Henry, Jun'r	--	--	--	--	330.0.0
Bercker, Valentine	--	--	1	1	3.0.0
Bollinger, Henry	100	--	2	2	3.0.0
Bachner, Daniel	--	--	--	1	10.0.0
Bricker, Stophel	160	--	1	3	12.0.0
Beckley, Henry	--	--	--	--	--
Doll, Daniel	50	--	2	1	--

Manhime Township	Acres	Negroes	Horses	Cattle	Tax
Dewalt, Henry	100	--	--	3	20.0.0
Dewalt, Valentine	--	--	2	2	12.0.0
Damy, Jacob	200	--	4	6	75.0.0
Danner, Henry	135	--	2	6	50.0.0
Danner, Michael	100	--	4	4	20.0.0
Dups, Daniel	200	--	3	3	90.0.0
Meredith, Rees	--	--	--	--	110.0.0
Derwechter, John	150	--	2	5	60.0.0
Davis, Richard	--	--	3	3	20.0.0
Drump, Abram	300	--	--	--	25.0.0
Demand, Frederick	--	--	--	1	5.0.0
Dubbs, Oswald	80	--	1	2	18.0.0
Dubbs, John	--	--	--	--	20.0.0
Ernst, John	200	--	3	5	80.0.0
Eichelberger, Lenard	44	--	--	--	9.0.0
Eichelberger, Adam	300	--	4	8	150.0.0
D'o to land	50	--	--	--	--
Ehrhard, Michael	100	--	--	2	6.0.0
Ebersolt, Jacob	200	--	3	5	55.0.0
Eppley, John	100	--	--	7	10.0.0
Eppley, Mathias	--	--	--	2	10.0.0
Eppley, Peter	--	--	--	2	10.0.0
Eyler, John	58	--	1	3	28.0.0
Fulford, Henry	--	--	1	1	--
Frank, David	50	--	--	5	7.10.0
Fowble, John	50	--	2	2	7.10.0
Fuhrman, Jacob	--	--	--	--	7.10.0
Fass, Christian	150	--	2	7	50.0.0
Fisher, Adam	--	--	--	1	4.0.0
Felger, Henry	50	--	2	4	20.0.0
Funk, Adam	--	--	--	6	7.10.0
Fucks, George	100	--	2	3	18.15.0
Flickinger, Jacob	150	--	2	3	27.10.0
Flickinger, Samuel	150	--	2	4	80.0.0
Fuhrman, Stephen	150	--	3	5	31.0.0
Furny, Nicholas	--	--	1	2	--
Furny, Mark	120	--	3	4	150.0.0
Furney, Philip	100	--	--	--	10.0.0
Felten, Conrad	130	--	3	3	65.0.0
Felton, John	--	--	1	1	8.0.0
Fisher, Valentine	186	--	2	7	65.0.0
Felix, John	150	--	2	3	22.10.0
Fehl, George	--	--	--	1	8.0.0
Fehl, Nicholas	--	--	--	1	8.0.0
Fickes, Martin	80	--	1	1	7.10.0
Galhoon, John	120	3	5	6	80.0.0
Gerrard, Wm.	100	--	2	3	15.0.0
Gramer, Andrew	60	--	1	2	15.0.0
Gramer, Adam	--	--	1	1	10.0.0
Gotty, George	40	--	--	2	10.0.0
Gunty, Peter	75	--	2	3	60.0.0
Gerber, John	140	--	3	3	35.0.0
Gich, Balzer	--	--	2	2	15.0.0
Gelwix, Frederick	150	--	2	4	20.0.0
Gelwix, Frederick, Sen'r	147	--	1	5	60.0.0

Manhime Township	Acres	Negroes	Horses	Cattle	Tax
Gelwix, Peter	--	--	2	3	5.0.0
Gminter, Martin	94	--	1	2	15.0.0
Gitt, Peter	150	--	1	2	20.0.0
Kelly, Thomas	100	--	1	2	10.0.0
Hank, Philip	160	--	2	1	30.0.0
Hauk, Jacob	50	--	--	--	5.0.0
Honer, Michael	50	--	--	2	--
Hetrick, Jacob	75	--	--	--	10.0.0
Hoffacher, Michael	100	--	--	1	10.0.0
Hinckel, John	275	--	--	--	50.0.0
Hinckel, Anthony	--	--	1	2	10.0.0
Hinckel, William	--	--	1	2	10.0.0
Herretter, John	200	--	2	4	20.0.0
Henry, Nicholas	--	--	--	1	--
Herring, Henry	150	--	2	4	30.0.0
Hoff, Henry	120	--	2	3	25.0.0
Hirshy, Christian	182	--	1	--	20.0.0
Hirshy, Christian, Jun'r	200	--	2	4	95.0.0
Hirshy, John	213	--	5	6	150.0.0
Hoff, Henry, doctor	100	--	2	1	--
Hubbert, Adam	150	--	3	5	70.0.0
Herr, Michael	180	--	1	1	5.0.0
Hofman, Peter	--	--	--	4	10.0.0
Harnish, Samuel	150	--	2	4	30.0.0
Hoke, Casper	44	--	--	2	40.0.0
Hime, Francis	10	--	--	--	3.0.0
Haselet, Francis	--	--	1	7	22.10.0
Henry, Frederick	140	--	2	2	18.0.0
Hegy, Jacob	--	--	--	1	35.0.0
Johnston, Jacob	--	--	--	--	5.0.0
Yeger, Henry	150	--	2	2	10.0.0
Yenewein, Leonard	93	--	2	6	25.0.0
Ickes, John	--	--	1	1	15.0.0
Young, Charles	100	--	2	3	20.0.0
Young, Adam	--	--	--	--	--
Jones, John	--	--	--	--	50.0.0
Youngblood, Daniel	--	--	2	2	--
Kaufelder's place	--	--	--	--	20.0.0
Karch, Andrew	182	--	1	1	10.0.0
Kock, Peter	--	--	--	1	10.0.0
Kock, George	--	--	--	--	5.0.0
Kraft, Jacob	200	--	2	5	65.0.0
Kline, Henry	100	--	2	4	25.0.0
Kroh, John	100	--	1	2	25.0.0
Kremer, Helfrich	200	--	2	3	27.10.0
Kreber, Adam	140	--	2	5	15.0.0
Kreber, Gerhard	100	--	2	3	5.0.0
Kreber, Gabriel	100	--	1	2	18.15.0
Krum, Peter	74	--	--	2	10.0.0
Kiefaber, Conrad	--	--	--	--	40.0.0
Kiefaber, Nicholas	250	--	2	4	125.0.0
Kochenauer, Jacob	--	--	--	1	4.0.0
Koch, George	--	--	--	--	--
Koch, Andrew	--	--	--	--	3.0.0
Kibinger, Peter	100	--	1	1	40.0.0

Manhime Township	Acres	Negroes	Horses	Cattle	Tax
Kitzmiller, John	150	--	4	7	55.0.0
Kitzmiller, George	150	--	4	6	100.0.0
Kerr, John	166	--	4	4	80.0.0
Karl, Michael	108	--	4	5	60.0.0
Kemerly, Christian	--	--	--	1	3.0.0
Long, Conrad	100	--	--	4	15.0.0
Lauer, Mathias	95	--	2	2	15.0.0
Long, Martin	120	--	1	2	15.0.0
Long, Frederick	120	--	1	2	15.0.0
Long, Jacob	--	--	2	2	--
Long, John	100	--	2	2	20.0.0
Lingle, Nicholas	60	--	2	2	15.0.0
Lininger, George	100	--	--	2	15.0.0
Liner, Henry	150	--	3	3	60.0.0
Liner, Henry, Jun'r	200	--	3	4	60.0.0
Leyer, Martin	--	--	--	1	--
Lischy, Henry	150	--	--	--	10.0.0
Martin, Henry	82	--	2	4	15.0.0
Mathias, Widow	50	--	--	--	--
Messemer, Yoder	100	--	3	7	80.0.0
Miller, Philip	100	--	2	3	17.10.0
Mathew, George	200	--	5	7	--
Ditto, for land	100	--	--	--	90.0.0
Meyer, Frederick	90	--	--	--	90.0.0
Michael, William	140	--	1	3	10.0.0
Muhlheim, George	80	--	1	11	20.0.0
Mushrush, Jacob	90	--	--	2	4.0.0
Meyer, George	--	--	2	2	6.0.0
Schneider's, Dewalt, land	100	--	--	--	--
Morningstar, Philip	108	--	3	6	90.0.0
Miller, James	180	--	2	3	70.0.0
Maul, Philip	200	--	2	5	45.0.0
Miller, Edward	200	--	--	--	50.0.0
Myer, John	--	--	--	--	10.0.0
Nuss, Jacob	200	--	2	3	15.0.0
Nunnemacher, Jacob	140	--	2	3	30.0.0
Newcomer, Jacob	100	--	2	6	15.0.0
Naas, Michael	50	--	1	5	15.0.0
Newman, Michael	94	--	2	4	30.0.0
Newman, Nicholas	100	--	1	4	30.0.0
Oberdier, Ludwig	90	--	2	2	15.0.0
Rabenstine, Widow	60	--	2	2	--
Reinyman, William	60	--	2	3	15.0.0
Ruleman, George	100	--	2	2	35.0.0
Ruleman, Christian	80	--	2	2	10.0.0
Raghy, Stophel	50	--	--	1	10.0.0
Raghy, Henry	50	--	--	4	15.0.0
Raghy, Wendel	--	--	--	1	--
Runckel, Jacob	150	--	2	3	40.0.0
Runckel, Ludwig	200	--	--	3	55.0.0
D'o for land	50	--	--	--	--
Rinehard, George	80	--	2	6	15.0.0
Rowenzahan, John	100	--	2	3	20.0.0
Reinecker, Casper	200	--	--	--	10.0.0
Rudisill, Ludwig	180	--	2	2	40.0.0

Manhime Township	Acres	Negroes	Horses	Cattle	Tax
Rudisill, Andrew	200	--	2	3	35.0.0
Reinhard, Conrad	50	--	2	2	--
Reighle, Henry	100	--	--	--	12.0.0
Sholl, Widow	150	--	2	3	5.0.0
Stephen, Widow	150	--	2	4	5.0.0
Stiess, Zachariah	--	--	1	1	10.0.0
Strauch, William	50	--	--	4	7.10.0
Schinck, John	140	--	5	6	200.0.0
Stumpf, Peter	50	--	--	1	--
D'o for land	15	--	--	--	--
Shuss, George	130	--	2	3	10.0.0
Schwartzbach, John	150	--	2	4	12.0.0
Schneider, Stophel	150	--	2	4	25.0.0
Sterner, Bernard	63	--	2	3	10.0.0
Sable, Leonard	150	--	--	--	40.0.0
Sable, Peter	150	--	2	4	25.0.0
Sherman, Jacob	160	--	--	--	30.0.0
Sherman, Conrad	300	--	5	6	110.0.0
Sower, Adam	90	--	2	3	15.0.0
Sherretz, Arnold	400	--	1	2	70.0.0
Sherretz, Conrad	400	--	1	2	70.0.0
Sherretz, Daniel	--	--	1	4	--
Sherretz, Ludwig	--	--	1	4	35.0.0
Sheirer, John	80	--	1	1	5.0.0
Summer, John	140	--	3	7	70.0.0
Schlotthauer, Nicholas	128	--	2	4	30.0.0
Stambach, Jacob	250	--	1	3	100.0.0
Shaack, John	--	--	1	2	10.0.0
Stamback, John	--	--	1	2	15.0.0
Schneider, John	70	--	--	2	5.0.0
Steinbrecher, Sebastian	--	--	--	--	10.0.0
Savage, Hill	140	--	--	--	15.0.0
Thron, John	160	--	3	6	100.0.0
Thron, Abraham	200	--	1	3	40.0.0
Uland, Michael	--	--	--	1	10.0.0
Wohlfart, Philip	150	--	4	5	60.0.0
Wercking, Nicholas	150	--	3	3	40.0.0
Wercking, Philip, Vance	100	--	2	3	10.0.0
Wercking, Philip	150	--	3	3	20.0.0
Wercking, Valentine	50	--	2	1	9.0.0
Walter, Ludwig	--	--	1	3	15.0.0
Werner, Melchior	200	--	2	3	5.0.0
Werner, George	--	--	--	2	5.0.0
Wolfgang, Nicholas	150	--	3	4	22.10.0
Willet, Stophel	180	--	2	3	20.0.0
Wampler, John	200	--	2	4	30.0.0
Wilkison, Jacob	95	--	2	4	40.0.0
Wilkison, Samuel	150	--	3	5	50.0.0
Weinbrecht, Michael	150	--	--	--	100.0.0
Welty, John	--	--	--	--	57.0.0
Wagner, Yost	150	--	--	2	40.0.0
Wagner, Peter	--	--	3	4	10.0.0
Wagner, Ludwig	--	--	--	1	5.0.0
Wagner, Conrad	--	--	--	2	--
Winter, John	50	--	2	1	5.0.0

Manhime Township	Acres	Negroes	Horses	Cattle	Tax
Wunder, Christian	50	--	2	2	7.10.0
Wentz, Valentine	150	--	2	5	50.0.0
Wentz, Frederick	--	--	1	1	--
Wattson, William	--	--	1	2	--
Weiss, John	100	--	--	--	5.0.0
Zacharias, George	65	--	2	3	30.0.0
Zimmerman, Christian	100	--	2	5	20.0.0
Zimmerman, John	80	--	1	2	5.0.0
Furnace, Mary Ann & Gwinn, William	5000	1	16	8	739.15.0
Campbell, William	--	--	2	--	118.0.0

Single Men

	Amount of Tax		Amount of Tax
Sower, John	15.0.0	Klein, John	15.0.0
Zimmerman, Stophel	15.0.0	Klein, Henry	--
Krugener, John	--	Pay, Philip	--
Bush, Michael	15.0.0	Fuhrman, Valentine	18.0.0
Long, John	15.0.0	Fuhrman, Jacob	15.0.0
Gillmeyer, Francis	20.0.0	Fuhrman, Michael	10.0.0
Elseroth, Nicholas	15.0.0	Nunemacher, Godlieb	15.0.0
Forney, Christian	15.0.0	Bricker, Anthony	15.0.0
Reidinger, Henry	15.0.0	Baum, Jacob	15.0.0
Buyer, Henry	15.0.0	Bauser, Christian	10.0.0
Wert, John	15.0.0	Bauser, Daniel	10.0.0
Stambach, Jacob	15.0.0	Gerrard, Christian	15.0.0
Emich, John	15.0.0	Werking, Philip	15.0.0
Hull, Andrew	12.0.0	Baumgartner, Jacob	15.0.0
Gelwix, George	10.0.0	Miller, Henry	15.0.0
Gelwix, Nicholas	15.0.0	Matter, George	15.0.0
Huppert, Adam	15.0.0	Argentant, John	--
Bucher, John	15.0.0	Schlotthaur, Michael	10.0.0
Shilling, John	10.0.0	Pfannebecker, William	15.0.0
Welty, Peter	15.0.0	Welty, Henry	15.0.0
Dorny, Henry	15.0.0	Bixler, Jacob	15.0.0
Gally, Moses	--	Forney, Adam	15.0.0

NEWBERRY TOWNSHIP

	Acres	Negroes	Horses	Cattle	Tax
Arthur, Thomas	95	--	2	1	1.13.4
Armor, Thomas	--	--	--	--	7.10.0
Allender, William	--	--	1	2	5.10.0
Aston, John	80	--	2	1	26.13.0
Atkinson, John	--	--	--	--	5.0.0
Alsop, John	200	--	2	1	16.13.4
Atticks, John	80	--	2	3	17.10.0
Armstrong, Henry	--	--	1	1	--
Atkinson, Caiphas	--	--	2	3	12.0.0
Anderson, James	150	--	--	--	15.0.0
Apply, Jacob	130	--	1	2	30.0.0

Newberry Township	Acres	Negroes	Horses	Cattle	Tax
D'o in Cumberland county	155	--	--	--	--
Appley, George	--	--	1	--	5.0.0
Aston, Wm.	--	--	--	--	60.13.4
Bennet, Isaac	--	--	--	1	7.10.0
Byard, George	100	--	3	3	30.12.0
Barton, Edward	100	--	--	1	10.0.0
Barnet, Charles	--	--	2	1	3.0.0
Braton, Wm.	--	--	--	1	--
Baumgartner, John	200	--	3	4	104.5.0
Bower, George	100	--	2	4	30.7.6
Beatman, Andrew	50	--	--	2	10.0.0
Baxter, William	60	--	1	1	15.0.0
Baxter, John	50	--	1	2	15.0.0
Baxter, Joseph	--	--	--	--	20.0.0
Bennet, Thomas	--	--	1	1	10.0.0
Borger, Michael	--	--	1	2	7.10.0
Bean, James	--	--	--	--	100.0.0
Biegler, John	100	--	2	2	45.0.0
Behmer, Jacob	--	--	1	3	10.0.0
Behmer, John	--	--	1	--	5.0.0
Broband, Ann, Jacob's widow	140	--	2	2	30.0.0
Bailey, Daniel	--	--	--	--	20.0.0
Broband, Ann, Christian's widow	200	--	2	1	40.0.0
Bonine, James	80	--	2	3	10.10.0
Bonine, Tho's	--	--	--	--	--
Barber, Samuel	--	--	--	--	7.10.0
Bear, Jacob	60	--	1	3	20.0.0
Bennet, Henry	--	--	--	--	15.0.0
Brewey, George	--	--	3	4	54.0.0
Cox, Jacob	--	--	2	2	5.0.0
Correll, Abraham	--	--	--	1	5.0.0
Crone, Simon	100	--	2	4	20.0.0
Craymer, Adam	300	--	--	--	--
Conser, Henry	--	--	1	1	3.0.0
Cobel, Christopher	150	--	4	3	40.0.0
Copland, Thomas	--	--	1	1	15.0.0
Chesney, William	400	--	6	10	300.0.0
Chesney, William	500	--	--	--	--
Chesney, William	--	--	--	--	--
Climson, John	--	--	--	--	40.0.0
Crull, John	--	--	--	2	5.0.0
Copeland, Davis	--	--	1	1	20.0.0
Citterman, Andrew	--	--	--	--	45.0.0
Cook, Joseph	--	--	--	--	60.0.0
Cline, Andrew	150	--	1	3	29.10.0
Dougherty, William	--	--	--	--	15.0.0
Davis, Benjamin	--	--	--	2	25.0.0
Drohrbach, Jacob	100	--	2	2	48.0.0
Driver, John, Cumberland co.	100	--	--	--	12.0.0
Doudle, Jacob, deceas'd	--	--	--	--	20.0.0
Donet, George	48	--	2	2	7.10.0
Davis, William	100	--	2	2	36.0.0
Davis, David	133	--	4	5	97.0.0

Newberry Township	Acres	Negroes	Horses	Cattle	Tax
Elliot, John	100	--	2	4	30.0.0
Edmundson	310	--	--	--	50.0.0
Evans, Evan, old man	--	--	--	1	--
Ensmenger, George	140	--	2	4	20.0.0
Ensmenger, Henry	--	--	1	1	3.0.0
Elliot, James	114	--	2	2	30.0.0
Eyers, Henry	--	--	2	1	35.0.0
Eshelman, Peter, deceased	150	--	--	--	--
Eyres, John	--	--	--	2	3.0.0
Elliot, Alexander, deceased	80	--	--	--	7.10.0
Ensmenger, David, living on Daniel Shelly's	130	--	--	--	84.0.0
Eshbaugh, Eve	25	--	1	1	3.0.0
Fisher, Godlieb	100	--	3	3	100.0.0
Fetterro, Joseph	--	--	--	--	5.0.0
Freeman, Nathaniel	80	--	2	--	20.0.0
Freeman, Nathaniel	--	--	--	--	10.0.0
Freeman, John	--	--	--	--	10.0.0
Forrey, John	350	--	2	3	200.0.0
Fisher, James	--	--	--	--	4.0.0
Feddero, Philip, Sen'r	150	--	1	4	10.0.0
Feddero, Philip, Jun'r	--	--	--	2	5.0.0
Forrey, Christian	200	--	4	6	290.0.0
Floyd, Samuel, old	--	--	--	2	--
Feddero, John	--	--	--	--	5.0.0
Griffith, Abraham	67	--	1	2	25.0.0
Gitson, Wm.	--	--	--	--	--
Grove, Samuel	--	--	2	2	5.0.0
George, William	--	--	2	2	10.0.0
Gold, Thomas	130	--	2	5	25.0.0
Garretson, Samuel	--	--	--	--	160.0.0
Gorman, James	--	--	--	1	3.0.0
Gibbons, William	100	--	2	2	7.10.0
Gibbon, Patrick	--	--	--	--	--
Grubb, Michael	--	--	--	--	5.0.0
Grubb, Israel	--	--	--	1	7.10.0
Glancey, Torrence	--	--	2	6	100.0.0
Glancey, Jesse	--	--	--	1	20.0.0
Glancey, Joseph	--	--	--	--	13.0.0
Grime, Daniel	--	--	--	--	--
Garretson, John	--	--	--	--	300.0.0
Garretson, Cornelius	--	--	--	--	160.0.0
Garretson, Joseph	--	--	--	--	20.0.0
Gottwalt, Jacob	--	--	--	--	15.0.0
Huzzey, George	--	--	--	--	20.0.0
Hummel, Frederick	--	--	--	--	5.0.0
Hart, Jacob	100	2	--	2	70.0.0
Hunter, Joseph	--	--	--	--	5.0.0
Hutton, Joseph	81	--	2	2	15.0.0
Hughs, Walter	--	--	--	3	7.10.0
Huff, Adam	100	--	--	2	17.0.0
Huff, Peter	100	--	--	2	17.0.0
Hoops, Daniel	--	--	1	3	25.0.0
Huland, Marks	--	--	--	--	10.0.0
Hollingsworth, Jehu	--	--	--	--	480.0.0

Newberry Township	Acres	Negroes	Horses	Cattle	Tax
House, Benjamin	--	--	1	1	10.0.0
Holmes, Edward	--	--	--	1	5.0.0
Hamersly, Robert	100	--	2	2	20.0.0
Hancock, James	--	--	--	--	30.0.0
Hoffman, John	50	--	1	2	20.0.0
Hoffman, John	100	--	1	1	25.0.0
Hoffman, Henry	50	--	--	--	10.0.0
Herrold, Peter	80	--	2	4	10.0.0
Hock, Michael	50	--	1	1	60.0.0
Hunter, William	--	--	--	2	3.0.0
Hays, Jesse	110	--	--	1	35.0.0
Humbel, Garret	100	--	2	2	18.15.0
Hingardner, Charles	--	--	--	1	3.0.0
Hare, James	--	--	--	--	--
Hinds, John	--	--	--	--	10.0.0
Harris, George	100	--	2	3	15.0.0
Hunter, William	200	--	5	7	75.10.0
D'o in Cumberland county	100	--	--	--	--
Huff, Daniel	100	--	1	1	5.0.0
Hire, Charles	--	--	--	--	3.0.0
Hire, Frederick	--	--	2	3	32.0.0
Heidelbach, Jacob	--	--	4	7	51.0.0
Jennings, Tho's, deceased	100	--	--	--	30.0.0
Jones, Samuel	--	--	--	--	120.0.0
Jenkins, David	100	--	2	1	25.0.0
John, Ebenezer	--	--	1	--	25.0.0
Johnston, John	--	--	1	2	7.10.0
Johnston, Thomas	--	--	--	--	8.0.0
Jones, David	--	--	--	2	--
Jones, Edward	--	--	--	--	100.10.0
Johnston, Stephen	50	--	--	1	5.0.0
Jones, Edward	160	--	2	4	15.0.0
John, Evan	--	--	--	1	5.0.0
Irwin, Arthur	100	--	3	3	15.0.0
Jameson, Enos	--	--	--	2	7.10.0
Johnston, James	--	--	--	--	5.0.0
Kirk, William	30	--	2	3	18.0.0
Kirk, Timothy, Jun'r	12	--	--	1	10.0.0
Kirk, Timothy	100	--	1	4	160.0.0
Kirk, Ezechiel	--	--	1	1	3.0.0
Kirk, Jonathan	--	--	--	--	15.0.0
Kirk, Jacob	95	--	2	3	25.0.0
Kister, George	--	--	--	--	15.0.0
Knertzer, Balzer	--	--	--	--	80.0.0
Keppler, Jacob	130	--	2	1	33.10.0
Kepler, Samuel	--	--	--	--	120.0.0
Kern, Michael	300	--	2	3	25.0.0
Kister, Henry	--	--	2	3	50.0.0
Kern, Michael	--	--	--	--	5.0.0
Lenhard, George	400	--	--	--	--
Lewis, Samuel, renter	150	--	2	3	45.0.0
Laird, Hugh	150	--	2	4	35.0.0
Love, James	300	--	1	--	75.0.0
Logan, James	--	--	2	5	12.10.0
Love, Samuel	--	--	--	--	37.10.0

Newberry Township	Acres	Negroes	Horses	Cattle	Tax
Lewis, Ellis	200	--	3	6	240.0.0
Lewis, Ely	--	--	--	--	40.0.0
Lewis, Wm.,	150	--	--	--	40.0.0
Logan, John	--	--	--	--	8.10.0
Love, William	60	--	--	--	162.10.0
Martin, Andrew	196	--	3	4	37.10.0
Moore, Anthony	120	--	1	2	33.0.0
Michael, William	200	--	3	2	40.0.0
Maulsby, Rosannah	70	--	2	2	5.0.0
McHenry, Daniel	143	--	--	2	3.0.0
McDearmond, William	--	--	2	1	--
McConnell, James	58	--	2	2	10.0.0
Maxwell, Conrad	74	--	--	2	10.0.0
Miller, Samuel	--	--	--	--	12.0.0
Mathews, William	70	--	3	4	200.0.0
McNees, Isaiah	150	--	1	2	3.0.0
McKiesh, George	200	--	1	2	25.0.0
Miller, Henry	200	--	2	4	100.0.0
McCreary, Jonathan	100	--	--	--	20.0.0
Miller, Robert	--	--	--	--	100.0.0
Meyer, George	230	--	2	3	50.0.0
McNealy, William	50	--	3	1	10.0.0
Mansberger, George	100	--	2	3	15.0.0
Mansberger, John	150	--	1	2	12.10.0
Meyers, Catharine	100	--	--	1	5.0.0
Mills, James	50	--	2	3	100.0.0
Morgan, Thomas	20	--	--	1	3.0.0
Murphy, Isaac	--	--	2	2	--
Miller, Robert	100	--	2	3	50.0.0
McAdams, Tho's	--	--	--	1	10.0.0
McMaster, John	--	--	--	--	22.10.0
Maulsby, Wm.	200	--	2	3	166.0.0
Mills, John	50	--	2	2	40.0.0
McQuire, Nathan	--	--	1	1	50.0.0
McGinnis, Samuel	--	--	2	--	--
Myer, Peter	10	--	--	1	20.0.0
Miller, Adam	--	--	--	1	--
Miller, George	220	--	2	3	55.0.0
Miller, Andrew	30	--	1	1	20.0.0
Myer, Jacob	--	--	--	--	6.0.0
Mathias, Henry	161 1/2	--	2	4	45.0.0
McConnell, Rob't	--	--	--	--	10.0.0
Maxwell, John	--	--	--	--	10.0.0
Mullen, Patrick	--	--	--	--	10.0.0
Nailer, Elizabeth	200	--	3	4	25.0.0
Nossett, Peter	--	--	--	--	10.0.0
Noblet, Agnes	--	--	--	--	12.10.0
Norbury, Jacob	--	--	--	--	56.0.0
Nichols, John	300	--	3	3	130.0.0
Noblet and Armor	--	--	--	--	25.0.0
Pike, Isaac	60	--	2	2	15.0.0
Pollinger, Peter	50	--	1	2	20.0.0
Prunch, John	175	--	1	8	250.0.0
Pentz, Philip	--	--	2	--	3.0.0
Plow, John	140	--	2	3	80.0.0

Newberry Township	Acres	Negroes	Horses	Cattle	Tax
Pike, John	--	--	--	--	132.0.0
Pearson, Mary	300	--	--	--	--
Pollinger, Mica'l	--	--	3	2	5.0.0
Philips, George	100	--	2	3	33.0.0
Plucket, William	--	--	--	--	60.0.0
Rumbo, Moses	200	--	--	--	10.0.0
Randalls, William, Se'r	44	--	2	2	5.0.0
Randalls, William, Ju'r	50	--	--	1	5.0.0
Rigg, Clement	100	--	2	4	15.0.0
Reiff, Jacob	100	--	2	3	300.0.0
Reiff, Jacob	--	--	--	--	5.0.0
Rankin, John	260	--	3	4	20.0.0
Robinson, George	--	--	--	2	15.0.0
Rogers, Laban	--	--	--	1	5.0.0
Richmond, John	70	--	2	2	30.0.0
Ross, John	--	--	1	2	5.0.0
Rogers, Ellis	--	--	--	--	12.0.0
Rankin, William	--	--	--	--	50.0.0
Rothenheiser, John	--	--	--	1	--
Robert, Jacob	70	--	2	3	15.0.0
Shetter, John	200	--	2	4	60.0.0
Shetter, Jacob	--	--	--	1	--
Shetter, Martin	170	--	3	4	80.0.0
Spade, John	100	--	2	--	15.0.0
Strein, Adam	--	--	2	3	50.0.0
Stoner, Frederick	154	--	3	6	100.0.0
Snyder, George	161 1/2	--	2	2	42.0.0
Sehlers, Peter	--	--	--	--	5.0.0
Stair, John	196	--	2	2	15.0.0
Shannon, James	--	--	--	1	10.0.0
Schuler, Christian	100	--	1	2	30.0.0
Smith, James	50	--	2	2	30.0.0
Scheffer, Henry	--	--	--	3	3.0.0
Sower, Andrew	80	--	2	3	33.0.0
Snyder, Jacob	80	--	2	2	40.0.0
Schreiner, William	135	--	--	2	7.10.0
Strein, George	155	--	2	3	55.0.0
Schultz, Valentine	30	--	1	1	20.0.0
Schelly, Abraham	100	--	1	--	10.0.0
Schettrone, Casper	--	--	1	2	5.0.0
Salgrove, James	54	--	2	1	7.10.0
Shenck, Christian	4	--	--	1	10.0.0
Schultz, Thomas	80	--	--	--	--
Scarlet, William	--	--	1	1	10.0.0
Stall, Jesse	--	--	--	--	--
Staley, Malachia	--	--	5	4	75.0.0
Spurr, Leonard	--	--	--	1	3.0.0
Slane, Daniel	--	--	2	2	79.0.0
Sier, Albright	--	--	--	1	15.0.0
Shoeman, John	250	--	--	--	166.0.0
Stoner, Christian	--	--	--	--	--
Spence, George	--	--	--	1	5.0.0
Sayres, James	470	--	3	6	40.0.0
Sharp, James	170	--	3	6	40.0.0
Ditto for Westm. co.	300	--	--	--	--

Newberry Township	Acres	Negroes	Horses	Cattle	Tax
Tate, Jacob	200	--	2	3	120.0.0
Tate, Isaac	--	--	--	--	5.0.0
Tate, Solomon	--	--	--	--	5.0.0
Thomas, Nathan	120	--	2	2	30.0.0
Todd, James	100	--	2	3	40.0.0
Toland, James	100	--	2	2	10.0.0
Thoreley, George, Sen'r	152	--	1	1	--
Thorely, William	--	--	2	2	30.0.0
Terr, John	100	--	2	2	15.0.0
Taylor, Joseph	50	--	1	2	12.10.0
Thoreley, Abraham	150	--	1	2	37.10.0
Thoreley, George, Jun'r	175	--	2	4	30.0.0
Tentzel, John	50	--	2	2	5.0.0
Tentzel, Daniel	--	--	--	--	5.0.0
Travillea, Ja's	--	--	--	--	10.0.0
Thornbrough, Robert	--	--	--	--	--
Takery, Thomas	--	--	--	--	10.0.0
Updegraff, Derick	110	--	4	4	80.0.0
Updegraff, Herman	10	--	1	2	5.0.0
Underwood, Zephaniah	--	--	2	1	10.0.0
Varnon, Aaron	--	--	--	--	10.0.0
Vore, Peter	--	--	--	--	30.0.0
Wright, Aaron	--	--	--	--	--
William, Hezekiah	--	--	2	2	10.0.0
Watkins, Thomas	--	--	1	1	--
West, Charles	100	--	1	1	10.0.0
West, Thomas	--	--	1	--	5.0.0
Wilson, William	65	--	2	3	20.0.0
Wilson, John	50	--	1	1	6.0.0
Wall, Absolom	50	--	1	1	12.0.0
Whinnery, Robert	50	--	--	1	40.0.0
Whinnery, William	--	--	2	1	5.0.0
Whinnery, Thomas	--	--	1	4	60.0.0
Wagner, Jacob	--	--	2	3	5.0.0
Welsh, James	300	--	3	5	75.0.0
Welsh, Andrew	--	--	--	--	5.0.0
Waron, David	--	--	--	--	25.0.0
Warren, Thomas	--	--	--	--	25.0.0
Wilt, Sebastian	--	--	--	--	7.10.0
Webb, John	50	--	2	3	65.0.0
Wilson, Alexander	--	--	1	1	--
Willis, Richard	120	--	2	3	80.0.0
Willis, William	80	--	2	1	100.0.0
Wickersham, James	130	--	--	1	20.0.0
Wickersham, Jesse	130	--	--	--	40.0.0
Welsh, Gerrard	--	--	2	--	5.0.0
Welsh, Margaret	50	--	--	2	10.0.0
Weyer, John	--	--	--	2	10.0.0
Weyer, Ludwig	100	--	2	3	20.0.0
Wilt, Peter	80	--	2	3	20.0.0
Wohlgemuth, Henry	--	--	2	2	50.0.0
Wilson, William	--	--	--	--	--
Wressler, Mathias	--	--	2	2	70.0.0
Yarnell, Jesse	--	--	--	--	8.0.0
Conelly, Hugh	--	--	--	--	--

Newberry Township	Acres	Negroes	Horses	Cattle	Tax
Myar, Peter	--	--	--	--	20.0.0
Zorger, Frederick	150	--	2	3	32.10.0
Lewis, Robert	--	--	--	--	100.0.0
Lewis, Lewis	--	--	--	--	10.0.0
Lewis, John	--	--	--	--	15.0.0
Michael, Wilhelm	--	--	--	--	2.5.0
McCready, John	--	--	--	--	15.0.0
Rambow, Wm.	--	--	--	--	16.0.0
Richards, Samuel	--	--	--	--	50.0.0
Roads, Peter	--	--	--	--	50.0.0
Richardson, on Millstone mountain	--	--	--	--	50.0.0
Sear, Halbert	--	--	--	--	10.0.0
Stewart, Robert	--	--	--	--	15.0.0
Todd, Joseph	--	--	--	--	30.0.0
Warton, Tho's, deceased	--	--	--	--	50.0.0
Welsh, Joseph	--	--	--	--	15.0.0
Weaver, Adam	--	--	--	--	10.0.0

WINDSOR TOWNSHIP

	Acres	Negroes	Horses	Cattle	Tax
Able, George	88	--	2	3	12.12.6
Able, John	--	--	--	--	15.0.0
Albright, Henry	--	--	--	2	3.0.0
Attick, George	200	--	3	6	31.4.0
Asdil, Aaron	50	--	1	3	3.7.2
Allison, William	100	--	2	2	21.0.4
Bradley, William	--	--	1	1	3.0.8
Bengel, Leonard	176	--	2	2	21.0.4
Boyer, Jacob	--	--	2	2	5.19.2
Beaver, Jacob	180	--	2	4	37.1.0
Becker, Nicholas	85	--	2	2	8.15.6
Becker, Frederick	--	--	--	--	2.5.0
Bartley, Widow	70	--	2	1	8.19.10
Brubacher, Conrad	150	--	2	2	103.15.0
Beaner, Fite	196	--	2	4	60.0.0
Blouse, John	160	--	--	4	12.0.0
Bodine, John	--	--	--	1	--
Boyer, Philip	76	--	2	3	90.0.0
Bair, John, at the river	122	--	1	3	179.3.8
Baymiller, Michael	--	--	2	2	4.11.0
Beanor, George	--	--	--	--	4.11.0
Bair, John, at the river	70	--	--	--	5.12.8
Cline, Peter	--	--	3	5	6.0.2
Caylor, Martin	170	--	1	5	26.19.6
Cemerly, Jacob	67	--	2	3	7.10.0
Croan, John	135	--	4	5	35.4.0
Christy, Samuel	--	--	1	1	2.5.6
Cellor, Anthony	70	--	2	2	20.11.8
Coarman, Michael	--	--	--	--	--
Caufelt, Michael	51	--	2	2	23.10.0
Cage, John	--	--	1	1	2.5.6

Windsor Township	Acres	Negroes	Horses	Cattle	Tax
Cross, Widow	106	--	1	1	5.0.0
Cross, Randle	--	--	--	1	10.0.0
Cross, John	66	--	--	--	10.0.0
Cross, James	--	--	--	--	15.0.0
Conner, Thomas	--	--	--	1	2.5.6
Collingwood, Richard	236	--	2	1	15.18.8
Carman, Philip	--	--	--	1	--
Day, Nicholas	--	--	4	5	9.15.0
Day, Jacob	--	--	--	--	12.0.0
Donoughah, John	--	--	--	2	2.5.6
Dellinger, Jacob	100	--	2	2	14.5.10
Dellinger, John	105	--	2	1	12.9.2
Dellinger, Joseph	100	--	--	--	8.2.6
Davis, Hugh	--	--	--	--	20.0.0
Eady, Bastian	150	--	2	2	132.7.8
Eady, Frederich	--	--	--	--	10.0.0
Ellenberger, Ulrich	150	--	2	4	59.11.8
Eaby, John	149	--	2	4	23.16.8
Eiler, Peter	90	--	1	3	9.0.7
Emenheiser, Adam	120	--	2	3	16.7.6
Emenheiser, John	--	--	--	1	3.0.8
Fister, Jacob	95	--	2	4	15.13.0
Eason, Archibald	--	--	1	1	2.2.8
Fersith, John	--	--	1	--	12.0.0
Fry, John	80	--	--	--	14.1.8
Fry, Barnet	108	--	2	3	13.10.10
Fry, Peter	54	--	--	2	7.11.2
Fry, Conrad	66	--	1	2	9.4.8
Fits, Frederick	123	--	1	4	14.0.0
Fry, Philip	--	--	--	2	2.17.5
Foster, Fidelis	150	--	2	3	16.7.2
Fry, Frederick	50	--	2	2	7.3.0
Forsythe, Nathaniel	100	--	3	5	99.6.10
Goss, George	--	--	1	3	2.5.6
Goss, John	--	--	--	2	2.6.3
Gilbert, Andrew	124	--	2	3	16.15.6
Good, David	50	--	1	2	6.8.1
Gollougher, Abraham	100	--	1	1	17.17.6
Gyger, Widow	172	--	2	1	5.18.0
Gyger, Paul	--	--	--	--	10.0.0
Gohn, Philip	--	--	--	--	15.0.0
Gonston, Robert	--	--	--	1	2.5.6
Gohn, Philip	--	--	1	3	6.6.0
Gohn, Adam	--	--	1	3	3.10.8
Gohn, Widow	152	--	--	2	20.18.4
Good, David	150	--	1	3	16.5.0
Griffith, John	--	--	1	1	15.0.0
Gruber, Godfrey	--	--	--	1	2.5.6
Grove, Francis	100	--	2	3	6.10.0
To land	--	--	--	--	86.13.4
Gyger, Conrad	--	--	--	--	10.0.0
Good, John	--	--	--	--	10.0.0
Garnor, George	--	--	1	1	3.0.8
Hindle, Laurence	--	--	--	--	10.0.0
Heckendorn, John	180	--	--	4	15.0.0

Windsor Township	Acres	Negroes	Horses	Cattle	Tax
Herkins, Daniel	140	--	4	5	62.5.10
Hinds, Anthony	50	--	2	6	10.16.8
Hinds, James	100	--	2	4	10.16.8
Hartman, Henry	100	--	2	2	13.13.0
Holder, Michael	138	--	2	4	55.5.0
Herman, Dewalt	--	--	--	1	1.1.8
Helsel, Henry	183	--	--	4	3.0.0
Hindle, Adam	210	--	2	7	28.5.6
Hindle, Adam	--	--	--	--	10.0.0
Henry, Michael	100	--	2	3	17.6.8
Henry, Michael	--	--	1	--	10.0.0
Houseman, Christian	--	--	--	--	20.0.0
Hersinger, Widow	212	--	3	3	40.5.6
Houseman, Jacob	--	--	--	--	2.0.0
Hindle, Stophel	125	--	3	6	18.15.7
Hamer, Frederick	--	--	1	3	2.5.6
Hermal, Craft	160	--	--	1	10.6.6
Helsel, Jacob	--	--	--	--	15.0.0
Hersinger, Widow	53	--	--	--	1.3.0
Henderson, Alexander	--	--	2	1	12.4.8
Herkins, Daniel	95	--	--	--	15.14.2
Leaphard, John	100	--	1	4	15.6.8
Lefever, George	250	--	3	3	62.3.8
Lever, Jacob	117	--	2	2	14.8.8
Lever, Conrad	--	--	--	--	15.0.0
Lampert, Frederick	50	--	--	1	6.1.4
Landis, Samuel	206	--	3	9	57.4.3
Lever, Nicholas	--	--	--	--	15.0.0
Landis, Christian	300	--	2	3	138.9.9
Landis, Christian, Ju'r	--	--	2	3	3.7.2
Landis, Samuel, Ju'r	--	--	2	3	3.18.0
Lantz, Andrew	100	--	1	3	26.17.4
Liggit, Widow	50	--	1	1	7.1.7
Liggit, Wm.	50	--	1	--	40.0.0
Leverknight, Frederick	40	--	--	3	6.18.0
Lantz, Philip	114	--	2	4	19.1.4
Lookup, Conrad	--	--	--	--	10.0.0
Liggit, George	--	--	--	1	14.11.0
Liggitt, Joseph	50	--	--	--	40.0.0
Lear, Conrad	--	--	--	2	2.5.6
Landis, John	--	--	3	3	6.8.4
Lutz, Christian	--	--	2	1	2.5.6
Lamberd, Michael	--	--	2	1	2.14.2
Land of John Strickler	300	--	--	--	16.17.8
Lever, John	--	--	--	--	15.0.0
Lutz, Widow	145	--	--	3	5.0.0
Myers, Henry	--	--	1	2	2.12.0
McGlaughlen, Owens	--	--	--	1	2.5.6
Maxfield, George	--	--	2	2	3.9.4
Miller, George	--	--	--	1	1.1.8
Myer, John	80	--	2	4	21.4.3
Morrow, George	281	--	3	4	34.7.10
McKisson, John	300	--	4	4	30.1.0
Manson, David	--	--	--	--	2.5.6
Miller, Michael	160	--	2	5	21.2.6

Windsor Township	Acres	Negroes	Horses	Cattle	Tax
McCoy, John	200	--	2	2	12.13.6
Maness, Charles	20	--	--	1	2.5.6
Morrow, Joseph	--	--	1	--	15.0.0
Milhoff, Philip	174	--	2	5	29.7.2
McGarrough, Henry	50	--	2	4	8.1.4
Moser, Abraham	140	--	1	2	20.7.7
McGavock, James	226	--	2	3	14.2.3
McNeary, James	200	--	2	1	25.7.8
McElroy, James	--	--	--	1	1.1.8
Murphy, James	--	--	--	1	1.0.0
McComb, George	100	--	2	2	23.16.8
Myers, Jacob	--	--	3	1	5.14.0
Miller Rudy	172	--	3	4	24.5.3
Miller, Henry	--	--	--	--	10.0.0
McHolland, John	--	--	--	1	1.1.8
Myers, Jacob	118	--	--	--	116.0.0
Oberdorf, George	100	--	--	1	6.5.11
Oulwiler, Jacob	30	--	1	2	8.15.6
Neaf, Jacob	--	--	--	1	2.5.6
Nicholson, James	--	--	--	--	2.5.6
Page, Nathaniel	150	--	2	3	38.16.0
Paulus, Adam	215	--	2	5	45.10.0
Poff, George	129	--	2	2	14.18.0
Peters, Christopher	--	--	1	1	3.0.8
Peterman, John	--	--	--	--	15.0.0
Peterman, Daniel	--	--	1	--	15.0.0
Peterman, Widow	200	--	--	1	15.13.4
Peterman, Michael	150	--	3	4	24.7.6
Pence, Nicholas	140	--	--	2	13.2.2
Paulus, Laurence	119	--	2	4	21.13.4
Rogers, Linens	--	--	1	1	6.1.4
Renberger, Henry	50	--	--	--	7.11.8
Ruby, Henry	--	--	3	3	8.0.4
Ruby, Widow	226	--	1	2	100.0.0
Raffsneider, Ernst	132	--	4	5	26.0.0
Rey, Joseph	85	--	--	1	8.9.6
Ruby, Widow	100	--	--	--	8.2.6
Rider, Daniel	15	--	--	1	2.5.6
Rider, Lawrence	174	--	3	4	25.3.4
Rinehart, George	75	--	--	2	2.5.6
To land	--	--	--	--	6.1.4
Reisinger, Peter	149	--	3	7	28.3.4
Raup, Peter	94	--	2	4	11.7.6
Ruby, Jacob	--	--	2	3	--
Roberson, John	--	--	--	--	10.0.0
Roberson, Tho's	80	--	1	--	20.0.0
Russel, John	--	--	1	1	1.1.8
Rathfang, Christian	100	--	3	6	136.5.8
Readyer, Augustus	--	--	--	--	1.1.8
Shafer, Samuel	--	--	--	--	40.0.0
Scantlin, Adam	--	--	--	1	1.1.8
Shanberger, John	200	--	1	1	73.6.11
Step, Peter	--	--	--	2	1.1.8
Simmerman, Michael	123	--	4	3	25.4.10
Smith, John	80	--	2	3	16.5.0

Windsor Township	Acres	Negroes	Horses	Cattle	Tax
Simson, John	--	--	--	1	--
Smith, Ludwig	105	--	2	2	13.13.10
Shafer, Paul	285	--	1	3	55.4.11
Strawmonger, Jacob	100	--	2	2	11.9.0
Strite, David	--	--	1	2	6.12.2
Sealis, John	--	--	--	3	1.6.8
Stagner, Jacob	140	--	2	3	19.18.9
Sayler, Henry	40	--	--	1	7.3.0
Shanberger, Balzer	150	--	1	3	25.10.2
Schmuck, John	108	--	2	5	17.6.8
Sayler, Ulry	--	--	2	1	2.5.1
Secatz, Peter	160	--	1	2	23.0.0
Shew, William	--	--	--	--	1.1.8
Saylor, Christian	315	--	2	2	32.10.0
Sigler, John Michael	--	--	1	2	2.5.6
Smelser, Philip	235	--	1	2	26.16.6
Shafer, Henry	90	--	2	3	17.6.8
Schmuck, John	58	--	--	--	6.5.8
Shafer, Stophel	140	--	2	5	20.0.10
Slifer, Peter	--	--	2	2	--
Slifer, Stophen	--	--	2	2	4.19.8
Slanker, Andrew	135	--	2	4	38.6.8
Stuart, William	133	--	2	3	16.3.0
Stuart, Robert	150	--	3	2	15.0.0
Scott, Archibald	400	--	3	5	50.0.0
Sigler, Michael	--	--	2	3	3.18.8
Smith, George	150	--	--	--	17.6.8
Siler, Bartley	--	--	1	2	3.1.5
Strouce, Michael	--	--	2	--	--
Scott, Moses	180	--	2	2	24.1.0
Skear, John	--	--	1	2	2.6.3
Steas, Philip	50	--	2	2	61.4.2
Sinkey, Ezeckiel	--	--	--	--	15.0.0
Schlemer, Peter	45	--	2	1	7.5.8
Tritt, Peter	--	--	--	2	2.0.0
Tritt, Jacob	138	--	1	3	149.12.2
Lands of James Strong	15	--	--	--	1.12.6
Tush, Michael	50	--	3	3	45.10.0
Tyson, Henry	214	--	3	4	66.19.0
Tyson, Benjamin	200	--	1	3	36.16.8
Tickert, Henry	130	--	1	2	11.18.4
Trump, Casper	--	--	1	3	2.5.6
Tice, George	100	--	2	3	14.1.8
Vambach, Michael	66	--	1	1	7.5.0
Vambach, Peter	151	--	2	2	14.4.0
Vambach, George	178	--	2	4	22.15.0
Vambach, Philip	--	--	--	--	10.0.0
Urt, Melchior	100	--	2	2	14.10.4
Imsweller, Peter	129	--	--	3	13.0.0
Imseller, Jacob	--	--	--	--	15.0.0
John, John	130	--	2	2	15.16.4
Jones, Richard	146	--	1	2	13.10.4
Wolf, Henry	95	--	2	2	13.13.6
Williams, Joseph	--	--	--	1	2.5.6
Wolpack, George	190	--	2	4	15.12.0

Windsor Township	Acres	Negroes	Horses	Cattle	Tax
Weber, Ulrick	130	--	1	2	25.1.0
Will, John	86	--	1	3	11.7.6
Wiant, David	--	--	--	2	3.0.8
Wisman, Godlieb	--	--	1	3	3.5.0
Winter, Peter	50	--	--	1	3.5.0
Wachtel, George	89	--	1	1	10.8.0
Weltner, John	--	--	5	3	9.10.8
Williams, Benjamin	--	--	--	1	1.1.8
Young, Abraham	63	--	1	5	13.6.6
Young, William	40	--	2	2	6.2.6
Young, Nicholas	200	--	3	5	43.6.8
Young, Nicholas	200	--	--	--	26.3.4
Kecheries, Christian	11	--	--	--	12.4.10
Marks, Gastner	--	--	--	--	12.4.10
Reingey, Antony	--	--	--	--	13.0.0
Clough, Charles	--	--	--	--	8.13.4
Arb, Jacob	--	--	--	--	135.7.4
Tush, George	--	--	--	--	374.8.0
Bair, Henry	--	--	--	--	130.0.0
Land Christian Sailer lives on	--	--	--	--	14.12.6
Douglass, Wm.	--	--	--	--	5.8.4
Gick, Balzer	--	--	--	--	8.12.0
Wineholt, George	--	--	--	--	16.5.0
Bryson, Andrew	--	--	--	--	15.0.0
Keiser, George	--	--	--	--	15.0.0
Sheffer, Henry	--	--	--	--	10.0.0

TYRONE TOWNSHIP

	Acres	Negroes	Horses	Cattle	Tax
Brown, Alexander	202	2	5	7	106.0.0
Blackburn, John	250	--	6	4	85.0.0
Blackburn, Ja's	--	--	--	1	--
Bower, Michael	--	--	2	1	8.10.0
Braim, Henry	100	--	1	2	62.10.0
Cooper, William	222	--	--	--	60.0.0
Clyne, Adam	200	--	2	3	30.0.0
Chambers, Joseph	424	--	--	--	90.0.0
Duffield, George	296 1/2	--	5	3	90.0.0
Dodds, John	250	--	3	2	50.0.0
Delap, William	500	--	5	4	231.0.0
Delap, John	--	--	--	--	5.0.0
Delap, Robert	--	--	3	2	15.10.0
English, Wm.	--	--	--	--	10.0.0
Elliot, James	196 1/2	--	3	3	50.0.0
Elliot, Widow	200	--	3	1	40.0.0
Elliot, John	--	--	4	2	14.5.0
Elliot, Wm.	--	--	--	--	10.0.0
Elliot, Oliver	--	--	--	1	12.10.0
Fullerton, Robert	--	--	3	3	7.10.0
Fullerton, Rob't	--	--	--	--	12.10.0
Fidler, Philip	209	--	4	3	153.5.0

Tyrone Township	Acres	Negroes	Horses	Cattle	Tax
Gallagher, Charles	80	--	1	1	20.0.0
Gallagher, Barney	--	--	--	2	--
Gallagher, James	--	--	2	2	8.0.0
Gallagher, Thomas	--	--	--	--	20.0.0
Gallagher, Wm.	--	--	--	--	10.0.0
Griffith, John	100	--	4	2	79.5.0
Herman, John	--	--	2	1	7.0.0
Hutton, John	80	--	3	2	50.0.0
Hammon, James	150	--	4	1	83.10.0
Job, John	--	--	1	--	--
Hammers, John	200	--	2	2	109.15.0
King, William	247	--	2	2	90.0.0
King, John	283	--	3	1	75.0.0
Knox, Ja's	--	--	--	1	7.10.0
Larimor, Hugh	--	--	2	1	--
Leech, James	60	--	4	3	15.0.0
Leech, Robert	--	--	--	--	5.0.0
Leech, Henry	--	--	--	--	10.0.0
Meenich, Jacob	150	--	2	1	45.0.0
Meenich, Jacob, Ju'r	--	--	2	--	2.0.0
McGrew, Alexander	200	--	7	3	134.0.0
McGrew, Finley	100	--	2	2	77.5.0
McGrew, Peter	--	--	1	--	1.0.0
McNight, Tho's	151 1/2	--	2	2	50.0.0
McCrue, Nathan	80	--	1	2	66.10.0
McKnight, John	151 1/2	--	3	3	50.0.0
Mate, George	240	--	7	5	188.10.0
Mate, William	--	--	--	--	20.0.0
Miller, Peter	100	--	5	3	69.10.0
McCall, Thomas	221 1/2	--	4	3	75.0.0
Maxwel, Henry	--	--	3	1	4.10.0
Mickle, Samuel	170	--	1	2	50.0.0
Mordach, Robert	278	--	5	4	70.0.0
Mordach, Mathew	--	--	--	--	5.0.0
Maxwel, John, Sen'r	100	--	4	3	10.0.0
Maxwel, John, Jun'r	--	--	--	1	6.10.0
Maxwel, James	100	--	5	3	96.0.0
Maxwel, James	--	--	--	--	7.10.0
Neel, Samuel	--	--	3	2	4.0.0
Neely, Widow	399	--	9	5	100.0.0
Neely, Samuel	218	--	3	2	75.0.0
Neely, William	196 1/2	--	1	3	60.0.0
Neff, Michael	--	--	2	--	2.0.0
Neely, Jonathan	200	--	--	--	20.0.0
Orr, Author	150	--	5	4	49.10.0
Prior, Thomas	--	--	1	--	1.0.0
Petty, John	--	--	--	--	7.10.0
Porter, Thomas	--	--	2	2	5.0.0
Porter, William	150	--	6	4	49.15.0
Porter, Samuel	--	--	1	1	10.0.0
Pope, John	250	--	4	3	75.0.0
Ray, Robert	302	--	3	3	50.0.0
Reed, James	80	--	8	3	45.15.0
Reed, John	100	--	3	4	55.0.0
Richey, Mathew	318	--	7	6	100.0.0

Tyrone Township	Acres	Negroes	Horses	Cattle	Tax
Richey, John	--	--	--	1	10.0.0
Say, John	--	--	1	1	3.0.0
Simotten, John	--	--	--	--	3.0.0
Snyder, John	--	--	2	1	7.5.0
Sitesinger, Leonard	--	--	2	1	20.0.0
Smith, William	--	--	--	--	6.0.0
Spare, John	50	--	4	2	17.15.0
Spangler, Peter, Switzer	100	--	3	2	68.15.0
Switzer, Anthony	140	--	4	4	92.15.0
Titrich, Nicholas	288	--	9	7	100.0.0
Titrich, Baltzer	--	--	--	1	5.0.0
Wilson, John	191	--	3	2	60.0.0
Walker, William	466 1/2	--	7	5	125.0.0
White, John	100	--	8	4	45.0.0
Walker, Joseph	500	--	5	4	125.0.0
Walker, Samuel	--	--	3	2	6.10.0
Walker, James	191	--	6	3	70.0.0
McGaw, John	--	--	--	--	12.10.0
Smith, James	--	--	--	--	4.0.0

HOPEWELL TOWNSHIP

	Acres	Negroes	Horses	Cattle	Tax
Blasser, Abraham	200	--	3	6	40.0.0
Brown, Andrew	45	--	3	1	13.0.0
Reed, Adam	--	--	1	2	12.10.0
Craighten, Alexander	50	--	--	--	25.0.0
Moore, Alexander	100	--	2	1	25.0.0
Slone, Andrew	--	--	--	1	10.0.0
Ramsey, Alexander	80	--	2	2	42.10.0
Thompson, Andrew	50	--	2	2	50.0.0
Shinard, Abraham	50	--	2	2	30.0.0
And to Crosses land	100	--	--	--	--
Fulton, Andrew	261	--	3	6	33.0.0
Proudfoot, Andrew	210	--	3	7	35.0.0
Osburn, Alexander	100	--	1	2	37.10.0
Liggit, Alexander	50	--	1	1	22.10.0
Finley, Andrew	100	--	1	1	40.0.0
Allison, Alexander	330	--	4	6	45.0.0
Duncan, Andrew	--	--	--	--	35.0.0
Smith, Alexander	--	--	--	--	7.10.0
Manifold, Benjamin	25	--	1	1	27.10.0
Lowrey, Conrad	50	--	1	1	21.0.0
Blinmyer, Christopher	150	--	1	3	37.0.0
Stevenson, Charles	--	--	--	--	15.0.0
Evey, Christian	100	--	1	2	42.10.0
Wishart, Christopher	--	--	1	--	18.0.0
Hoy, Charles	--	--	2	1	15.0.0
Proudfoot, David	48	--	2	2	32.10.0
Lathan, David	--	--	--	--	6.0.0
Miller, Daniel	130	--	--	1	12.10.0
Fulton, David	50	--	1	1	35.0.0
Griffith, David	179	--	3	3	25.0.0

Hopewell Township	Acres	Negroes	Horses	Cattle	Tax
Anderson, David	170	--	2	2	27.0.0
Wiley, David	150	--	2	2	42.0.0
Jameson, David	--	--	1	1	15.0.0
Stone, David	--	--	1	1	15.0.0
Gemmil, David	100	--	2	2	26.0.0
Divine, Daniel	--	--	1	--	6.0.0
Kennedy, David	50	--	2	2	35.0.0
Fuget, Edward, Maryland	--	--	--	--	12.10.0
Griffith, Evan	30	--	1	--	23.0.0
Pugh, Elisha	30	--	1	1	15.0.0
Richey, Elijah	100	--	1	1	25.0.0
Pain, Elizabeth	30	--	1	1	1.2.6
Sicrist, Francis	100	--	1	2	26.0.0
Sadler, Frederick	100	--	--	1	24.0.0
Swartz, Frederick, Lancaster	50	--	--	--	7.10.0
Bross, Frederick	20	--	--	--	7.10.0
Delong, George	--	--	1	1	15.0.0
Gasper, Clemer	144	--	1	2	18.0.0
Householder, Henry	100	--	2	3	22.10.0
McClorge, Hugh	--	--	1	1	10.0.0
Cunningham, Henry	50	--	1	2	15.0.0
Galagher, Hugh	--	--	--	--	18.0.0
Stair, Henry	--	--	--	--	18.0.0
Weast, Henry	100	--	1	2	36.0.0
Cornelius, John	50	--	1	--	21.0.0
Noland, Joseph	--	--	--	--	18.0.0
Griffith, Evan	--	--	--	--	7.10.0
Leaper, James	263	--	2	3	24.0.0
Cornelius, Justa	40	--	--	2	15.0.0
Sheldon, James	--	--	--	--	10.0.0
Laird, John	--	--	1	--	18.0.0
Blasser, John	150	--	2	5	35.0.0
Kesey, John	--	--	--	--	15.0.0
Griffith, John	--	--	--	--	18.0.0
Purdy, James	100	--	--	2	10.10.0
Steel, James	--	--	--	--	18.0.0
Nelson, John	--	--	2	3	18.0.0
Travis, John	190	--	2	2	30.0.0
Householder, Jacob	50	--	1	2	22.10.0
McAllisters, James	30	--	1	1	15.0.0
St. Clair, James	100	--	--	--	10.0.0
Fisterland, Jacob	63	--	--	--	10.0.0
Griffith, John	50	--	1	2	35.0.0
Smith, Joseph	100	--	1	2	35.0.0
Smith, John, Sen'r	--	--	--	--	10.0.0
Adams, John	--	--	1	3	16.10.0
Smith, James	100	--	1	3	37.10.0
Smith, James	--	--	--	--	18.0.0
Smith, John	--	--	--	--	18.0.0
Smith, John, curly	50	--	1	1	27.10.0
McDonnel, James	50	--	2	4	35.0.0
Easting, Jacob	252	--	1	2	22.10.0
Young, James	--	--	1	1	10.0.0
Weldon, Jacob	--	--	2	1	12.0.0

Hopewell Township	Acres	Negroes	Horses	Cattle	Tax
Shearer, Jacob	80	--	2	2	25.0.0
Yont, Jacob	--	--	--	--	24.0.0
Carswell, James	100	--	2	4	35.0.0
Muphet, James	222	--	1	4	38.10.0
Shearer, John	50	--	1	1	--
Sadler, Jacob	50	--	1	2	27.10.0
Alt, Jacob	30	--	1	1	12.10.0
Gordon, John	250	--	2	2	40.0.0
Orr, John	150	--	2	3	38.0.0
Buchannon, John	--	--	1	1	15.0.0
Anderson, James	100	--	2	5	35.0.0
Anderson, James	--	--	1	--	21.0.0
Anderson, John	--	--	1	--	20.0.0
Anderson, John	--	--	1	3	35.10.0
Mickel, John	--	--	--	--	18.0.0
Herring, John	100	--	1	3	22.10.0
Harper, James	50	--	1	3	36.10.0
Gemmil, John	40	--	1	1	32.10.0
Wilson, John	124	--	2	2	24.0.0
Shinard, John	50	--	1	--	23.0.0
Manifold, Joseph	50	--	2	2	37.10.0
McCollough, John	--	--	--	1	15.0.0
McKatrick, John	--	--	1	1	12.0.0
Miller, John	--	--	1	2	25.0.0
Cross, John	30	--	3	2	33.10.0
McIsaac, Isaac	50	--	1	1	28.0.0
Marshall, Isaac	100	--	2	3	30.0.0
Meads, John	--	--	--	2	10.0.0
Hutcheson, James	--	--	1	1	15.0.0
Shavour, Jacob	150	--	2	3	32.10.0
Richey, John, Sen'r	50	--	2	2	35.0.0
Richey, John	--	--	--	--	10.0.0
Gibson, John	200	--	2	2	40.0.0
Montgomery, John	100	--	1	2	32.10.0
Reaney, John	--	--	1	2	12.10.0
McGlaughlin, James	--	--	2	2	18.0.0
Mitchel, John, land in Lancaster	100	--	--	--	12.10.0
Duncan, John	100	--	2	2	35.0.0
Rush, Jane	--	--	1	1	--
Wilson, James	50	--	1	2	35.0.0
McClary, John	263	--	2	2	25.0.0
McSwine, James	100	--	--	--	15.0.0
Morris, Israel, to land in Philadelphia	100	--	--	--	12.10.0
Lewdin, John, to land in Nottingham	100	--	--	--	12.10.0
Patterson, James	100	--	--	--	18.0.0
Richey, John & Griffy, John	--	--	--	--	--
McClorge, Mark	--	--	--	--	18.0.0
Wallace, Mary	--	--	--	1	7.10.0
Reed, Emanuel	100	--	--	--	18.0.0
Ewing, Mathew	100	--	1	1	12.10.0
Pennington, Moses	100	--	--	--	7.10.0

Hopewell Township	Acres	Negroes	Horses	Cattle	Tax
Overmiller, Martin	176	--	1	2	27.10.0
Morrison, Michael	--	--	1	1	16.10.0
Steeple, Nicholas	50	--	1	2	15.0.0
Strair, Nicholas	50	--	--	--	25.0.0
Henry, Nicholas	144	--	2	2	25.0.0
Douglass, Patrick	--	--	1	1	22.0.0
Roberts, Peter	--	--	1	1	7.10.0
Taylor, Philip	70	--	1	1	18.0.0
Stair, Peter	100	--	1	1	22.10.0
Pryfogle, Peter	50	--	1	2	22.10.0
Pins land	--	--	--	--	12.10.0
Atkins, Robert	130	--	2	2	30.10.0
Strawford, Robert	160	--	1	2	15.0.0
Cunningham, Robert	--	--	--	--	18.0.0
Proudfoot, Robert	100	--	2	4	28.0.0
Swan, Robert	25	--	1	2	20.0.0
Yost, Rudy	100	--	2	3	45.0.0
Stuart, Rowland	100	--	1	1	15.0.0
Dickeson, Robert	100	--	1	1	27.0.0
Atkinson, Richard	--	--	--	1	5.0.0
McDonnell, Richard	200	--	2	4	47.10.0
Richey, Robert	50	--	2	2	20.0.0
McMullin, James	200	--	--	--	15.0.0
Anderson, Robert	--	--	1	--	20.0.0
Carswell, Robert	--	--	--	--	18.0.0
Hively, Stophel	100	--	2	2	35.0.0
Smith, Samuel	100	--	1	2	26.0.0
Harper, Samuel	200	--	1	2	32.10.0
Martin, Samuel	80	--	2	2	32.10.0
Moore, Samuel	--	--	1	1	15.0.0
Watson, Samuel	100	--	2	3	20.0.0
Roseborough, Samuel	50	--	2	1	33.0.0
Fulton, Samuel	--	--	1	--	25.0.0
Heslet, Samuel	--	--	--	--	18.0.0
Cornelius, Stephen	--	--	1	4	10.10.0
Dickonson, Samuel	100	--	2	2	36.10.0
Mosser, Samuel	50	--	1	1	18.0.0
Patterson, Samuel	50	--	1	1	15.10.0
Elliot, Samuel	50	--	--	1	10.0.0
Ray, Thomas	--	--	2	2	18.0.0
Evans, Thomas	50	--	--	--	30.0.0
To Orphans land	50	--	--	--	--
Mickel, Thomas	180	--	1	3	28.0.0
Shinard, Thomas	--	--	1	--	21.0.0
Litten, Thomas	--	--	1	1	10.0.0
Jameson, Thomas	50	--	2	2	18.0.0
Dickson, Thomas	68	--	1	2	18.0.0
Jameson, William	30	--	1	1	18.0.0
Miller, William	150	--	--	--	10.0.0
Boyd, William	50	--	1	1	10.0.0
Gemmil, William	100	1	2	2	42.10.0
Ramsay, William	--	--	1	--	--
Morrow, William	80	--	1	3	18.0.0
Wilson, William	179	--	3	4	25.0.0
Douglass, William	80	--	1	1	22.10.0

Hopewell Township	Acres	Negroes	Horses	Cattle	Tax
Smith, William	100	1	2	2	45.0.0
Ligget, William	100	--	2	2	40.0.0
Ligget, William	--	--	--	--	18.0.0
Edgar, William	139	--	2	3	27.0.0
Shinard, Widow	--	--	1	1	7.10.0
Widow and Saak to land	100	--	--	--	--
Edy, William	70	--	1	2	37.10.0
Hart, Widow	50	--	1	--	5.0.0
Ferris, William	40	--	1	1	20.0.0
Godfrey, William	30	--	--	1	12.0.0
Spitler, William	50	--	1	1	25.0.0
Pollock, William	7	--	1	3	12.0.0
Good, William	--	--	2	2	18.0.0
McClorge, William	50	--	2	2	35.0.0
Griffith, Evan	--	--	--	--	--
McClorge, Mark	--	--	--	--	--
Smith, John	--	--	--	--	--

FAWN TOWNSHIP

	Acres	Negroes	Horses	Cattle	Tax
Alexander, James	40	--	--	--	37.10.0
Adams, Williams	100	--	2	4	30.15.0
Alexander, John	100	--	1	2	24.15.0
Alexander, Thomas	--	--	2	2	9.15.0
Alexander, Isaac	201	--	2	2	42.11.3
Alexander, Henry	--	--	--	2	--
Andrews, Humphrey	298	--	1	1	22.10.0
Adair, Robert	--	--	1	1	4.17.6
Allen, Thomas	210	--	1	3	42.18.9
Anderson, William	100	--	1	--	48.15.0
Andrews, John	--	--	--	--	--
Alloways, Stephen	--	--	1	2	3.0.0
Armstrong, Robert	--	--	3	2	6.15.0
Best, Sarah, widow	50	--	--	--	4.13.9
Best, John	--	--	1	1	4.17.6
Brennan, Thomas	200	--	2	4	40.0.0
Baldwin, Joseph	--	--	--	1	1.10.0
Bradley, Hannah	25	--	--	--	4.13.9
Baders, George	--	--	--	1	1.10.0
Brown, Joshua	130	--	2	3	35.5.0
Buchanon, Thomas	190	--	2	3	23.5.0
Buchanon, Samuel	100	--	1	--	12.3.9
Buchanon, James	185	--	2	2	30.15.0
Beard, John	140	--	1	6	31.10.0
Benson, James	--	--	2	2	3.7.6
Brown, Thomas	173 1/2	--	4	4	35.16.3
Breckenridge, William	--	--	1	1	1.10.0
Cooper, Thomas	300	4	3	3	250.2.6
Cooper, Nicholas	130	--	3	5	73.18.0
Cooper, Alexander	600	--	3	8	113.5.0
Cooper, William	175	--	2	4	30.11.3
Cooper, Archibald	420	--	3	5	67.10.0

Fawn Township	Acres	Negroes	Horses	Cattle	Tax
Carson, William	--	--	2	2	2.5.0
Campble, John	--	--	2	2	4.17.6
Caldwell, Robert	200	--	4	3	37.10.0
Commons, John	70	--	2	3	12.0.0
Crow, Samuel	201	--	2	5	33.15.0
Clerk, Ja's, Maryland	332	--	--	--	46.13.9
Colvin, William	273	--	3	5	33.18.9
Clemens, Patrick	83	--	2	3	11.5.0
Catterwood, John	--	--	3	1	6.3.9
Cunning, Samuel	50	--	2	2	22.17.6
Day, John	140	--	3	2	27.11.3
Duncan, Robert	400	--	3	5	50.0.0
Doran, John, Maryland	180	--	--	--	25.6.3
Dougherty, John	--	--	--	2	2.5.0
Duval, Samuel	--	--	--	1	--
Dunlap, Robert	150	--	--	--	28.2.6
Dull, Joseph	--	--	--	--	3.15.0
Dunlap, James	--	--	2	2	9.15.0
Duncan, Jacob	--	--	1	7	2.8.9
Eager, James	286	--	4	4	52.17.6
Ewings, Alexander	74	--	3	3	17.12.6
Fulton, William	200	--	2	2	66.0.0
Frew, Alexander	140	--	3	7	25.0.0
Fundrews, Adam	--	--	--	--	14.1.3
Flanagan, James	3	--	1	1	--
Flowers, John	--	--	2	2	3.0.0
Gordon, Widow	--	--	--	2	--
Galagher, James	50	--	1	3	7.10.0
Gibson, Robert	50	--	1	2	20.1.3
Gibson, James	--	--	--	--	3.15.0
Gilcrist, Agnes	138	--	1	1	43.10.0
Guist, John	150	--	1	2	16.2.6
Gordon, James	200	--	3	4	36.0.0
Gordon, John	--	--	2	5	5.12.6
Graham, Henry	--	--	--	1	1.10.0
Giles, James, in Maryland	228	--	--	--	42.15.0
Grey, William	200	--	3	4	30.0.0
Gordon, Rob't, Maryland	200	--	--	--	18.15.0
Hamilton, John	100	--	3	5	25.6.3
Heaton, Jeremiah	--	--	1	2	6.0.0
Hopkin, Levins, Maryland	400	--	--	--	56.5.0
Harbison, John	--	--	1	1	2.8.9
Hartford, Matthew	150	--	2	4	46.17.6
Jones, Theophilus	167 3/4	--	2	8	30.18.9
Johnson, Charles	--	--	--	1	1.10.0
Jones, Isaac	--	--	2	1	2.8.9
Kincade, Samuel	270	--	3	4	45.15.0
Kithcart, Joseph	265	--	3	5	46.0.0
Kaurts, Martin	200	--	3	5	82.2.6
Kelly, James	--	--	--	--	--
Levinston, John	60	--	2	2	11.8.9
Long, Henry	--	--	1	1	1.10.0
Lemmon, John	--	--	1	2	3.0.0
Lockhead, John	--	--	--	--	1.10.0
Latimore, George	--	--	--	1	--

Fawn Township	Acres	Negroes	Horses	Cattle	Tax
Doob, Joseph	--	--	--	--	--
Manifold, Joseph	50	--	--	--	4.14.3
Manifold, Edward	200	--	2	4	68.5.0
McCollough, Peter	--	--	--	--	3.15.0
Milligan, James	185	--	1	4	23.5.0
Mitchel, George	250	--	3	4	31.6.3
Mitchel, George	200	--	6	4	30.0.0
McCurley, Patrick	--	--	--	--	3.15.0
McCaskey, William	200	--	1	3	35.0.0
Mandle, William	150	--	2	1	25.6.3
Mooberry, Robert	100	--	3	4	21.15.9
McMullen, James	282	--	2	4	45.11.3
McMullen, George	--	--	--	--	3.15.0
Matson, Thomas	20	--	2	5	7.10.0
Major, John	274	--	2	6	36.0.0
Land in the name of Morris	370	--	--	--	45.0.0
Morris, Thomas	--	--	2	1	2.8.9
McPherson, Frederick	--	--	2	2	3.0.0
McMullin, James, Muddy Creek	50	--	1	2	6.15.0
McCord, James	90	--	2	1	16.17.6
McMullen, John	--	--	2	2	4.17.6
McCandless, James	756	--	7	8	152.1.3
McCollough, James	160	--	2	2	26.5.0
McCandless, William	--	--	2	2	12.7.6
McFaden, Hugh	85	--	3	4	16.17.6
Miller, Robert	76	--	1	3	12.0.0
McCleary, William	183	--	3	5	30.7.6
McCrea, David	--	--	--	1	1.10.0
Nichol, George	600	--	1	5	106.17.6
Neale, Thomas	67	--	2	4	50.0.0
Neal, John	127	--	--	--	18.15.0
Ohara, John	--	--	1	1	3.0.0
Parker, John	236	--	--	--	22.2.6
Porter, Wm., Lanc'r county	300	4	2	9	123.0.0
Parks, John	75	--	2	5	17.16.3
Ritchey, Samuel	--	--	--	--	1.10.0
Ralston, John	100	--	2	3	19.10.0
Ross, Joseph	222	--	3	3	38.8.9
Rowlands, Margaret	300	--	1	1	38.7.9
Richey, Andrew	120	--	2	4	16.17.6
Robison, James	116	--	1	2	18.0.0
Robison, William	35	--	2	--	17.5.0
Russel, John	--	--	--	--	3.15.0
Ramsay, James	381	--	4	6	84.7.6
Rowan, Andrew	245	--	4	3	43.10.0
Rowan, William	245	--	--	--	34.6.3
Reed, William	148	--	2	6	15.0.0
Ramsey, Alex'r, in Hopewell	100	--	--	--	28.0.0
Snodgress, Wm.	--	--	2	4	4.2.0
Suter, George	120	--	1	2	10.2.1
Smith, Barney	10	--	2	1	3.7.6
Scott, John	--	--	--	--	--

Fawn Township	Acres	Negroes	Horses	Cattle	Tax
Smith, James	299	--	2	3	47.16.3
Smith, Wm.	--	--	1	--	3.15.0
Smiley, Wm.	310	--	5	4	55.2.6
Scott, Patrick	272	--	2	3	55.0.0
Semple, John	760	--	6	6	159.0.0
Semple, Cunningham	268	--	5	9	90.0.0
Smith, Joseph	--	--	2	1	20.0.0
Steel, Rachel	160	1	2	5	20.0.0
Steel, Thomas	288	--	2	4	46.10.0
Taggart, John	50	--	1	1	7.10.0
Taylor, John	250	--	3	1	41.5.0
Tarbert, Robert	204	--	3	5	30.0.0
Tarbert, James	--	--	--	1	1.10.0
Twiggs, John	--	--	1	1	1.10.0
Waram, Abraham	--	--	1	1	--
Woods, Samuel	120	--	2	3	14.16.3
Wiley, Joseph, Sen'r.	100	--	--	--	28.2.6
Wilson, Elizabeth, widow	--	--	2	2	--
Webb, James	97	--	2	5	19.13.9
Webb, John	--	--	1	2	3.0.0
Webb, Richard	133	--	1	4	22.15.9
West, Samuel	215	--	1	2	68.12.6
White, Joseph	--	--	1	1	2.8.9
West, Isaac	--	--	1	1	4.17.6
Wilson, Thomas	--	--	1	2	6.0.0
Wilson, James	--	--	1	2	2.1.3
Wiley, Joseph, Jun'r	300	--	2	5	58.6.3
Whiteford, Hugh, Mary'l	50	--	--	--	6.18.0
Wiley, Nathaniel	68	--	--	--	18.8.9
Wilson, Benjamin	--	--	--	--	1.10.0
Wilson, John	--	--	2	--	7.10.0
Wilson, John	450	--	3	6	145.0.0
Wallace, William	140	--	3	8	26.16.3

Freemen

	Acres	Negroes	Horses	Cattle	Tax
Dawney, Patrick	--	--	--	--	12.10.0
Dame, Joseph	--	--	--	--	10.0.0
Beaty, Wm.	--	--	--	--	10.0.0
Savage, Henry	--	--	--	--	10.0.0
White, Andrew	--	--	--	--	10.0.0
Guest, Robert	--	--	--	--	12.10.0
Curry, Joseph	--	--	--	--	12.10.0
Gordon, Thomas	--	--	--	--	15.0.0
Armstrong, David	--	--	--	--	10.0.0
McMullen, Michael	--	--	--	--	10.0.0
Ballendine, William	--	--	--	--	12.10.0
West, George	--	--	1	--	12.0.0
Johnston, Jacob	--	--	--	--	10.0.0
Latimore, James	--	--	--	--	10.0.0
Roberts, John	--	--	--	--	10.0.0
Smith, Ebenezer	--	--	--	--	10.0.0

Fawn Township	Acres	Negroes	Horses	Cattle	Tax
McCarrol, Thomas	--	--	1	--	12.10.0
McFaden, Samuel	--	--	--	1	12.10.0
Cooper, John	--	--	--	--	10.0.0
Puff, Christopher	--	--	--	--	10.0.0
Wiley, Mathew	--	--	--	--	15.0.0
Fitzgerald, James	--	--	--	1	--
Wilson, Samuel	--	--	--	--	10.0.0
Millichan, William	--	--	--	--	10.0.0
Jones, Benjamin	--	--	1	--	10.0.0
Reed, James	--	--	--	--	15.0.0
Leard, James	--	--	--	--	12.10.0
Davison, John	--	--	--	--	12.10.0
Cunningham, Benjamin	100	--	--	--	62.5.0
Thomson, Samuel	--	--	--	--	12.10.0

HELLAM TOWNSHIP

	Acres	Negroes	Horses	Cattle	Tax
Alexander, William	--	--	--	--	225.0.0
Alexander, Andrew	--	--	7	2	22.10.0
Ament, John	50	--	2	4	6.15.0
Allebach, Frederich	--	--	--	2	8.10.0
Anderson & Lowrey	--	--	--	--	45.0.0
Baum, Adam	180	--	2	2	95.1.0
Beyer, Peter	200	--	3	6	110.0.0
Bahn, John	20	--	1	--	20.0.0
Bellet, Craft	150	--	2	2	18.15.0
Balzer, Jacob	100	--	3	3	59.0.0
Bruckhart, Jacob	100	--	2	3	51.5.0
Bowman, John	70	--	2	1	26.10.0
Bidler, Peter	100	--	2	5	150.6.3
Bidler, Barbara	240	--	4	6	172.4.0
Bernhart, John	--	--	--	1	15.0.0
Blessinger, Michael	140	--	2	7	49.0.0
Craft, Conrad	--	--	--	2	6.0.0
Cloper, George	25	--	1	2	12.10.0
Carman, Mathias	10	--	--	2	8.0.0
Cobler, Adam	--	--	--	--	--
Cobel, Abraham	100	--	1	3	17.10.0
Coltrider, Henry	--	--	--	1	12.10.0
Clayton, Daniel	--	--	--	2	25.0.0
Crow, Alexander	160	--	3	4	85.0.0
Cauffman, Jacob	270	--	2	2	180.0.0
Cann, Henry	237	--	4	6	105.17.0
Crow, Michael	50	--	2	2	105.17.0
Comfort, Jacob	12	--	1	2	17.0.0
Decker, Philip	104	--	3	4	100.0.0
Dellinger, Joseph	100	--	1	2	20.0.0
Deeds, George	230	--	4	7	99.15.0
Dronnon, David	--	--	1	1	4.0.0
Destein, Michael	73	--	2	3	52.6.2
Dorman, John	50	--	4	8	27.0.0
Diddy, Peter	--	--	4	3	--

Hellam Township

	Acres	Negroes	Horses	Cattle	Tax
Demuth, Widow	50	--	2	2	15.10.0
Daron, Adam	75	--	3	2	27.0.0
Ewing, James, Gen'l	162	--	2	7	115.0.0
Flory, Abraham	30	--	1	3	37.0.0
Flory, Isaac	330	--	2	4	108.0.0
Flory, Jacob	40	--	1	2	40.0.0
Fox, John	51	--	1	2	5.0.0
Frees, David	120	--	3	4	75.0.0
Frees, George	200	--	3	2	48.10.0
Frees, Jacob	--	--	--	2	12.10.0
Fits, Balzer	150	--	3	5	106.10.0
Foncanora, Michael	--	--	1	1	8.0.0
Fritz, Philip	117	--	2	2	26.5.0
Gartner, Philip	200	--	3	3	111.18.9
Gartner, Martin	200	1	4	5	93.14.9
Gipe, Peter	--	--	--	--	8.1.9
Gipe, Henry	60	--	2	2	11.12.6
Hamilton, Thomas	--	--	--	1	2.10.0
Hunsinger, Simon	--	--	--	1	2.10.0
Hunsinger, William	--	--	--	1	2.10.0
Herr, John	360	--	5	10	220.0.0
Huber, Martin	190	--	3	8	204.15.0
Hoyer, Jacob	14	--	--	1	15.0.0
Hivel, Stophel	100	--	1	4	22.10.0
Hivel, Jacob	--	--	--	1	24.5.0
Hool, John	98	--	--	3	30.4.6
Hoyer, George	90	--	2	3	25.12.6
Isaac, John	--	--	2	2	6.15.0
Jordan, John	--	--	3	2	25.0.0
Isenhauer, Leonard	--	--	--	1	6.15.0
Kindich, Henry	200	--	2	4	116.19.0
Kunckel, Christian	--	--	--	2	12.7.6
Kunckel, Balzer	100	--	2	3	41.11.0
Kunckel, Godlieb	100	--	2	3	81.2.0
King, Charles	100	--	--	3	7.10.0
Liebhart, Valentine	180	--	2	4	79.16.3
Liebhart, Henry	168	--	4	7	100.0.0
Lanius, Jacob	150	--	3	4	84.10.0
Leedy, Jacob	150	--	3	5	78.17.6
Lanius, Henry	150	--	3	7	94.10.9
Leaman, Christian	140	--	2	3	40.10.6
Mate, Casper	--	--	--	2	10.0.0
Mollison, Samuel	--	--	1	1	--
Mate, John	303	--	4	4	197.1.0
Mate, John, Jun'r	--	--	--	--	12.0.0
Mantle, George	5	--	--	3	30.17.6
Marks, Joseph	--	--	4	3	22.10.0
Mellinger, David	125	--	2	5	64.0.0
Mose, Jacob	--	--	2	2	--
Miller, Michael	243	--	3	4	186.15.0
Mosser, Michael	243	--	3	4	186.15.0
Mosselbach, John	10	--	1	4	8.10.0
Mosser, Christian	80	--	2	2	18.10.0
Morgan, John	200	--	2	4	87.0.0

Hellam Township	Acres	Negroes	Horses	Cattle	Tax
Neff, Daniel, in the Barrens	312	1	2	2	77.15.0
Newcomer, Chris'r	150	--	3	3	38.0.0
Newcomer, Ulrich, Jun'r	--	--	2	2	5.5.0
Newcomer, Christ'r, Jun'r	--	--	--	4	4.10.0
Newcomer, Ulrich, Se'r	50	--	2	3	10.0.0
Pile, Peter	--	--	--	2	3.10.0
Roop, Christian	80	--	2	2	25.10.6
Rup, Stephen	100	--	3	4	40.10.0
Rudy, Michael	196	--	3	5	80.18.0
Rup, Yost	10	--	--	2	25.10.0
Reist, John	--	--	--	--	25.0.0
Stoner, Christian	177	--	4	9	140.0.0
Swope, John	--	--	--	1	3.10.0
Strickler, Henry	150	--	3	4	175.10.6
Strickler, Jacob, Jun'r	--	--	1	4	6.15.0
Strickler, Henry, Jun'r	--	--	--	2	6.15.0
Staulfer, Jacob	30	--	--	2	5.0.0
Swope, Adam	50	--	--	2	5.0.0
Shultz, Jacob	94	--	3	5	7.1.0
Sultzback, Philip	184	--	2	8	82.2.6
Shaller, George	115	--	--	2	50.5.6
Strickler, John	190	--	3	5	142.10.0
Strickler, Conrad	--	--	--	--	32.19.0
Strickler, Henry	125	--	2	6	76.10.0
Shroll, John	50	--	2	3	15.10.0
Shroll, Christian	--	--	--	--	7.10.0
Shroll, John, Jun'r	150	--	2	2	20.0.0
Snideman, Daniel	--	--	--	--	6.10.0
Strickler, Jacob	182	--	4	5	191.5.10
Thomas, Philip	90	--	--	4	15.10.0
Truck, George	--	--	1	2	2.0.0
Welshover, Jacob	170	--	4	6	99.18.0
Wendle, Wolf	--	--	--	2	5.10.0
Willis, William	--	--	1	1	6.10.0
Williams, Solomon	120	--	4	4	50.0.0
Wright, John	500	--	1	2	457.10.10
Wiland, John	90	--	4	8	25.10.0
Wright, Samuel	300	--	--	--	175.0.0
Weston, Joseph	--	--	--	1	5.0.0
Yessley, Michael	--	--	4	5	--

Single Men

	Amount of Tax		Amount of Tax
Cauffman, Michael	20.0.0	Jordan, John	22.10.0
Conn, John	20.0.0	Young, Edward	22.10.0
Erp, Joseph	25.0.0	Stentz, Jacob	30.0.0
Ewing, John, Col'l	20.0.0	Smeltzer, Michael	22.10.0
Flory, Daniel	25.0.0	Mathews, Thomas	22.10.0
Fits, John	25.0.0	Shultz, Jacob	20.0.0
Geiss, Elias	22.10.0	Shaller, George	20.0.0
Gipe, George	22.10.0	Thompson, Wm.	10.0.0
Hoover, Martin	20.0.0	Stoner, John	25.0.0

DOVER TOWNSHIP

	Acres	Negroes	Horses	Cattle	Tax
Albert, Charles	80	--	2	3	14.0.0
Besenour, Anthony	100	--	2	2	18.0.0
Bigler, Joseph	--	--	--	1	2.1.8
Bear, Ludwig	--	--	1	1	8.6.8
Bitzel, Laurence	--	--	--	1	8.6.8
Bigler, Jacob	--	--	--	1	4.10.0
Bear, Jeremiah	100	--	3	3	37.10.0
Berbower, Philip	50	--	1	1	4.2.6
Bob, Jacob	100	--	2	2	16.13.0
Bonix, George	--	--	--	1	1.1.8
Bellet, Thomas	160	--	3	5	50.0.0
Berbower, Casper	50	--	1	1	2.1.8
Boblitz, Michael	160	--	2	4	41.13.4
Bitzel, Jonathan	200	--	2	5	41.13.4
Brunner, Peter	70	--	2	2	16.13.4
Bitzel, John	450	--	4	6	80.0.0
Barten, James	300	--	2	3	47.13.4
Bentzel, Philip	150	--	2	3	37.10.0
Bentzel, Henry	75	--	1	2	12.10.0
Becker, Philip	200	--	2	3	47.13.8
Benedick, Melchior	120	--	2	3	20.16.8
Beltzhuber, Conrad	40	--	2	2	--
Browl, William	100	--	1	2	20.0.0
Cox, Jacob	--	--	1	1	8.6.8
Davis, Henry	80	--	--	1	6.0.0
Devise, Joseph	80	--	2	1	2.11.8
Deardorf, Anthony	200	--	3	5	100.0.0
Danner, Casper	75	--	2	2	4.0.0
Davis, John	--	--	1	1	10.13.4
Donaldson, John	100	--	2	3	14.0.0
Dundore, Henry	80	--	1	2	4.13.0
Demint, John	120	--	2	2	10.13.4
Deer, Ulrich	--	--	--	1	4.1.8
Eiger, Joseph	200	1	2	3	140.0.0
Evans, Jonathan	--	--	--	1	1.17.6
Elgenfritz, George	300	--	2	6	150.0.0
Evans, Thomas	100	--	1	--	12.10.0
Evans, Able	--	--	--	1	--
Elgenfritz, George, Ju'r	--	--	1	2	2.18.4
Eicholtz, Mathias	115	--	2	2	29.3.4
Eicholtz, Frederick	212	--	3	3	50.0.0
Eichholtz, Frederick, Ju'r	--	--	--	2	4.0.0
Flohr, Leonard	150	--	3	4	50.0.0
Fischel, John	--	--	--	1	6.0.0
Fischel, Adam	100	--	3	4	41.13.4
Flind, Michael	50	--	--	2	10.13.4
Fry, Tobias	150	--	2	4	41.13.4
Fieser, John	200	--	3	4	40.0.0
Fink, George	100	--	2	2	25.0.0
Fink, Bastian	150	--	3	4	40.0.0
Flohr, Valentine	110	--	--	1	29.3.4
Gross, John	--	--	--	1	2.1.8
Gantley, George	--	--	--	--	120.0.0
Gross, Michael	--	--	--	--	2.1.8

Dover Township	Acres	Negroes	Horses	Cattle	Tax
Gauff, George	150	--	2	2	25.0.0
Gartner, Henry	250	--	2	3	37.10.0
Gayer, George	213	--	2	4	45.0.0
Gross, George	70	--	2	2	4.13.4
Gross, Wendel	160	--	2	2	29.13.4
Grim, Charles	--	--	--	--	6.0.0
Hoss, John	--	--	2	2	--
Holles, William	70	--	1	1	3.11.8
Herbolt, William	130	--	2	3	50.0.0
Herbolt, Michael	120	--	2	3	41.13.4
Herbolt, George	70	--	2	1	26.0.0
Haselet, Andrew	50	--	--	1	3.0.0
Hanss, Andrew	150	--	2	5	45.13.6
Hoffman, Nicholas	450	--	4	6	160.0.0
Hoffman, Charles	--	--	1	1	6.0.0
Hellman, Herman	--	--	1	1	12.10.0
Hetzer, Adam	--	--	--	1	5.1.8
Huber, Conrad	100	--	2	2	40.0.0
Ham, Balzer	150	--	2	3	41.13.4
Hoffman, Philip	60	--	1	2	29.3.9
Hoffman, Jacob	169	--	2	4	37.10.0
Heck, Conrad	160	--	--	1	37.10.0
Hoffman, Nicholas	--	--	2	2	12.10.0
Henisen, John	150	--	4	4	33.6.8
Julius, Jacob	250	--	3	3	60.16.8
Kooch, George	150	--	2	3	37.10.0
Kimmel, Anthony	150	--	4	4	174.0.0
Kober, Andrew	50	--	1	1	4.10.0
Konn, George	160	--	2	4	50.0.0
Kochinower, Joseph	120	--	2	3	35.6.8
Kronbach, Jacob	200	--	2	2	41.13.4
Kron, Philip	162	--	2	4	30.0.0
Leonhart, William	200	--	2	3	60.0.0
Leonhart, Stophel	--	--	5	3	25.0.0
Leather, Frederick	200	--	4	6	100.0.0
Leather, Frederick, Jun'r	--	--	--	2	4.13.4
Lambert, Casper	100	--	2	4	50.0.0
Lambert, Jacob	140	--	3	3	100.0.0
Leinbauch, Conrad	200	--	3	4	41.13.4
Leinbauch, Felix	60	--	1	2	10.13.4
Lower, Jacob	150	--	2	2	37.10.0
Lininger, George	90	--	2	2	22.10.0
Leyser, George	60	--	1	2	3.0.0
Leidig, Michael	100	--	2	3	25.0.0
Messerly, Daniel	300	--	4	5	75.0.0
Meyer, Nicholas	115	--	2	1	12.10.0
Miller, John	--	--	--	1	2.1.8
Mittman, Charles	--	--	--	--	8.6.8
Messenkop, Jacob	--	--	--	1	6.0.0
Miller, Andrew	80	--	--	3	3.0.0
March, Jacob	60	--	2	2	12.10.0
Martorf, Conrad	--	--	--	1	4.0.0
Meyer, Simon	100	--	3	2	25.0.0
May, John	15	--	--	2	3.0.0
Mayer, Peter	120	--	3	3	33.6.8

Dover Township	Acres	Negroes	Horses	Cattle	Tax
Mayer, Jacob	200	--	3	4	58.6.8
Miller, Barnet	300	--	4	5	100.0.0
Mayer, Frederick	100	--	2	1	20.16.8
Michael, Adam	100	--	2	2	29.3.4
Michael, Nicholas	15	--	1	1	10.13.4
Martin, David	200	--	2	3	60.0.0
McAllisters, John	300	--	--	--	45.13.4
Moorè, Widow	100	--	2	2	10.13.0
Melhorn, Andrew	93	--	2	2	7.10.0
Miller, Jacob	100	--	2	3	16.13.4
Maurer, Herman	170	--	4	5	46.13.4
March, George	--	--	--	--	25.0.0
Metzler, Thomas	--	--	--	1	1.0.10
Morris, Joseph	--	--	--	2	--
May, Daniel	200	--	3	6	53.0.0
Northen, Isaac	200	--	2	2	50.0.0
Nerbass, Francis	80	--	2	3	25.0.0
Neaf, Abraham	112	--	3	2	6.0.0
Nelson, William	100	--	2	4	25.0.0
Orban, John	--	--	--	1	--
Opp, Jacob	250	--	1	3	16.13.4
Opp, Peter	--	--	2	2	16.13.4
Oberdier, John	100	--	2	2	33.6.8
Quickel, Michael	100	--	1	2	33.6.8
Quickel, George	100	--	1	2	22.3.4
Quickel, Philip	--	--	1	2	3.0.0
Riginger, Stephen	--	--	--	1	4.0.0
Richter, George	--	--	--	1	6.0.0
Reisinger, Martin	100	--	2	2	20.0.0
Reisinger, Conrad	--	--	--	1	2.1.8
Richter, Paul	60	--	2	2	60.0.0
Regan, Daniel	150	--	2	3	100.0.0
Rambow, Andrew	150	--	3	3	16.13.8
Rudy, George	100	--	--	1	25.0.0
Rudy, George, Ju'r	--	--	2	2	6.0.0
Rudy, Henry	60	--	2	2	10.13.0
Ridinger, Stephen	100	--	--	--	10.13.0
Romig, George	--	--	--	1	2.1.8
Ramsay, Alexander	270	--	4	5	30.0.0
Rudisill, John	250	--	2	3	95.0.0
Rudrauff, John	195	--	3	5	25.0.0
Ramsey, Alexander	--	--	--	1	8.0.0
Rahauser, Daniel	90	--	2	4	20.16.8
Rahauser, Jacob	100	--	3	6	20.0.0
Stouch, George	150	--	4	4	45.13.4
Stouch, Frederick	30	--	3	4	45.13.4
Spahr, Adam	--	--	2	4	--
Shown, John	130	--	2	3	36.0.0
Schneider, John	37	--	1	2	10.13.4
Shetron, John	200	--	2	3	40.10.0
Spangler, Joseph	--	--	--	--	37.10.0
Spahr, Frederick	270	--	2	4	50.0.0
Sheffer, John	180	--	2	4	41.13.0
Shatron, Jacob	100	--	2	4	75.0.0
Siffert, Adam	99	--	2	3	33.6.8

Dover Township	Acres	Negroes	Horses	Cattle	Tax
Spahr, Casper	150	--	2	3	37.10.0
Spahr, George	100	--	2	2	20.0.0
Siffert, Michael	--	--	--	1	4.0.0
Streher, Peter	150	--	3	6	50.0.0
Streley, Stephen	30	--	1	2	8.6.4
Strehr, Jacob	100	--	2	3	20.16.0
Schwartz, Mathias	100	--	2	3	20.0.0
Spies, Peter	200	--	3	3	120.0.0
Spies, Peter	100	--	--	--	8.6.8
Schnellbecher, George	115	--	2	2	37.10.0
Sipe, Philip	100	--	2	2	16.13.4
Shettley, George	50	--	2	2	12.10.0
Smith, Jacob	242	--	3	6	33.6.8
Sipe, Andrew	--	--	--	1	2.1.8
Sipe, Emanuel	--	--	--	1	2.10.0
Strine, Peter	100	--	2	2	25.0.0
Smith, Peter	--	--	--	1	4.3.4
Tryne, Peter	--	--	--	--	65.0.0
Tomey, Thomas	--	--	--	--	2.1.8
Vartin, Richard	--	--	--	1	6.0.0
Wethrow, John	--	--	1	1	4.13.4
Wilt, Samuel	--	--	--	1	4.13.4
Wolk, John	70	--	1	2	16.13.4
Wolk, Philip	70	--	1	1	12.10.0
Worley, Samuel	300	--	2	3	150.0.0
Wolf, Conrad	--	--	2	2	6.0.0
Weaver, Martin	170	--	2	4	25.0.0
Doudle, Widow, a location	200	--	--	--	10.0.0
Wigel, Jacob	50	--	1	1	25.0.0
Wentz, Philip	130	--	2	3	25.0.0
Wilte, Paul	250	--	4	4	70.0.0
Wilte, John	--	--	--	1	2.1.8
Welty, Philip	100	--	2	3	10.13.0
Welty, George	120	--	2	2	16.13.4
Witcock, Ambrose	50	--	--	2	3.0.0
Wintermeyer, Anthony	80	--	2	2	10.0.0
Yoner, Jacob	150	--	2	2	152.0.0
Yeke, Peter	--	--	3	2	8.6.8
Yeke, Adam	100	--	2	3	33.6.8
Young, Peter	--	--	--	1	6.0.0
Yoner, Nicholas	25	--	1	1	2.0.0
Yoner, John	--	--	--	--	2.1.8
Zinn, Philip Jacob	140	--	3	4	100.0.0
Zinn, Nicholas	30	--	2	3	12.10.0
Zimmerman, Jacob	80	--	--	2	5.1.8

Single Men

	Amount of Tax		Amount of Tax
Messerly, Abraham	10.0.0	Welty, Jacob	7.10.0
Kooch, John	10.0.0	Sipe, Tobias	7.10.0
Ham, Christian	15.0.0	Miller, Henry	6.0.0
Spahr, Michael	20.0.0	Quickel, Adam	2.1.8
Pew, Joseph	20.0.0	Ramsey, Oliver	12.1.8
Rudisill, John	5.0.0	Detter, Mathias	25.0.0
Welty, Michael	10.0.0	Gantley, William	24.0.0
Bitzel, John	8.0.0	Hiner, John	10.6.8
Sheffer, Jacob	10.0.0	Stauch, Andrew	2.1.8
Deerdorf, Paul	20.0.0	Spahr, Philip, for Prop'rs	6.0.0
Miller, Jacob	3.0.0	Spahr, Philip, for land	10.13.0
Miller, George	--	Willis, Wm.	6.0.0
Miller, Michael	12.0.0	Wills, John, for Fred'k	
Julius, Philip	10.0.0	Myers' land	25.0.0
Kochenour, Jacob	20.0.0	Urban, John	4.13.0
Goodwin, Seth	10.0.0		

MOUNT JOY TOWNSHIP

	Acres	Negroes	Horses	Cattle	Tax
Aspough, Andrew	109	--	4	5	40.0.0
Adair, William	240	--	4	6	70.0.0
Adair, John	239	--	3	6	67.0.0
Bigham, Hugh	--	--	--	1	3.15.0
Bigham, Patrick	248	--	3	6	77.5.0
Breckenridge, Rob't	132	--	4	4	25.0.0
Breckenridge, Wm.	--	--	--	--	7.10.0
Barr, James	180	--	4	6	50.0.0
Barr, James	--	--	--	--	15.0.0
Boyl, Widow	150	--	--	2	30.0.0
Beaty, James	130	--	1	4	35.0.0
Bainter, Valentine	140	--	4	4	55.0.0
Correthers, James	--	--	2	3	7.10.0
Diar, John	--	--	2	2	7.10.0
Doran, John	--	--	3	1	3.0.0
Davydal, John	209	--	4	6	65.0.0
Dillow, John	--	--	3	3	4.10.0
Eickart, Peter	130	--	2	3	110.0.0
Fleming, James	163	--	2	2	45.0.0
Guinn, Wm. Sen'r	150	--	5	7	55.0.0
Guinn, Wm., Jun'r	--	--	3	2	6.0.0
Gualt, Thomas	280	--	4	4	55.0.0
Gibson, Widow	100	--	2	2	22.10.0
Gibson, William	--	--	--	--	7.10.0
Guinn, Andrew	--	--	--	--	10.0.0
Guinn, Hugh	--	--	--	--	10.0.0
Grier, Patrick	--	--	1	1	10.0.0
Hunter, Samuel	100	--	2	3	30.0.0
Horner, Robert	460	1	4	3	190.0.0
Horner, Robert	200	--	--	--	--
Horner, David	400	3	4	6	140.0.0
Helms, Francis	121	--	--	10	35.0.0

Mount Joy Township	Acres	Negroes	Horses	Cattle	Tax
Hunter, Joseph	200	--	3	2	55.0.0
Hunter, James	--	--	--	--	7.10.0
Hutcheson, James	80	--	3	5	30.0.0
Hutcheson, Robert	--	--	--	--	15.0.0
Hunter, Alexander	200	--	3	3	45.0.0
Hughs, John	70	--	1	3	22.10.0
Hope, Augustus	250	--	3	4	70.0.0
Houghdelin, Wm.	131 1/2	--	3	3	35.0.0
Hughs, Barney	--	--	2	--	--
Hughs, Daniel	--	--	--	--	10.0.0
Johnston, James	--	--	--	1	5.0.0
Jefferies, John	--	--	3	3	--
Little, Henry	--	--	--	--	7.10.0
Little, Jacob	--	--	1	1	15.0.0
Little, Henry, Sen'r	323	--	2	3	80.0.0
Little, Andrew	--	--	--	--	7.10.0
Little, David	--	--	2	3	7.10.0
Little, Casper	413	--	2	3	100.0.0
Little, George	--	--	--	--	10.0.0
Larmor, Thomas	250	--	3	4	70.0.0
Linn, William	135	--	3	5	40.0.0
Linn, Samuel	200	--	3	3	50.0.0
Larmor, John	--	--	--	--	10.0.0
Larmor, John	--	--	2	2	7.10.0
Lawson, David	--	--	--	--	--
Lawson, Robert	--	--	1	1	4.0.0
Lawson, Isaac	--	--	--	--	--
McKenney, Robert	300	--	4	4	80.0.0
McKenney, John	--	--	--	--	10.0.0
McKenney, Andrew	--	--	--	--	10.0.0
Manford, Francis	141	--	3	4	40.0.0
Manford, Peter	139	1	3	6	50.0.0
McBride, Daniel	300	--	5	3	70.0.0
Michael, Jacob	49 1/2	--	--	3	7.10.0
McMaughan, James	170	--	--	--	22.10.0
McCreery, Widow	100	--	--	1	15.0.0
McAllister, James	168	--	3	3	48.0.0
McElhenny, James	200	--	3	3	55.0.0
McAnulty, Charles	50	--	1	2	15.0.0
McElhenny, William	200	--	4	7	50.0.0
McCune, Thomas, Sen'r	20	--	1	2	5.0.0
McCune, Thomas, Jun'r	30	--	2	2	15.0.0
McGowan, William	--	--	2	1	7.0.0
McGowan, Widow	100	--	1	3	15.0.0
McGowan, Rob't	--	--	2	2	8.0.0
Miller, Nicholas	150	--	1	3	37.10.0
Miller, Ludwig	162	--	--	--	37.10.0
Myers, Henry	162	--	2	6	55.0.0
McElhenny, Samuel	200	3	3	--	58.0.0
McKellip, John	--	--	1	1	8.0.0
Miller, James	250	2	4	4	85.0.0
McCush, Samuel	200	1	3	1	72.0.0
Orbison, Thomas	100	--	3	3	25.0.0
Paxton, John	200	--	2	5	55.0.0
Richoson, James	--	--	--	--	15.0.0

Mount Joy Township	Acres	Negroes	Horses	Cattle	Tax
Routbough, John	--	--	--	--	30.0.0
Routbough, Zacharias	130	--	3	2	30.0.0
Robison, Isaac	100	--	3	4	33.0.0
Rice, John	--	--	--	--	7.10.0
Ringland, John	316	--	6	5	90.0.0
Stoner, Frederick	155	--	3	7	50.0.0
Sheely, Nicholas	130	--	2	3	35.0.0
Shown, Nicholas	--	--	2	3	9.0.0
Sheely, Jacob	230	--	4	5	70.0.0
Simerman, Michael	--	--	2	3	9.0.0
Stewart, Robert	100	--	2	3	30.0.0
Stewart, William	120	--	--	--	30.0.0
Smith, Andrew	--	--	--	--	10.0.0
Smith, James	--	--	--	--	10.0.0
Smith, Samuel	188	--	2	1	40.0.0
Stewart, James	160	--	3	5	69.0.0
Thomson, Joseph	36	--	2	2	72.15.0
Thomson, Wm.	145	--	3	3	37.10.0
Townsley, John	285	1	3	6	90.0.0
Townsley, George	--	--	--	--	15.0.0
Timmons, Charles	--	--	--	--	10.0.0
Vance, Urban	100	--	1	1	20.0.0
Timmons, Paul	163	--	3	3	45.0.0
Wilson, Charles, Sen'r	150	--	2	6	22.10.0
Willson, Robert	--	--	--	--	22.10.0
Wilson, Charles	--	--	--	--	5.0.0
Wilson, Joseph	314	--	6	3	80.0.0
Wilson, Daron, town	500	--	--	--	150.0.0
Wilson, John	--	--	2	3	9.0.0
Wilson, Samuel	--	--	2	2	8.0.0
West, James	--	--	1	2	--
Wisdel, Widow	236	--	4	6	60.0.0
Weems, Thomas	315	--	3	5	90.0.0
Weems, John	--	--	--	--	15.0.0
Young, Robert	141	--	3	6	40.0.0
	--	--	--	--	--

MANALLEN TOWNSHIP

	Acres	Negroes	Horses	Cattle	Tax
Anderson, John	--	--	1	3	27.0.0
Adams, Hugh	50	--	2	2	21.0.0
Apple, Vendel	--	--	--	1	0.10.0
Abercromey, John	--	--	--	--	10.0.0
Armstrong, Thomas	150	--	2	3	34.0.0
Black, John	--	--	1	--	15.0.0
Bleckley, William	--	--	--	--	10.0.0
Bender, Jacob	261	--	5	5	137.11.8
Bender, Jacob	--	--	1	--	20.0.0
Bowan, Thomas	100	--	2	1	25.3.4
Bowan, Jonathan	30	--	1	1	27.13.4
Bleckley, James	100	--	3	5	15.15.0
Blackburn, Thomas	100	--	2	3	91.6.8

Manallen Township	Acres	Negroes	Horses	Cattle	Tax
Bracken, Thomas	100	--	1	2	53.3.4
Biggar, William	128	--	3	6	36.10.0
Baldwin, Thomas	100	--	2	4	105.15.0
Barnet, John	143	--	2	2	45.0.9
Beaker, Philip	140	--	3	3	28.18.4
Bowsman, Laurence	200	--	2	2	43.0.0
Burntregger, Andrew	150	--	3	4	79.13.4
Bender, Conrad	--	--	2	4	5.0.0
Brandon, William	--	--	2	1	1.1.8
Brown, Hugh	--	--	1	2	0.13.4
Bowan, Thomas	--	--	--	--	10.0.0
Bracken, Widow	100	--	2	2	55.0.0
Clark, Henry	45	--	2	1	4.18.4
Colmery, William	209	--	4	6	45.12.6
Colmery, John	--	--	--	--	10.0.0
Chambers, Robert	280 1/2	--	5	6	70.3.4
Chambers, Robert	--	--	1	--	15.0.0
Chambers, James	--	--	2	3	4.10.0
Cochran, William	247	--	4	7	66.16.6
Cord, John	18	--	2	3	6.3.4
Carson, William	170	--	3	3	35.1.8
Carstiman, Christian	100	--	3	4	82.0.0
Carlisle, Henry	--	--	2	--	--
Davis, Joseph	--	--	2	2	14.13.4
Darborough, Isaac	60	--	2	4	16.6.8
Domi, George	50	--	2	2	--
Elliot, Robert	--	--	--	--	20.0.0
Fleming, Archibald	94	--	2	2	9.0.0
Fink, Casper	60	--	2	2	10.15.0
Ferguson, Widow	190	--	1	2	--
Graham, James	716	--	--	--	--
Grudy, Elisha	--	--	--	--	10.0.0
Griffith, Widow	7	--	1	1	12.0.0
Griffith, William	100	--	2	4	114.0.0
Gilliland, John	200	--	2	5	55.4.2
Gilliland, Samuel	--	--	1	--	15.0.0
Gilliland, William	--	--	1	2	2.8.4
Good, Charles	80	--	2	3	15.16.8
Graham, Robert	200	--	3	5	50.16.8
Graham, William	80	--	2	3	17.8.4
Glasgow, James	209	--	4	6	48.1.8
Glasgow, Nathaniel	--	--	--	--	10.0.0
Gilbreath, John	300	2	6	5	106.9.2
Graham, William	--	--	1	--	--
Gilbert, George	243	--	4	5	50.3.4
Glass, Mathias	100	--	2	4	13.1.8
Hammer, William	--	--	1	--	10.0.0
Hickenlooper, Andrew	80	--	2	2	27.16.8
Hickenlooper, Andrew	--	--	--	--	--
Holms, Thomas	100	--	2	4	23.5.0
Hutton, William	200	--	3	4	235.13.4
Hutton, Levy	--	--	--	--	20.0.0
Hoobley's land	150	--	--	--	25.0.0
Hammons, James	50	--	--	--	16.13.4
Hammer, Baltis	100	--	2	4	5.16.8

Manallen Township	Acres	Negroes	Horses	Cattle	Tax
Hamilton, James	200	--	2	3	--
Hendricks, Samuel	100	--	3	4	289.6.8
Hendricks, Nathan	--	--	1	2	6.0.0
Hamilton, Wm.	300	--	2	3	83.13.4
Hamilton, William	--	--	1	2	--
Hewet, George	--	--	1	2	1.6.8
Hewet, Joseph	100	--	2	2	--
Harlon, Samuel	80	--	1	--	54.0.0
Hampton, Robert	--	--	--	2	0.10.0
Hussey, Christopher	--	--	2	1	1.1.8
Hutton, John	--	--	--	--	20.0.0
Hopson, Joseph	100	--	1	2	13.6.8
Hopson, Francis	--	--	--	--	10.0.0
Hamilton, William	114	--	2	5	3.5.0
John, Abel	100	--	2	3	107.0.0
John, Joseph	--	--	--	--	20.0.0
Johnston, John	201 3/4	--	3	5	55.0.0
Johnston, Ephraim	230	--	4	6	60.6.8
Knouse, Francis	160	--	4	4	46.0.4
Light, Jacob	128	--	2	4	32.16.8
Lawrence, Joseph	120	--	2	5	32.5.0
Lawrence, Ephraim	150	--	1	3	16.0.0
Long, John	222	--	2	5	50.8.4
Lomask, Conrad	140	--	2	2	10.8.4
Leney, Joseph	100	--	3	4	20.13.4
Latshaw, Joseph	90	--	3	5	144.6.6
Lincey, James	--	--	--	--	--
Morrison, Hugh	300	--	1	1	68.16.8
Meals, Jacob	--	--	1	2	4.13.4
McConoughy, David	444	--	9	13	117.10.0
McCaslin, Thomas	371	1	4	5	91.5.0
McConoughy, Sam'l	310	--	6	9	99.6.10
McConoughy, Robert	191	--	5	6	81.5.10
Machlin, Alexander	120	--	2	4	33.10.0
McGrail, Owen	50	--	2	3	46.10.0
McGrail, James	100	--	1	3	59.13.4
McGrail, William	--	--	--	--	4.6.8
McQuown, John	100	--	2	4	24.6.8
Morton, John	200	--	2	4	52.11.8
McClean, John	--	--	--	1	5.0.0
Mickle, John	165	--	2	4	43.18.4
Moore, James	98	--	4	3	86.18.4
McGrew, James	150	--	2	2	108.13.4
McGrew, James, Jun'r	--	--	--	1	0.10.0
McBride, William	150	--	2	4	42.11.8
McNaught, James	140	--	3	7	42.13.4
McNaught, William	--	--	--	--	15.0.0
McNaught, Joseph	--	--	1	--	10.0.0
Mays, Charles	150	--	3	4	34.5.0
Mays, Samuel	--	--	1	1	10.0.0
McNutt, Widow	200	--	3	3	40.13.4
McNutt, Francis	--	--	3	2	15.0.0
McCleary, James	150	--	2	2	40.8.4
McFerron, Andrew	196	--	3	3	52.15.0
McKinley, Isaac	171	--	4	4	47.18.4

Manallen Township	Acres	Negroes	Horses	Cattle	Tax
Montgomery, John	130	--	3	3	35.15.0
McQuown, Lawrence	100	--	2	3	15.13.4
McQuown, Thomas	50	--	1	--	15.0.0
McQuown, Wm.	--	--	1	--	10.0.0
McElhenny, William	150	--	3	3	38.11.8
McCleave, Robert	--	--	--	--	15.0.0
Mickle, Elijah	--	--	--	3	5.0.0
Money, John	50	--	2	2	8.8.4
Moore, Widow	200	--	4	3	50.3.4
Moore, Robert	--	--	--	--	10.0.0
Moore, William	--	--	--	--	10.0.0
McCleary, George	45	--	1	2	--
McCreary, John	--	--	--	--	22.10.0
Mays, William	--	--	--	--	15.0.0
McEntire, Robert	--	--	--	--	--
Newel, Andrew	50	--	3	2	8.8.4
Newland, William	94	--	1	1	--
Newland, Elijah	--	--	1	1	1.16.8
Oyler, Felty	154	--	3	7	47.10.0
Oyler, Felty	--	--	--	--	10.0.0
Oyster, George	50	--	--	--	12.10.0
Patterson, William, Jun'r	--	--	2	1	--
Potts, David	88	--	3	4	25.10.0
Patterson, William	124 1/4	--	2	3	11.13.4
Pollock, William	105	--	2	2	20.16.8
Pollock, Joseph	105	--	1	--	27.10.0
Pollock, Richard	--	--	1	--	15.0.0
Pollock, John	100	--	2	2	17.0.0
Pillow, Henry	--	--	--	--	10.0.0
Pope, John	--	--	2	5	3.5.0
Rynolds, Anthony	170	--	3	3	45.5.0
Rynolds, John	--	--	1	--	10.0.0
Russel, William	128	--	4	6	36.16.8
Rish, William	60	--	2	5	40.0.0
Reymer, John	--	--	2	3	20.8.4
Reymer, Frederick	148	--	2	4	37.3.4
Blackburn, Moses	50	--	2	3	9.0.0
Selicks, Thomas	--	--	--	--	--
Selicks, Thomas, Sen'r	150	--	3	2	56.8.4
Stewart, David	130	--	4	6	30.0.0
Stewart, John	148	--	2	4	58.6.8
Spencer, Widow	200	--	1	1	25.13.1
Spencer, Isaac	--	--	3	1	2.15.0
Snider, John	150	--	2	4	82.0.0
Stockton, Joseph	--	--	1	4	--
Stockton, David	200	--	4	6	50.10.0
Stockton, John	--	--	1	2	--
Snider, Abraham	150	--	3	4	80.0.0
Snider, John	--	--	2	4	--
Shafer, Frederick	100	--	2	4	81.0.0
Simpson, John	90	--	1	--	7.18.4
Simpson, James	90	--	--	--	15.0.0
Stoobs, Robert	--	--	2	2	--
Stanover, Frederick	150	--	3	4	41.10.4
Stuart, William	100	--	1	3	42.16.8

Manallen Township	Acres	Negroes	Horses	Cattle	Tax
Thomson, William	--	150	2	4	55.6.8
Trosbough, Peter	80	--	2	4	9.6.8
Taylor, Joseph	100	--	2	3	10.8.4
Townsend, Benjamin	150	--	2	3	143.13.4
Taylor, Benjamin	20	--	--	2	1.11.8
Tarr, Peter	20 1/2	--	1	2	12.0.0
Williams, Thomas	80	--	3	6	37.6.8
Warrington, Frederick	50	--	2	3	19.16.8
Wright, John	160	--	2	4	143.0.0
Wright, Benjamin	100	--	1	2	55.6.8
Wright, Jonathan	100	--	2	2	92.0.0
Wright, Widow	150	--	2	4	200.13.4
Williams, William	--	--	--	--	--
Wright, William	--	--	2	3	20.0.0
Wright, John	--	--	--	--	20.0.0
Weaver, Adam	--	--	2	1	1.5.0
Wright, Henry	--	--	--	--	12.10.0
Wright, James	--	--	--	--	20.0.0
Watson, James	--	--	--	--	3.13.4
Yager, John	--	--	1	2	2.13.4
Young, William	150	--	3	3	41.5.0
Young, Samuel	--	--	--	--	10.0.0
Young, Francis	--	--	--	--	10.0.0
Frederick, Andrew	--	--	--	--	23.15.0
Hammond, Nathan	--	--	--	--	57.0.0
Hasty, Able	--	--	--	--	1.11.8
Hewet, Jonathan	--	--	--	--	2.0.0
McQuown, David	--	--	--	--	15.13.4
Patton, David	--	--	--	--	10.0.0
Sims, Jacob	--	1	--	--	33.6.8
Stewart, James	--	--	--	--	15.0.0

PARADISE TOWNSHIP

	Acres	Negroes	Horses	Cattle	Tax
Appleman, John	250	--	1	3	37.10.0
Ammon, Jacob	200	--	3	3	52.15.0
Arnold, Samuel	150	--	2	3	42.0.0
Aumor, Daniel	130	--	--	3	52.10.0
Aumor, Daniel, Jun'r	--	--	2	1	10.0.0
Altland, Philip	197	--	2	4	42.10.0
Bernard, Ulrich	--	--	1	2	10.0.0
Becher, John	70	--	2	2	15.0.0
Becher, David	--	--	--	1	7.10.0
Becher, Jacob	12	--	1	--	7.10.0
Brighner, Godlieb	100	--	1	--	25.0.0
Balsley, Henry	50	--	1	2	16.0.0
Blyer, Adam	80	--	2	2	20.10.0
Balsley, Joseph	50	--	--	--	11.5.0
Bouser, Abraham	--	--	--	1	5.0.0
Bouser, Jacob	--	--	2	2	10.0.0
Bittinger, Nicholas	300	--	--	--	45.0.0
Brighner, Peter	77	--	1	--	19.10.0

Paradise Township	Acres	Negroes	Horses	Cattle	Tax
Berkheimer, Valentin	150	--	3	4	32.10.0
Becher, Jacob	--	--	--	1	--
Bouser, Daniel	200	--	--	--	50.0.0
Bouser, Daniel	--	--	3	3	10.0.0
Boursax, Valentine	--	--	--	1	--
Beck, George	100	--	2	4	29.15.0
Brenner, Adam	40	--	1	2	5.0.0
Christ, Adam	250	--	2	3	50.0.0
Decker, Frederick	--	--	--	1	15.0.0
Dicks, Peter	300	1	5	6	130.0.0
Dicks, John	--	--	--	--	10.0.0
Doll, Conrad	150	--	2	4	52.0.0
Dello, Nicholas	90	--	2	3	29.15.0
Doll, John	160	--	3	4	52.0.0
Dewalt, Peter	--	--	--	1	10.0.0
Dierdorf, Peter	250	--	3	4	56.0.0
Dierdorf, John	250	--	4	4	72.0.0
Entras, Nicholas	150	--	2	3	26.0.0
Fischel, Wendel	100	--	2	3	27.10.0
Fischel, John	100	--	2	3	26.0.0
Fischel, Michael	120	--	2	4	26.0.0
Fishel, Henry	35	--	1	3	5.0.0
Foerst, Adam	160	--	2	3	48.10.0
Foerst, Martin	100	--	2	2	17.10.0
Fegley, Paul	100	--	--	2	32.10.0
Finks, Michael	82	--	2	2	22.10.0
Frankenberger, Philip	150	--	2	1	20.10.0
Frankenberger, Wm.	--	--	--	1	7.10.0
Frederick, Michael	100	--	3	3	29.25.0
Frankenberger, John	100	--	2	--	7.10.0
Frederick, Andrew	150	--	2	3	27.0.0
Graff, Matthias	100	--	4	5	37.10.0
Geiss, Peter	--	--	3	3	15.0.0
Graff, Henry's widow	150	--	--	1	15.0.0
Greaver, Werner	50	--	2	2	27.0.0
Geyger, Wendle	150	--	2	2	32.10.0
Graff, Michael	100	--	1	1	25.0.0
Griffith, David	150	--	2	4	30.0.0
Hershy, Andrew	200	--	4	8	85.0.0
Hershy, Peter	200	--	2	3	59.5.6
Hershy, Joseph	200	--	4	5	77.0.0
Heller, Martin	30	--	1	2	10.10.0
Heiner, Henry	--	--	--	--	5.0.0
Heltzel, Tobias	180	--	3	4	47.10.0
Heiner, Ludwig	--	--	2	2	9.0.0
Haverstock, Andrew	--	--	2	3	12.15.0
Heidler, John	200	--	3	3	52.0.0
Hailey, Patrick	50	--	2	2	16.0.0
Henry, Conrad	150	--	2	3	20.0.0
Heffner, William	120	--	3	2	40.0.0
Haverstock, Tobias	70	--	2	2	30.0.0
Hairing, Philip	70	--	2	2	20.0.0
Hourey, Jacob	110	--	2	3	23.10.0
Heiner, Yost	--	--	--	1	15.0.0
Haverstock, Philip	100	--	2	2	20.0.0

Paradise Township	Acres	Negroes	Horses	Cattle	Tax
Heim, Charles	80	--	2	2	26.0.0
Heim, Christian	80	--	2	2	23.10.0
Joseph, John	150	--	2	3	22.10.0
Jacobs, George	250	--	2	4	90.0.0
Keepers, Joseph	--	--	1	1	12.0.0
Konrad, George	250	--	4	6	60.0.0
Kerver, Casper	200	--	--	--	45.0.0
Kell, Christian	15	--	--	1	2.10.0
Kell, John	--	--	--	1	5.0.0
Kleinpeter, Rudolph	100	--	2	3	30.0.0
Kulp, Valentine	150	--	1	3	22.10.0
Krone, Laurence	100	--	2	3	19.15.0
Kemp, Christopher	50	--	1	1	13.15.0
Leas, Alexander	--	--	1	1	8.10.0
Leinbach, Christian	100	--	1	3	22.10.0
Lamuth, John	100	--	1	3	12.0.0
Long, Henry	200	--	2	4	40.0.0
Lane, John	100	--	2	3	50.0.0
Leshey, Jacob	100	--	--	--	15.0.0
Moyer, John	200	--	2	3	33.15.0
Moore, Peter	150	--	2	4	31.10.0
Meyer, John	--	--	--	2	8.10.0
Meyer, Philip	100	--	2	3	21.10.0
Marx, Jacob	130	--	2	3	19.0.0
Mease, John	400	--	2	3	85.0.0
Mummert, John	20	--	--	1	12.10.0
Mummert, Matthias	13	--	--	1	19.15.0
Mummert, Richard	--	--	--	1	15.15.6
Mummert, William	100	--	2	3	33.10.0
Nelson, John	--	--	1	2	10.0.0
Nagle, John	--	--	2	4	16.10.0
Pensil, Casper	100	--	1	3	27.10.0
Palley, Andrew	250	--	2	3	32.10.0
Puse, Peter	200	--	4	4	50.0.0
Pentz, Nicholas	100	--	2	2	20.0.0
Pussel, Thomas	50	--	--	2	16.10.0
Plonk, Michael	--	--	2	2	11.5.0
Peifer, Adam	80	--	1	2	11.5.0
Philip, Jacob	100	--	2	3	39.15.0
Raimer, Francis	181	--	3	3	60.0.0
Roads, Jacob	100	--	3	3	48.10.0
Roads, Abraham	100	--	2	3	33.15.0
Roads, Christian	--	--	1	1	--
Roads, George	--	--	--	2	10.0.0
Roffelsberger, Martin	100	--	1	2	24.15.0
Roffersberger, Christian	150	--	--	--	28.15.0
Rots, Peter	80	--	2	3	18.0.0
Rudey, George	180	--	2	6	86.15.6
Rentzler, Widow	100	--	2	4	27.15.0
Spring Forge	800	--	--	--	250.0.0
Spangler, Rudolph	250	--	4	4	100.0.0
Spengler, Henry	150	--	4	4	75.0.0
Spangler, Bernard	150	--	3	3	75.0.0
Stover, Jacob	100	--	3	3	37.10.0
Stofer, John	270	--	3	3	135.0.0

Paradise Township	Acres	Negroes	Horses	Cattle	Tax
Shirk, John	250	--	4	5	88.10.0
Shafer, Philip	200	--	4	4	43.10.0
Strasback, Michael	126	--	1	2	13.10.0
Schmeltzer, Adam	--	--	--	1	8.10.0
Shapman, William	--	--	--	2	7.10.0
Sneider, Anthony	100	--	2	2	23.15.0
Sneider, Jacob	--	--	--	--	14.0.0
Stifler, Jacob	100	--	2	2	14.0.0
Stover, Frederick	250	--	3	6	70.0.0
Speece, Christopher	100	--	--	1	23.15.0
Sweisguth, Laurence	80	--	2	3	32.10.0
Sunday, John	80	--	2	3	30.0.0
Sweigert, Jacob	--	--	1	1	--
Sarbach, Jacob	200	--	--	--	25.0.0
Tucker, Tempest	--	--	--	--	12.10.0
Turner, Peter	--	--	--	1	7.10.0
Tressler, George	70	--	2	3	20.0.0
Trump, Peter	100	--	2	3	22.10.0
Tumpf, Mathas	50	--	1	2	18.0.0
Trimmer, Andrew	150	--	2	3	32.15.0
Trimmer, John	100	--	2	2	31.10.0
Wiest, John	150	--	3	4	90.0.0
Wilson, Joseph	5	--	4	6	85.0.0
Wiest, Christian	150	--	4	3	58.0.0
White, Thomas	--	--	1	2	8.10.0
White, William	--	--	2	3	15.10.0
White, George	150	--	1	1	23.15.0
Wollet, George	80	--	1	2	17.10.0
Weinand, Philip	138	--	1	2	26.0.0
Wolst, Philip	--	--	1	2	13.15.0
Wailer, Henry	200	--	4	4	14.10.0
Wagner, Yost	--	--	--	2	9.0.0
Wolf, Peter, Esq'r	250	--	--	--	35.0.0
Winkler, Francis	180	--	1	3	20.0.0
Walder, Adam	100	--	2	3	25.0.0
Walder, Henry	70	--	2	3	25.0.0
Zollinger, Peter	150	--	2	3	32.10.0

Single Men

	Amount of Tax		Amount of Tax
Puse, John	10.0.0	Slonicher, Christian	15.0.0
Berkheimer, Martin	--	Long, Jacob	10.0.0
Fissel, Adam	15.0.0	First, Adam	48.10.0
Hirshy, Christian	15.0.0	Ashliman, David	20.0.0
Haverstock, Conrad	15.0.0	Brown, James	3.0.0
Henry, Jacob	15.0.0	Bentz, Andrew	3.0.0
Spengler, Henry	15.0.0	Geip, Peter	3.0.0
Spengler, Bernard	15.0.0	Emig, Paul	3.0.0
Stover, Nicholas	15.0.0	Maulsback, Peter	3.0.0
Kleinpeter, Adam	15.0.0	Sunday, Jacob	3.0.0
Kleinpeter, Rudolph	15.0.0	Lamuth, Francis	15.0.0
Worst, Jacob	15.0.0	Young, Christian	3.0.0

Single Men

Studebaker, Clementz	15.0.0	Wolf, Peter, Esq'r	10.0.0
Zollinger, Peter	15.0.0	Sarback, Jacob	26.10.0
Berkheimer, Valentine	15.0.0	Winemiller, Stophel	8.10.0
Sunday, Joseph	15.0.0	Mummert, Richzrd	24.10.0

CODORUS TOWNSHIP

	Acres	Negroes	Horses	Cattle	Tax
Albright, Henry	119	--	--	--	11.18.0
Alt, Valentine	45	--	--	1	10.0.0
Amspoker, George	40	--	2	3	10.0.0
Almeroth, George	--	--	--	--	--
Bauman, John	80	--	2	2	25.0.0
Bailey, Jacob	10	--	1	--	5.0.0
Bortner, George	50	--	2	2	75.0.0
Brunneman, Benjamin	57	--	2	2	13.0.0
Brannam, William	200	--	2	3	18.15.0
Brunneman, Samuel	200	--	2	4	25.0.0
Baker, William	50	--	--	4	15.0.0
Bope, Mathias	100	--	2	3	20.0.0
Baker, Henry	--	--	1	2	3.0.0
Beyer, John	100	--	1	4	13.7.0
Brodbeck, John	--	--	--	2	10.0.0
Bear, Jacob	200	--	4	5	90.0.0
Bealer, Jacob	50	--	--	2	6.13.0
Bealer, Michael	100	--	3	3	40.0.0
Baker, William, Jun'r	--	--	3	4	10.0.0
Brillhard, Peter	200	--	5	2	80.0.0
Bollinger, Abraham	100	--	1	2	10.0.0
Bacler, Jacob	150	--	3	4	45.0.0
Dahofe, George	225	--	2	3	45.0.0
Dahofe, Henry	25	--	4	5	1.13.0
Dahofe, Nicholas	100	--	1	2	16.10.0
Diel, George	300	--	5	4	10.0.0
Dentlinger, Adam	6	--	1	--	2.5.0
Diel, Charles	300	2	4	8	150.0.0
Egy, Michael	300	4	11	20	175.0.0
Egy, Michael	200	--	--	--	10.0.0
Everhart, John	--	--	--	1	6.14.0
Ehrman, Michael	175	--	2	4	20.0.0
Donaldson, Joseph	150	--	--	--	13.15.0
Epply, Jacob	180	--	3	7	27.10.0
Emich, George	170	--	2	2	17.10.0
Emich, Philip	200	--	2	3	40.0.0
Eichelberger, Frederick	100	--	--	--	16.13.0
Fischel, Henry	100	--	2	1	--
Fulkner, Jacob	70	--	--	6	13.7.0
Fraser, Frederick	129	--	2	6	30.0.0
Foltz, Adam	40	--	--	1	6.13.0
Farnsler, George	20	--	--	1	5.0.0
Getz, Martin	--	--	2	2	5.0.0
Gerberich, Peter	70	--	2	3	20.0.0
Gantz, Francis	200	--	2	8	60.0.0

Codorus Township	Acres	Negroes	Horses	Cattle	Tax
Gentzler, Philip	--	--	--	2	7.10.0
Glasick, Samuel	100	--	2	2	20.0.0
Gramer, Widow	150	--	3	3	20.0.0
Grier, David	100	--	--	--	15.0.0
Henry, Jacob	80	--	1	2	33.7.0
Hoseler, Michael	60	--	1	2	13.7.0
Hosler, Joseph	150	--	2	3	25.0.0
Huber, George	200	--	2	10	40.0.0
Henich, Peter	200	--	2	4	40.0.0
Hinchel, Anthony	100	--	--	--	12.10.0
Hederich, Jacob	150	--	2	4	85.0.0
Hillman, Philip	100	--	1	3	11.7.0
Hillman, John	120	--	2	3	26.13.0
Herleman, Sebastian	213	--	2	5	10.0.0
Hoober, Ulrich	300	--	3	8	135.0.0
Ham, Daniel	228	--	2	6	33.7.0
Ham, John	--	--	2	2	7.10.0
Haffner, Jacob	100	--	4	3	33.7.0
Houser, John	150	--	2	5	15.0.0
Henry, Nicholas	144	--	--	--	10.0.0
Killcanon, John	10	--	--	1	2.5.0
Hirshy, Andrew	100	--	--	--	10.0.0
Hauser, Peter	150	--	2	1	7.10.0
Hellman, Sebastian	86	--	2	2	10.0.0
Hofe, Francis	75	--	1	2	20.0.0
Hofe, Andrew	80	--	3	2	60.0.0
Hoffman, Adam	130	--	4	3	50.0.0
Hossler, Christian	--	--	--	1	7.10.0
Hirshy, John	200	--	--	--	12.10.0
Hirshy, Peter	100	--	--	--	10.0.0
Hoke, John	100	--	--	--	10.0.0
Jonas, Daniel	50	--	1	2	10.0.0
Kleindienst, David	300	--	3	6	55.0.0
Kroll, John	280	--	2	5	56.13.0
Kleindienst, Godfrey	150	--	2	3	10.0.0
Kerker, Jacob	50	--	--	4	12.10.0
Kreps, Ludwig	450	--	2	8	55.0.0
Kreps, Peter	311	--	3	2	20.0.0
Keller, George, Jun'r	50	--	2	2	10.0.0
Kreiss, Jacob	95	--	2	4	13.7.0
Kuhn, Henry	80	--	1	2	10.0.0
Keller, Jacob	170	--	2	4	55.0.0
Kirsh, Jacob	75	--	--	--	10.0.0
Kneyer, Leonard	60	--	2	3	12.10.0
Keller, George	200	--	2	3	130.0.0
Kyser, Jacob	200	--	--	--	50.0.0
Kessler, Henry	50	--	--	2	7.10.0
Kessler, Michael	50	--	1	1	10.0.0
Kuntz, Abraham	100	--	2	2	20.0.0
Kuntz, Peter	75	--	2	2	20.0.0
Kindlein, John	--	--	--	2	3.7.0
Klatfelter, Felix	200	--	2	4	43.7.0
Klatfelter, Michael	--	--	--	--	5.0.0
Ligget, James	128	--	3	3	20.0.0
Liggett, James	190	--	--	--	29.3.0

Codorus Township	Acres	Negroes	Horses	Cattle	Tax
Leshy, Jacob	180	--	3	7	40.0.0
Lorick, Jacob	50	--	2	2	15.0.0
Lear, Valentine	--	--	1	1	--
Leonard, Charles	--	--	--	1	7.10.0
Law, Peter	150	--	3	4	95.0.0
Law, Andrew	--	--	2	2	10.0.0
Law, George	--	--	--	1	10.0.0
Law, Michael	200	--	--	--	10.0.0
Law, Philip	100	--	--	--	10.0.0
Lawson, Widow	140	1	2	3	40.0.0
Lechner, Michael	--	--	--	1	5.0.0
Lohman, Atony	--	--	--	1	7.10.0
Miller, Peter	210	--	2	4	--
Mourer, John	121	--	2	3	17.10.0
Marchel, Henry	388	--	2	5	40.0.0
Meyer, John	300	--	4	4	93.7.0
Miller, George	100	--	2	2	22.10.0
Miller, Andrew	20	--	--	1	7.10.0
Miller, Widow	50	--	1	2	8.7.0
Matz, Jacob	--	--	--	1	2.5.0
Meyer, Frederick	--	--	2	2	--
Neyman, George	240	--	2	2	17.10.0
Neff, Henry	100	--	--	4	12.10.0
Neycomer, Henry	50	--	--	2	5.0.0
Noll, Jacob	100	--	2	1	5.0.0
Ott, John	--	--	3	3	--
Ollinger, Peter	50	--	2	2	15.0.0
Ortman, John	50	--	1	1	6.13.0
Peter, Stephen	300	--	6	2	50.0.0
Peter, Michael	--	--	--	--	5.0.0
Rohrbough, Christian	259	--	3	8	18.17.0
Ripold, George	50	--	1	1	5.0.0
Ripold, Adam	10	--	--	1	2.5.0
Ross, Michael	40	--	--	1	5.0.0
Ripold, Andrew	100	--	4	2	16.13.0
Ruhl, John	100	--	2	4	3.0.0
Ruhl, William	200	--	2	6	18.17.0
Rigel, Ludwig	160	--	2	2	16.13.0
Rohrbach, Lawrence	159	--	2	3	16.13.0
Renoly, Daniel	300	--	5	6	100.0.0
Renoly, Daniel, Ju'r	--	--	--	1	--
Runk, Yost	100	--	2	3	22.10.0
Rudisill, Jacob	100	--	2	2	40.0.0
Rever, John	100	--	2	2	40.0.0
Ruhl, John	30	--	--	--	33.7.0
Simon, Casper	50	--	2	2	13.6.0
Simon, John	50	--	2	3	13.6.0
Senft, Philip	40	--	1	2	5.0.0
Senft, Philip, Ju'r	15	--	1	1	7.10.0
Souer, Leonard	60	--	--	3	10.0.0
Sabough, Jacob	100	--	--	3	9.13.0
Skills, Henry	180	--	2	4	33.7.0
Spossart, Michael	100	--	1	2	20.0.0
Snider, Henry	--	--	1	2	--
Shultz, Lawrence	300	--	2	2	40.0.0

Codorus Township	Acres	Negroes	Horses	Cattle	Tax
Stambach, Philip	50	--	4	2	20.0.0
Stambach, Peter	--	--	--	1	5.0.0
Smelzer, Widow	80	--	1	2	15.0.0
Strickhouser, Widow	50	--	1	1	5.0.0
Spengler, Balzer	149	--	--	--	55.0.0
Stoufer, Daniel	200	--	--	--	30.0.0
Stambach, Jacob	116	--	3	4	18.7.0
Stuck, Peter	200	--	3	4	30.0.0
Shafer, Jacob	100	--	2	4	45.0.0
Sherer, John	25	--	--	2	10.0.0
Shnider, Martin	100	--	1	2	15.0.0
Sherer, Jacob	150	--	2	4	80.0.0
Smith, George	150	--	2	4	40.0.0
Snider, Dewald	100	--	2	5	20.0.0
Smith, Mathias	--	--	2	2	--
Snider, Michael	--	--	1	3	7.10.0
Sholl, Jacob's widow	213	--	2	3	12.10.0
Shadler, Andrew	150	--	2	5	22.10.0
Shyrer, Martin	130	--	2	4	13.7.0
Schlessman, George	100	--	2	3	16.3.0
Schultz, Michael	100	--	2	2	11.13.0
Shyrer, Michael	--	--	1	1	--
Shwing, Dennis	--	--	2	2	10.0.0
Shoe, Zachariah	70	--	2	2	15.0.0
Spenckel, Peter	--	--	--	--	10.0.0
Shank, Henry	200	--	3	4	27.0.0
Wertz, John	--	--	--	1	5.0.0
Walter, John	90	--	1	3	10.0.0
Wideman, Sebastian	192	--	4	2	25.0.0
Winemiller, Francis	260	--	5	3	27.10.0
Winter, Jacob	--	--	2	2	8.7.0
Wilhelm, Henry	256	--	2	4	20.0.0
Werner, John	50	--	--	4	10.0.0
Wiant, Nicholas	53	--	1	1	8.7.0
Werley, Henry	100	--	--	1	8.7.0
Werley, George	100	--	4	2	20.0.0
Walter, Jacob	200	--	3	5	60.0.0
Walter, George	--	--	1	3	10.0.0
Wideman, Henry	--	--	--	--	5.0.0
Ziegler, Nicholas	130	--	2	4	30.0.0
Ziegler, Jacob	80	--	2	4	20.0.0
Ziegler, Barnet	400	--	3	13	90.0.0
Pflieger, Jacob	--	--	--	--	10.0.0

Single Men

Weaver, John	30.0.0		Renolly, Peter	--
Deeds, Jacob	--		Shank, Michael	10.0.0
Kreps, George	15.0.0		Brillhart, Jacob	20.0.0
Rohrbach, John	8.0.0		Freyter, John	5.0.0
Shultz, Michael	8.0.0		Harris, Thomas	8.0.0
Ripolt, Nicholas	--		Klatfelter, Henry	8.0.0
Kaltrider, George	20.0.0		Fischel, Henry	15.0.0

Single Men

Gramer, Helfrey	12.0.0	Copp, John	10.0.0
Bear, Jacob	20.0.0	Decker, John	2.5.0
Keller, Jacob	20.0.0	Blillhart, Peter, Jun'r	2.5.0
Runk, Valentine	8.0.0	Beltz, Michael	2.5.0
Ham, Daniel	10.0.0	Bechtel, Jacob	2.5.0
Helman, Laurence	20.0.0	Fonhover, Jacob	15.0.0
Woods, Elias	28.0.0	Peters, Richard	16.13.0
Miller, George	20.0.0	Wertz, Daniel	5.0.0
Miller, Jacob	20.0.0	Keller, Abraham	20.0.0
Rubel, Christian	35.0.0	Reibold, Michael	5.0.0
Klin, John	5.0.0		

MOUNT PLEASANT TOWNSHIP

	Acres	Negroes	Horses	Cattle	Tax
Andrew, John	150	--	3	4	35.15.0
Ammerman, Henry	100	--	2	4	22.17.6
Burnet, George	--	--	1	3	7.10.0
Brinkerhoof, James	257	--	4	11	78.6.8
Buchanon, Henry	182	--	3	4	52.18.4
Brinkerhoof, Gilbert	214	--	3	6	40.1.8
Brinkerhoof, Raliff	270	--	4	5	64.7.6
Brinkerhoof, Jacob	--	--	2	2	10.0.0
Brillhart, Joseph	--	--	3	5	20.0.0
Baker, Mathias	179	--	3	3	39.7.6
Bealey, William	--	--	3	4	50.0.0
Burgan, Peter	76	--	3	3	10.18.4
Banta, Peter	140	--	2	4	1.13.4
Bolten, Robert	--	--	3	--	7.10.0
Camp, George	6	--	1	2	9.0.0
Cochenauer, John	100	--	3	3	21.17.6
Cooper, William	350	--	2	3	60.0.0
Cooper, James	150	--	1	3	10.0.0
Cannine, Peter	173	--	2	4	35.0.0
Clapsaddle, Michael	150	--	3	5	74.3.4
Cannon, Thomas	--	--	1	1	10.0.0
Chambers, John	50	--	2	7	25.18.3
Cline, John	100	--	2	2	44.3.4
Chamberlain, Niviath	167	--	--	--	36.9.3
Degraff, Michael	270	--	4	6	71.5.10
Degraff, Abraham	--	--	2	2	7.10.0
Degraff, William	119	--	2	2	26.0.10
Damaree, David	152	--	5	6	45.3.4
Duff, John	--	--	2	4	12.19.0
Dotter, Conrad	200	--	--	--	35.0.0
Ewing, Isaac	100	--	2	3	24.7.6
Eichelberger, Ludwig	200	--	2	3	35.0.0
English, David	--	--	--	--	20.0.0
Ewing, John	100	--	4	5	47.1.8
Ewing, Samuel, Esq'r	200	--	4	5	90.0.0
Ewing, Robert	100	--	--	--	41.13.4
Fonasdelin, Simon	--	--	--	--	14.3.4
Foller, Adam	125	--	2	1	27.1.8

Mount Pleasant Township	Acres	Negroes	Horses	Cattle	Tax
Flemon, Robert	--	--	--	--	--
Faris, George	279	--	5	5	40.5.0
Freed, Peter	130	--	3	5	69.16.8
Freed, Christian	130	--	3	5	69.16.8
Forney, Henry	100	--	1	2	25.5.0
Fonasdelin, Simon	130	--	3	1	30.0.0
Fandike, Henry	100	--	3	1	22.10.0
Fonasdelin, Lukens	100	--	1	4	22.0.0
Gettis, William	200	--	--	--	41.13.8
Graham, Nathan	--	--	2	2	3.0.0
Gelwix, Daniel	150	--	2	5	33.2.6
Galbraith, Robert	120	--	3	5	40.0.0
Garrey, James	122	--	--	--	25.5.6
Garrey, John	121	--	--	--	25.4.2
Hagon, Patrick	--	--	2	2	20.0.0
Hagan, to heirs	350	--	--	--	72.18.4
Hagon, Henry	--	--	2	1	10.0.0
Haughdelin, Ezechiel	272	--	6	6	74.3.4
Hunter, John	--	--	1	1	12.0.0
Houts, John	198	--	4	7	106.10.9
Huppert, Catharine	200	--	2	4	40.0.0
Haggy, John	100	--	2	5	30.19.2
Haggy, George	--	--	1	1	15.0.0
Halebach, Christoph	93	--	2	2	20.12.6
Hear, Christian	200	--	--	--	58.6.8
Johnson, Thomas	234	--	3	5	61.5.0
Kipp, John	94	--	2	3	21.0.10
Karr, Joshua, Sen'r	350	--	3	3	75.4.2
Karr, Joshua, Jun'r	--	--	--	--	7.10.0
Lilly, Thomas	30	--	--	--	--
Lacky, George	260	--	4	6	57.1.8
Little, John	100	--	2	2	44.3.4
Lockart, Moses	200	--	1	4	35.18.4
Lindsay, James	--	--	2	2	40.3.4
Lilley, John	206	--	5	6	63.0.10
Laudebach, Henry	--	--	3	3	10.0.0
McAllister, Abdil	100	--	--	--	25.16.10
McCherry, Patrick	600	--	--	--	130.0.0
Morton, John	100	--	--	--	2.1.8
Miller, James	--	--	3	4	7.10.0
Marsdill, Edward	260	--	3	3	87.9.4
McClure, John	20	--	2	2	7.0.0
McCurdy, Samuel	80	--	2	3	15.2.6
McCutchen, James	53	--	1	--	22.0.3
McElvain, Moses	--	--	3	2	12.0.0
McElvain, Andrew	218	--	2	4	100.0.0
Mouse, George	248	--	2	2	51.13.4
Morningstar, John	160	--	3	2	30.0.0
Myers, Martin	150	--	1	--	35.1.8
Myers, Michael	100	--	1	2	21.17.6
McCarter, Alexander	366	--	4	5	97.0.0
Monfort, James	193	--	4	5	40.10.0
Maxwell, John	42	--	1	1	10.6.8
McElvain, John	482	--	3	3	80.3.4
Mouse, Ludwig	209	--	3	5	48.2.6

Mount Pleasant Township	Acres	Negroes	Horses	Cattle	Tax
McMacing, Patrick	--	--	1	1	--
McElvain, William	--	--	2	3	1.10.0
McCreery, John	150	--	1	7	40.5.0
McCreery, Amos	--	--	1	1	7.10.0
Neely, Thomas, Se'r	--	--	2	3	7.10.0
Orr, William	175	--	4	10	50.4.2
Orr, Robert	219	--	2	4	35.0.0
Patterson, Garrett	--	--	--	--	--
Patterson, Thomas	200	--	4	3	59.6.8
Potter, John	149	--	2	4	26.0.4
Parks, John	175	--	3	9	33.0.0
Patton, James	--	--	1	2	7.10.0
Ranger, John	--	--	2	3	25.0.0
Rudolfh, Stephen	30	--	--	--	7.13.4
Reynolds, William, Sen'r	209	--	3	5	50.19.2
Ross, William	--	--	--	--	--
Smock, John	100	--	2	5	25.14.2
Slench, Philip	128	--	2	3	28.0.0
Shelly, Widow	120	--	2	3	20.0.0
Shelly, Jacob	150	--	2	5	33.2.6
Spitler, Jacob	280	--	2	6	61.5.0
Smock, Mathias	50	--	--	3	15.10.0
Sturgeon, Henry	180	--	2	6	44.11.4
Shupe, Jacob	245	--	3	3	105.0.0
Shupe, Martin	--	--	1	1	20.0.0
Smock, Barney	85	--	2	3	15.9.4
Skakeley, William	528	--	5	11	100.0.0
Shriver, John	132	--	2	2	68.10.0
Swigert, John	150	--	3	3	40.6.0
Stuart, James	100	--	--	--	26.16.8
Theobat, Shollas	190	--	1	3	100.0.0
Teeter, Joseph	140	--	3	4	40.0.0
Torrens, William	173	--	3	3	76.13.4
Tickerhuff, Frederick	--	--	3	4	5.0.0
Vantine, Javish	200	--	4	2	43.10.10
Vantine, Charles	--	--	4	4	7.10.0
Vestervelt, Abraham	--	--	2	3	7.10.0
Watson, William	170	--	4	7	38.10.10
Winemiller, Christian	160	--	7	3	36.17.6
Whitley, Benjamin	200	--	5	3	40.9.6
Wilford, Peter	286	--	4	11	80.0.0
Young, Peter	300	--	7	7	186.13.4
Young, Frederick	220	--	1	7	50.0.0
McGuffy, Joseph	446	--	3	3	134.9.9

Single Men

	Amount of Tax		Amount of Tax
Lachy, George	7.10.0	Clapsaddle, Daniel	20.0.0
Lindsay, John	12.0.0	Camper, Michael	10.0.0
Lindsay, Joseph	7.10.0	Sheakley, George	7.10.0
Brady, Nicholas	15.0.0	McAllister, John	15.0.0
Bailey, James	10.0.0	Weaver, Boston	15.0.0
Clapsaddle, Francis, Ju'r	20.0.0	McCreary, Thomas	15.0.0

Mount Pleasant Township   Single Men

	Amount of Tax		Amount of Tax
McCracken, James	7.10.0	Duff, John	10.0.0
Houghdelin, Abraham	7.10.0	Vandine, Charles	7.10.0
Degraff, Samuel	7.10.0	Barr, Charles	20.0.0
Bryan, Jeremiah	10.0.0	Vandike, Peter	26.3.4
Mixel, Peter	15.0.0	Graham, James	10.0.0
Marsden, Mathew	15.0.0	Lacky, Alexander	7.10.0
Marsden, James	20.0.0	McNight, Thomas	37.10.0
Kerr, James	15.0.0	Oar, Charles, Ju'r	10.0.0
Neely, Thomas	7.10.0	Rynolds, Wm., Ju'r	10.0.0
McCollough, Rob't	15.0.0	Sturgeon, Jeremiah	20.0.0
Smith, Charles	20.0.0	Steel, Samuel	15.0.0
Cochenauer, Garret	30.19.0	Vintner, Savage	43.10.10
Panton, David	7.10.0	Dumeree, Garret	7.10.0
Stergeon, William	7.10.0	Hagon, Edward	15.0.0
Wattson, John	7.10.0	Kiegler, Cornelius	7.10.0
Duff, James	10.0.0	McCreary, John	36.5.0

WARRINGTON TOWNSHIP

	Acres	Negroes	Horses	Cattle	Tax
Ayres, David	--	--	3	4	12.0.0
Atherton, Thomas	350	--	2	4	188.0.0
Atherton, Thomas	100	--	--	--	--
Atherton, Henry	--	--	2	1	8.15.0
Atherton, Richard's widow	--	--	--	--	--
Alcock, John	--	--	--	2	4.0.0
Alcock, Francis	20	--	--	1	7.10.0
Aker, Michael	--	--	2	1	11.11.0
Brugh, John	150	--	3	3	70.0.0
Brugh, Jacob	150	--	2	3	67.18.0
Brouster, Charles	--	--	--	2	5.8.0
Brunton, Thomas	--	--	2	3	4.0.0
Beam, Henry	50	--	2	2	13.2.6
Binder, Martin	300	--	3	5	106.0.0
Bower, Michael	150	--	3	6	111.7.6
Bauman, Jacob	150	--	3	6	72.0.0
Blackford, Mary	80	--	1	1	5.0.0
Blair, Brice	100	--	2	1	50.5.3
Blair, John	50	--	2	1	14.0.0
Boyd, George	--	--	--	--	40.0.0
Brumagim, John	2	--	1	2	3.0.0
Brindley, Jacob	150	--	3	4	109.7.6
Brindley, Jacob	--	--	--	--	10.0.0
Brunton, John	100	--	2	4	18.15.0
Bower, Peter	100	--	2	4	50.10.0
Cookis, Adam	--	--	--	1	6.0.0
Cloudy, Martin	125	--	2	4	44.0.0
Cook, Jacob	100	--	1	1	51.0.0
Cook, Samuel	90	--	2	4	51.10.0
Cook, Peter	100	--	1	3	52.10.0
Coxan, William	--	--	2	1	5.7.0
Cadwallader, James	180	--	3	4	87.15.0

Warrington Township	Acres	Negroes	Horses	Cattle	Tax
Crouss, Daniel	100	--	2	5	65.12.0
Cleaver, Peter	150	--	3	5	67.12.0
Cashady, Nicholas	--	--	1	1	3.4.0
Cooper, Samuel	100	--	1	2	7.10.0
Cramer, Adam	180	--	4	6	95.10.0
Cramer, John	--	--	--	--	7.10.0
Cramer, Henry	--	--	--	--	7.10.0
Cramer, Adam	50	--	--	--	95.0.0
Cox, Nathaniel	90	--	2	3	104.19.0
Cox, Abraham	95	--	2	3	25.0.0
Cox, Richard	100	--	--	1	16.7.0
Cough, George	--	--	--	--	15.0.0
Cuntry, William	20	--	1	--	13.4.0
Crafford, John	25	--	1	--	2.3.0
Conelly, James	--	--	--	--	3.0.0
Cimple, Nicholas	200	--	3	4	60.0.0
Cough, Widow	100	--	2	3	27.5.0
Cox, William	250	--	3	6	262.8.0
Cox, Wm.	--	--	1	1	3.7.6
Dennison, James	263	--	2	4	50.0.0
Drack, Wm.	--	--	1	--	--
Davis, John	170	--	3	4	91.18.0
Davis, Daniel	--	--	--	--	10.0.0
Driver, James	100	--	2	3	20.0.0
Dougherty, Richard	--	--	--	1	--
Davis, Lewis	--	--	--	1	--
Davis, Joshua	3	--	2	2	61.15.0
Dean, Nehemiah	40	--	--	1	4.10.0
Davis, John	--	--	1	3	3.0.0
Dunn, William	--	--	5	3	--
Dickeson, Joshua	--	--	--	2	6.0.0
Evans, Cadwalleder	--	--	--	--	6.0.0
England, Joseph	--	--	--	--	15.0.0
Ealy, George	150	--	3	3	85.0.0
Eurey, Michael	150	--	2	4	55.0.0
Eurey, Widow	100	--	2	3	20.0.0
Elliot, Widow	--	--	--	--	7.10.0
Edmondson, Thomas	150	--	4	9	245.0.0
Edmundson, John	200	--	3	7	256.18.9
Evans, Azariah	--	--	--	--	--
Fogelgesong, Stophel	--	--	--	2	8.15.0
Fogelgesong, Philip	50	--	2	3	37.0.0
Fonastock, Boras	100	--	--	2	280.0.0
Fonastock, Benjamin	100	--	1	2	52.0.0
Fonastock, Daniel	100	--	1	3	53.0.0
Flory, Henry	--	--	1	2	6.7.6
Fulwiler, John	100	--	2	2	65.12.0
Fulwiler, Michael	50	--	2	3	37.0.0
Farra, William	100	--	2	5	20.0.0
Feagon, James	--	--	1	1	8.0.0
Frazier, Ezechiel	45	--	1	2	43.14.9
Faster, Henry	50	--	2	3	37.0.0
Garrison, William	250	--	2	4	126.17.6
Graft, John	200	--	2	3	46.18.9
Gray, James	83	--	2	--	15.0.0

Warrington Township	Acres	Negroes	Horses	Cattle	Tax
Garrison, John	--	--	2	2	21.17.6
Grist, John, Sen'r	200	--	4	8	280.0.0
Grist, John	--	--	2	4	35.0.0
Garrison, John	200	--	3	7	231.10.0
Green, Joseph	80	--	1	1	23.17.6
Griffey, Widow	250	--	2	3	37.10.0
Griffey, Jacob	200	--	--	--	37.3.9
Griffey, Jacob, Prop'y	--	--	2	--	111.11.3
Green, John	--	--	1	1	3.0.0
Gallesby, John	--	--	--	--	3.0.0
Garwood, Mideon	--	--	1	1	6.7.0
Gardner, Peter	427	3	4	6	102.16.3
Holland, Henry	90	--	--	1	23.16.6
Henry, Peter	125	--	2	3	37.2.0
Howe, William	45	--	--	1	5.0.0
Herbach, Casper	--	--	2	2	--
Hool, Samuel	57	--	1	2	26.5.0
Hool, Jacob	100	--	1	3	41.9.6
Holapeter, Mathias	200	--	--	26	384.0.0
Hess, Dewalt	150	--	2	3	126.14.0
Horseman, Ebenezer	90	--	1	--	35.0.0
Jones, John	--	--	1	2	3.7.6
Jordan, David	250	--	3	4	--
Jordan, Lewis	--	--	--	--	10.0.0
Jordan, Jarman	--	--	1	1	3.7.6
Jones, Amos	--	--	1	2	4.7.6
Kennedy, William	--	--	1	--	6.0.0
Kelly, William	--	--	--	1	--
Kirk, Thomas	--	--	1	2	8.15.0
Kennedy, James	--	--	1	1	2.3.0
Kennedy, Hugh	153	--	2	3	18.15.0
King, Michael	200	--	3	2	25.5.0
Leamer, John	100	--	3	7	142.2.0
Larkin, George	--	--	--	--	--
Latshaw, Peter	150	--	3	6	91.16.0
Leech, Thomas	150	--	3	5	35.0.0
McMullen, John	180	--	2	5	89.12.0
McMullen, Thomas	--	--	1	--	10.0.0
McMullen, William	100	--	3	5	58.19.6
Myers, George	--	--	1	3	15.2.0
McMullin, George	160	--	3	4	112.0.0
Mash, John	250	--	3	4	109.13.0
Mash, Jonathan	150	--	3	7	95.8.0
Maughlin, William	150	--	3	6	157.8.0
Moddy, Samuel	--	--	--	--	7.10.0
Miller, Samuel	--	--	--	--	1.10.0
Mundle, John	179	--	2	2	3.0.0
McClellan, William	285	--	5	6	50.0.0
Maughlin, Samuel	150	--	1	5	78.15.0
Minehart, Peter	25	--	--	--	62.6.0
Myers, John	--	--	--	--	10.0.0
Myers, Peter	--	--	--	--	10.0.0
Minehart, Philip	200	--	2	5	40.0.0
McElway, Samuel	--	--	--	--	10.0.0
McElway, Charles	100	--	2	2	20.0.0

Warrington Township	Acres	Negroes	Horses	Cattle	Tax
McElway, James	50	--	1	3	7.10.0
McMullen, Mathew	--	--	2	4	3.0.0
McMullen, Samuel	400	--	4	6	7.0.0
Moody, John	150	--	2	3	16.0.0
Myers, John	--	--	2	2	12.0.0
Mask, Jonathan	--	--	--	--	12.3.0
Mask, Peter	200	--	4	7	236.1.0
Macklin, William	50	--	--	--	3.0.0
Macklin, Widow	100	--	1	--	10.0.0
May, John	--	--	--	--	15.0.0
Measebough, George	50	--	1	2	7.10.0
Millhouse, Peter	--	--	--	2	6.0.0
Miller, Henry	--	--	1	1	--
Mash, Gravener	250	--	2	3	60.0.0
McElroy, Samuel	--	--	--	--	15.0.0
Maughlin, Hugh	150	--	2	4	120.0.0
Miller, Abraham	80	--	1	2	10.0.0
Morrison, William	200	--	2	6	40.0.0
Matson, Richard	--	--	--	2	--
McQuown, David	--	--	2	2	--
Nisley, Anthony, Ju'r	--	--	1	1	8.15.0
Nisley, John	--	--	2	2	6.11.0
Nisley, Anthony	300	--	3	3	48.2.0
Nelson, Samuel	25	--	--	--	4.7.6
Nelson, Robert	150	--	5	5	25.0.0
Nelson, Lazarus	--	--	--	--	7.10.0
Nelson, Thomas	--	--	--	--	10.0.0
Nelson, James	--	--	--	--	10.0.0
Nebitt, John	323	--	4	8	50.0.0
Nebitt, John	54	--	--	--	--
Nevett, William	100	--	2	3	82.14.9
Nesbitt, Alexander	--	--	1	1	10.0.0
Neucomer, George	--	--	--	--	--
Neucomer, Christian	170	--	3	5	131.5.0
Pream, Jacob	100	--	2	3	55.0.0
Pream, Jacob	--	--	--	--	10.0.0
Pisler, Daniel	--	--	--	--	--
Parks, Robert	10	--	2	3	20.0.0
Pence, John	10	--	2	3	40.7.6
Pisle, Joseph	--	--	--	--	10.0.0
Pisle, Peter	150	--	2	3	80.15.0
Pleaser, Herman	--	--	--	--	10.0.0
Parkinson, James	190	--	3	5	44.15.0
Pisle, Philip	90	--	--	1	15.0.0
Pencely, Felix	150	--	2	2	100.12.0
Parker, Moses	150	--	2	4	87.10.0
Pence, Joseph	150	--	2	4	45.0.0
Pue, David	60	--	1	3	10.0.0
Penrose, Thomas	300	--	4	7	287.4.0
Philips, Nathan	40	--	1	3	15.0.0
Phillips, John	50	--	2	2	30.12.0
Portmesser, Philip	150	--	2	3	30.12.0
Reed, David	--	--	--	1	--
Reed, John	--	--	--	1	--
Reed, Robert	--	--	1	1	--

Warrington Township hip	Acres	Negroes	Horses	Cattle	Tax
Ruce, Frederick, Sen'r	150	--	1	1	59.0.0
Ruce, Frederick	--	--	2	2	13.2.0
Ruce, Andrew	120	--	3	4	78.14.0
Rooper, Martin	--	--	--	--	--
Rider, Frederick	150	--	3	3	50.0.0
Rigg, John	--	--	1	3	3.7.6
Ross, Alexander	170	--	4	6	30.0.0
Stickel, Jacob	100	--	3	3	36.1.0
Stickel, Peter	100	--	2	1	22.0.0
Stickel, Christopher	25	--	1	2	--
Stickel, George	100	--	2	2	25.12.0
Smith, Balzer	100	--	2	4	62.0.0
Shanks, Thomas	100	--	3	4	37.3.9
Stofer, John	200	--	2	2	83.2.0
Smith, Samuel	--	--	--	--	15.0.0
Smith, Henry	--	--	--	--	15.0.0
Smith, Gabriel	--	--	--	--	11.5.0
Smith, Peter	170	--	4	5	122.10.0
Stuart, John	--	--	--	1	3.0.0
Steel, James	60	--	2	2	15.6.3
Switzer, Jacob	--	--	--	--	--
Shatoe, Nicholas	50	--	2	2	35.0.0
Shade, John	--	--	2	2	4.7.0
Shearer, Philip	105	--	2	3	35.0.0
Stevenson, Widow	160	--	3	3	22.10.0
Smith, John	170	--	3	5	122.10.0
Stevenson, Joseph	--	--	1	1	3.0.0
Thomas, Jehu	20	--	1	2	35.0.0
Thomas, John	35	--	1	1	26.4.0
Thomas, Mary	55	--	2	1	--
Thomas, Ja's & Christ'r Vear, to land	220	--	--	--	87.0.0
Taylor, Joseph	100	--	2	3	20.0.0
Tudro, Michael	153	--	2	2	30.0.0
Underwood, Elihu	100	--	--	3	40.1.0
Underwood, Elihu	100	--	1	4	64.8.0
Underwood, William	200	--	3	5	148.3.0
Underwood, Benjamin	200	--	3	2	78.15.0
Underwood, Mary	250	--	2	3	36.0.0
Updegraff, Wm.	70	--	--	2	17.10.0
Underwood, Nehemiah	--	--	--	1	--
Uppa, Teeter	150	--	2	2	83.2.0
Voar, Jacob	--	--	--	1	6.0.0
Voar, Jesse	--	--	--	--	--
Voar, Isaac	--	--	--	--	10.0.0
Veal, Wm.	--	--	--	1	4.7.0
Veal, Robert	80	--	1	2	60.10.0
Veal, Robert, Sen'r	150	--	2	6	174.15.0
Webb, Wm.	--	--	1	1	--
Walker, Able	100	--	2	2	56.16.0
Williams, Jacob	--	--	1	3	8.15.0
Withero, Wm.	118	--	2	2	15.0.0
Willey, Adam	100	--	2	3	39.7.0
Wikersam, Widow	50	--	--	1	7.12.0
Wickersham, Isaac	15	--	1	2	--

Warrington Township

	Acres	Negroes	Horses	Cattle	Tax
Williams, Abraham	85	--	--	--	7.12.0
Williams, Abram	--	--	--	1	--
Wright, John	200	--	3	8	47.2.0
Withero, John	100	--	--	--	15.0.0
Wright, Aron	100	--	--	--	8.15.0
Withero, Jn'o in Barrens	186	--	--	--	8.15.0
Weaver, Henry	150	--	3	4	35.0.0
Williams, Benjamin	50	--	2	2	21.17.0
Walker, Benjamin	150	--	2	4	122.8.0
Westler, Joseph	--	--	--	--	--
William, Mordicai	100	--	2	3	50.16.0
Bower, Andrew	170	--	2	3	80.15.0
Butt, Wm.	70	--	--	--	71.0.0
Huzzy, Riccord	225	--	3	5	202.16.0
Hoober, John	130	--	2	3	45.0.0
Herman, George	140	--	3	4	37.0.0
Underwood, Jacob	--	--	--	--	10.0.0
Huber, John	--	--	--	--	23.0.0
Blair, John	--	--	--	--	10.0.0
Blair, Brice	--	--	--	--	10.0.0

SHREWSBURY TOWNSHIP

	Acres	Negroes	Horses	Cattle	Tax
Albright, John	--	--	1	--	10.3.0
Allison, Mathew	120	--	1	4	15.18.0
Anderson, William	--	--	1	2	6.0.0
Blymeyer, Bernard	--	--	2	3	16.0.0
Bailey, Daniel	100	--	2	2	25.0.0
Bailey, George	100	--	2	1	12.10.0
Baumgartner, Henry	--	--	--	3	6.0.0
Beard, John	--	--	--	2	6.0.0
Buzzard, Jacob	--	--	1	3	11.16.0
Bailey, Jacob	70	--	2	2	15.0.0
Brillhart, Peter	500	--	4	7	71.16.0
Beaker, Peter	100	--	2	2	84.0.0
Boyer, Tobias	100	--	2	2	220.0.0
Chryst, Andrew	100	--	2	1	24.0.0
Croud, Anna	50	--	1	1	5.0.0
Coller, Balzar	163	1	2	2	30.0.0
Coller, Christian	--	--	2	5	9.10.0
Crouse, Christian	3	--	1	2	4.0.0
Geisey, Christian	80	--	1	2	7.16.0
Corpman, Daniel	202	--	3	5	37.10.0
Cleinfelter, George	300	--	2	2	32.16.0
Casselman, George	180	--	2	4	18.0.0
Corpman, Henry	--	--	--	5	10.0.0
Celler, John	140	--	3	4	70.0.0
Celler, Jacob	150	--	1	3	40.0.0
Coller, Jacob	100	--	2	3	18.0.0
Cleinfelter, John	200	--	3	6	35.0.0
Conner, John	100	--	2	2	20.0.0
Caffelt, Jacob	200	--	--	1	45.0.0

Shrewsbury Township	Acres	Negroes	Horses	Cattle	Tax
Cersey, Jacob	100	--	2	4	16.0.0
Corpman, Jacob	150	--	1	5	25.0.0
Clatfelter, Jacob	240	--	2	2	35.0.0
Coller, John	257	--	2	5	35.0.0
Clanfelter, Laurence	212	--	2	3	17.0.0
Courts, Martin	150	--	--	--	35.0.0
Congell, Michael	200	--	2	9	60.0.0
Clanfelter, Michael	219	--	3	9	45.0.0
Carberry, Michael	--	--	2	2	11.0.0
Casselman, Michael	300	--	4	7	80.0.0
Clanfelter, Peter	--	--	1	2	6.0.0
Celler, Samuel	200	--	--	--	18.0.0
Caffman, Solomon	64	--	--	--	8.0.0
Deel, Adam	150	--	1	3	36.0.0
Deel, Charles	300	--	2	6	90.0.0
Downs, Henry	30	--	2	--	12.0.0
Dickens, John	100	--	2	2	60.0.0
Deelman, Jacob	157	--	2	3	22.10.0
Deifinger, Killian	--	--	2	2	30.0.0
Dias, Thomas	20	--	--	4	5.0.0
Deidenhefer, George	--	--	1	1	12.0.0
Harman, George	200	--	2	4	35.0.0
Eberhard, Vendle	100	--	--	1	8.0.0
Eichelberger, Adam	150	--	--	--	11.0.0
Fischel, Frederick	370	--	--	--	90.0.0
Ferree, Conrad	100	--	1	5	15.0.0
Flowers, Catharine	200	--	1	1	--
Fiffer, George	--	--	--	2	--
Ferree, Henry	66	--	2	2	15.0.0
Freelein, John	50	--	1	1	20.0.0
Fisher, John	60	--	1	2	14.0.0
Fry, John, shoemaker	72	--	4	3	15.0.0
Grove, Francis	200	--	2	3	70.0.0
Gerdan, Jonas	25	--	--	1	30.0.0
Gobble, John	100	--	2	2	15.0.0
Gramer, Laurence	100	--	2	2	15.0.0
Hendrixon, Adam	280	--	2	3	80.0.0
Kurtz, Conrad	170	--	1	3	20.0.0
Hanover, Christopher	--	--	2	2	8.0.0
Hoshburn, Alexander	100	--	--	--	10.0.0
Holp, Ernst	125	--	2	4	90.0.0
Homspoker, Valentine	50	--	1	1	28.0.0
Hildenbrand, Felix	180	--	2	3	25.0.0
Hildenbrand, John	100	--	2	2	20.0.0
Hoveis, Frederick	50	--	2	3	15.0.0
Homspoker, George	70	--	--	--	6.0.0
Heiderick, Jacob	50	--	1	1	14.0.0
Heibely, Jacob	150	--	2	4	45.0.0
Heiss, Jacob	150	--	2	2	25.0.0
Hildenbrand, Jacob	--	--	2	3	25.0.0
Hendrix, Isaac	70	--	2	4	12.0.0
Heart, Martin	108	--	--	5	14.0.0
Herman, Michael	150	--	2	2	20.0.0
Henry, Nicholas	185	--	3	5	37.10.0
Halfpenny, Patrick	10	--	1	1	5.0.0

Shrewsbury Township	Acres	Negroes	Horses	Cattle	Tax
Hearhart, Thomas	280	--	2	5	72.0.0
Herms, Thomas	--	--	2	1	--
Hartman, Tobias	100	--	--	--	7.10.0
Heist, Vinald	50	--	1	3	12.0.0
Hess, Ulrich	300	--	1	1	50.0.0
HeartHart, Wm.	300	--	4	6	240.0.0
Heinsler, Michael	50	--	2	2	12.0.0
Lice, Peter	100	--	2	4	25.0.0
Lauch, Philip	250	--	--	--	35.0.0
Long, Henry, in Maryland	50	--	--	--	8.0.0
Lowe, Joshua	192	--	2	5	60.0.0
Lawson, John	100	--	--	--	10.0.0
Lowbridge, Joseph	50	--	--	2	7.0.0
Landmesser, Jacob	--	--	--	1	10.0.0
Lowe, John	150	--	2	2	80.0.0
Meyer, Andrew	140	--	1	6	56.0.0
Miller, Andrew	100	--	--	2	17.0.0
Meyer, Christian	117	--	1	5	52.0.0
Michley, Christian	80	--	2	4	25.0.0
Miller, Frederick	--	--	1	1	14.0.0
Miller, Frederick	70	--	2	3	12.0.0
Meyer, George	123	--	2	4	18.0.0
Miller, Herman	100	--	2	2	40.0.0
Marickel, Henry	70	--	--	--	10.0.0
McSwine, James	200	--	3	4	27.0.0
Marshall, James	214	--	2	5	30.0.0
McDonnald, John	--	--	2	1	6.0.0
Meyer, John	200	--	--	--	30.0.0
McMahoney, John	120	--	1	1	18.0.0
Meyer, Jacob	25	--	--	1	10.0.0
Moore, James	125	--	2	2	18.0.0
Miller, John	100	--	--	--	36.0.0
Miller, John, Captain	166	--	1	5	20.0.0
Miller, Martin	150	--	4	5	40.0.0
Meyer, Martin	--	--	--	--	--
Miller, Tobias	130	--	2	4	40.0.0
Nuss, Jacob	210	--	--	--	24.0.0
Ness, Jacob	235	--	4	3	55.0.0
Nunemaker, Solomon	120	--	2	3	34.0.0
Peary, Abraham	152	--	3	6	70.0.0
Pope, Bernard	211	--	--	1	20.0.0
Peckley, Christian	200	--	--	--	20.0.0
Peterman, Daniel	173	--	1	4	35.0.0
Peaffer, John	--	--	--	1	6.0.0
Peary, George	100	--	2	2	36.0.0
Pick, Jacob	80	--	1	3	8.0.0
Pope, Ludwig	200	--	2	2	25.0.0
Patterson, William	150	--	2	3	30.0.0
Quarterman, John	--	--	1	1	4.0.0
Roaser, Adam	182	--	1	4	60.0.0
Reaver, Abraham	200	--	2	2	70.0.0
Rule, Frederick	96	--	1	4	24.0.0
Roaser, John	--	--	--	1	8.0.0
Rush, Christian	100	--	2	3	120.0.0
Roaser, Laurence	50	--	--	1	7.0.0

Shrewsbury Township	Acres	Negroes	Horses	Cattle	Tax
Reaman, Jacob	103	--	--	--	20.0.0
Reip, Nicholas	173	--	2	4	27.0.0
Rothiherse, Nicholas	177	--	2	1	30.0.0
Smith, Andrew	--	--	1	1	10.0.0
Shilling, Bastian	100	--	2	3	15.0.0
Swartz, Andrew	150	--	2	2	100.0.0
Stibler, Christian	350	--	2	3	45.0.0
Shindler, Christopher	--	--	--	1	18.0.0
Shafer, Catharine	200	--	2	4	20.0.0
Swartz, Conrad	80	--	2	3	25.0.0
Shinnerman, David	--	--	--	--	--
Sides, John	129	--	1	3	15.0.0
Sheffer, Philip	350	--	--	3	85.0.0
Sword, George	--	--	2	3	10.0.0
Swartz, Henry	50	--	2	2	20.0.0
Seickly, Jacob	92	--	2	1	12.0.0
Sparks, Thomas	--	--	1	2	5.0.0
Sides, Joseph	200	--	2	3	39.0.0
Spitler, Jacob	150	--	--	--	35.0.0
Stone, Jacob	112	--	2	1	15.0.0
Smith, John	100	--	3	4	28.0.0
Swartz, Jacob	100	--	2	3	15.0.0
Shiery, Jacob	--	--	1	2	--
Studden, Joseph	150	--	--	--	35.0.0
Zeich, Michael	--	--	--	1	5.0.0
Smith, Peter	150	--	2	5	85.0.0
Stormer, Rosanna	80	--	2	2	3.0.0
Taylor, Abraham	100	--	--	3	11.0.0
Taylor, Philip	210	--	3	3	40.0.0
Taylor, John	86	--	--	2	10.0.0
Tinkey, John	150	--	3	2	40.0.0
Tommack, John	--	--	2	2	12.0.0
Taylor, John	132	--	2	1	15.0.0
Trorbach, Mathias	--	--	2	2	7.0.0
Taylor, George	--	--	--	3	4.0.0
Teigel, John	125	--	--	5	34.0.0
Waltemeyer, Henry	100	--	2	3	14.0.0
Wilhelm, Henry	100	--	--	--	14.0.0
Wildgoose, James	100	--	1	1	10.0.0
Willey, Wm.	100	--	2	1	15.0.0
Welsch, John	100	--	--	--	10.0.0
Willey, Aquilla	325	--	2	5	50.0.0
Wagner, Henry	85	--	--	--	--
Einghell, Henry	--	--	--	--	16.8.0
Conrad, Corpman	50	--	--	1	5.0.0
Smith, John	270	--	1	2	21.0.0
Leib, Ulry	198	--	3	9	60.0.0
Miller, Henry	75	--	--	1	10.0.0
Sheirer, John	--	--	2	3	--
Shafer, David	--	--	--	--	--
Henry, Adam	--	--	--	--	25.0.0
Hershy, Andrew	--	--	--	--	20.0.0
Harris, Thomas	--	--	--	--	20.0.0
Kelley, Francis	--	--	--	--	20.0.0
Byer, Henry	--	--	--	--	20.0.0

Shrewsbury Township	Acres	Negroes	Horses	Cattle	Tax
Celler, Henry	--	--	--	--	25.0.0
Myer, Michael, smith	--	--	--	--	7.10.0
Hess, Henry	--	--	--	--	20.0.0
Shefer, Henry	--	--	--	--	20.0.0
Shelly, John	--	--	--	--	20.0.0
Stebley, John	--	--	--	--	20.0.0
Beck, Jacob	--	--	--	--	15.0.0
Graham, John	--	--	--	--	15.0.0
Olp, John	--	--	--	--	20.0.0
Feigely, Martin	--	--	--	--	30.0.0
Moyer, Michael	--	--	--	--	25.0.0
Neiss, Michael	--	--	--	--	20.0.0
Motts, Henry	--	--	--	--	20.0.0
Wagner, Melchior	--	--	--	--	20.0.0
Peary, Nicholas	--	--	--	--	20.0.0
Clatfelder, Casper	--	--	--	--	20.0.0
Hildenbrand, Casper	--	--	--	--	20.0.0
Lantz, John	--	--	--	--	20.0.0
Bouser, John	25	--	--	2	5.0.0
Shoemaker, Peter	--	--	--	--	4.0.0
Meyreiss, John	--	--	--	--	4.0.0
Eisenhart, George	120	--	2	3	25.0.0
Miller, Henry	--	--	--	--	8.0.0
Sheyrer, John	--	--	--	--	20.0.0

HEIDELBERG TOWNSHIP

	Acres	Negroes	Horses	Cattle	Tax
Adams, Widow	265	--	4	6	80.0.0
Aulebach, Nicholas	5	--	--	1	12.0.0
Bauman, John	150	--	4	4	105.0.0
Ballance, James Rev'd.	500	2	7	16	255.0.0
Beltz, Jacob	--	--	--	1	14.0.0
Benmer, Henry	--	--	1	1	37.0.0
Brillhart, John	9	--	--	2	23.0.0
Bradley, Wm.	--	--	--	1	7.10.0
Berkgold, Michael	--	--	--	--	7.10.0
Barnitz, Daniel	--	--	1	1	47.0.0
Beer, Michael	92	--	2	4	45.0.0
Beateman, Henry	--	--	--	1	12.0.0
Blintzinger, George	--	--	--	1	12.0.0
Bear, Christian	100	--	3	3	75.0.0
Bixler, Samuel	200	--	3	4	72.0.0
Byer, Martin	--	--	--	--	320.0.0
Chambers, Arthur	--	--	1	1	21.0.0
Cunnings, James	--	--	--	--	12.10.0
Decker, Joseph	--	--	--	--	8.10.0
Diggs, Wm.	--	--	--	--	35.0.0
Detterer, Conrad	390	--	3	5	105.0.0
Ehrman, Joseph	--	--	--	2	6.0.0
Etzler, George	150	--	4	5	95.0.0
Etzler, Andrew	160	--	3	5	77.0.0
Erwin, Robert	--	1	1	1	21.0.0

Heidelberg Township	Acres	Negroes	Horses	Cattle	Tax
Eyler, Frederick	--	--	--	1	19.0.0
Eckart, Conrad	--	--	--	--	60.0.0
Riddle, Widow	--	--	--	--	7.10.0
Eckart, John	--	--	--	--	145.0.0
Eichelberger, Leonard	44	--	2	3	21.0.0
Eichelberger, Jacob	6	--	--	2	10.0.0
Emlet, Michael	200	--	1	1	17.0.0
Fleshman, Martin	10	--	--	2	9.0.0
In Manheim township	100	--	--	--	--
Forney, Philip	110	--	4	7	105.0.0
Fuller, John	--	--	--	1	20.0.0
Flickinger, Peter	180	--	3	4	75.0.0
Fletter, George	--	--	--	--	5.10.0
Fersithe, Alexander	--	--	1	2	40.0.0
Geitzel, Leonhart	125	--	3	3	80.0.0
Grove, Christian	190	--	2	3	110.0.0
Gallentine, John	--	--	--	1	--
Genswiler, Andrew	5	--	1	--	--
Grove, Christian	--	--	--	1	15.0.0
Grate, John	176	--	3	4	110.0.0
Gitt, Wm.	--	--	1	2	19.0.0
Geiwix, Charles	--	--	--	1	30.0.0
Heiser, Tietrich	--	--	--	--	7.10.0
Hostetter, Francis	5	--	1	1	16.0.0
Hegy, Adam	--	--	--	1	6.0.0
Hostetter, Henry	40	--	1	2	11.0.0
Helman, Jacob	--	--	--	1	10.0.0
Hinckel, John	275	1	1	2	18.15.0
Hauck, Jacob	--	--	--	1	9.0.0
Hime, Francis	11	--	2	3	65.0.0
Hofman, Mathias	--	--	--	1	4.10.0
Heins, John	--	--	1	1	8.10.0
Hauck, David	--	--	--	1	8.10.0
Humes, Solomon	--	--	--	1	8.10.0
Hoobman, Jacob	--	--	--	--	10.10.0
Hauck, Michael	--	--	--	1	15.0.0
Hock, Conrad	--	--	1	1	83.0.0
Hoofman, Christian	--	--	--	1	10.10.0
Hauck, Barnet	--	--	--	1	11.10.0
Horn, Henry	10	--	--	2	12.15.0
Johnston, Jacob, Jun'r,	5	--	1	1	25.0.0
Johnston, Jacob	--	--	--	1	10.10.0
Karl, George	130	--	2	4	70.0.0
Klein, Jacob	5	--	--	1	6.0.0
Keller, Wendel	--	--	1	2	90.0.0
Kurtz, Frederick	--	1	--	1	12.0.0
Kraft, John	4	--	1	1	50.0.0
Kloy, Jacob	--	--	--	1	9.0.0
Koppenhefer, Michael	--	--	--	1	20.0.0
Keller, John	--	--	--	--	25.0.0
Klar, Simon	30	--	2	1	27.0.0
Keagy, John	100	--	4	8	30.0.0
Keagy, Jacob	216	--	1	4	95.0.0
Klein, William	--	--	--	--	7.10.0
Kehler, Michael	--	--	--	--	7.10.0

Heidelberg Township	Acres	Negroes	Horses	Cattle	Tax
Logan, Hugh	--	--	3	4	--
Lamuth, Daniel	--	--	1	1	50.0.0
Lauteman, Peter	--	--	--	1	8.10.0
Lutz, Widow	200	--	--	1	4.0.0
Miller, Paul	--	--	--	1	22.0.0
Meyer, Philip	--	--	1	1	49.0.0
McCallister, Richard	220	--	7	6	210.0.0
McClean, James	--	--	--	--	6.10.0
McCherry, Patrick	619	2	2	3	280.0.0
Milhime, Christian	10	--	2	2	15.0.0
Martin, Andrew	--	--	1	1	6.10.0
Middlehauf, Leonard	247	--	4	6	112.10.0
Miller, John	4	--	--	2	12.0.0
Melhorn, Simon	25	--	2	3	18.0.0
Melhorn, Simon, Jun'r,	25	--	2	3	18.0.0
Metzger, Paul	--	--	1	1	25.0.0
Noaser, Jacob	--	--	--	1	19.0.0
Neuman, David	--	--	--	1	34.0.0
Ness, George	--	--	--	--	7.0.0
Ness, Mathias	--	--	1	2	115.0.0
Owens, Thomas	--	--	--	2	5.10.0
Owens, William	150	--	3	5	95.0.0
Owens, Roberts	150	--	4	4	95.0.0
Obold, Bastion	150	--	3	4	115.0.0
Obold, Joseph	197	--	4	5	75.0.0
Owens, John	--	--	--	1	--
Reisinger, John	--	--	--	1	9.0.0
Rudisil, Jacob	--	--	1	1	25.0.0
Reinecker, Casper	57	1	3	3	195.0.0
In Manheim t'w'p	240	--	--	--	--
Rule, George	--	--	1	1	--
Shorp, John	150	--	3	5	100.0.0
Shultz, Frederick	--	--	--	1	25.0.0
Shultz, Peter	100	--	3	5	86.0.0
Shultz, Henry	--	--	--	1	20.0.0
Swane, Benjamin	--	--	1	1	50.0.0
Slentz, Philip	5	--	--	1	8.0.0
Shreiber, Conrad	50	--	3	3	35.0.0
Shuy, Peter	125	--	3	4	55.0.0
Smeltzer, John	--	--	--	--	7.10.0
Shreyer, George	--	--	2	2	35.0.0
Spitler, John	--	--	--	1	20.0.0
Swoope, Conrad	--	--	--	1	77.0.0
Sites, Benjamin	176	--	4	7	115.0.0
Stauter, George	--	--	1	1	18.0.0
Shreiber, Ludwig	85	--	2	5	100.0.0
Shreiber, Peter	130	--	2	2	50.0.0
Shreiber, Andrew	150	--	4	5	95.0.0
Shreiber, Jacob	125	--	2	2	53.0.0
Staub, Adam	20	--	2	3	15.10.0
Staub, Philip	60	--	2	3	27.0.0
Sholl, Philip	--	--	1	1	15.0.0
Stoner, George	50	--	1	4	40.0.0
Stemy, Christian	--	--	1	1	6.15.0
Stoll, Godfrey	--	--	--	1	4.0.0

Heidelberg Township	Acres	Negroes	Horses	Cattle	Tax
Staub, Jacob	60	--	2	2	27.10.0
Syfort, John	--	--	1	1	4.10.0
Timmons, Philip	--	--	--	1	6.10.0
Trine, Jacob	10	--	1	1	12.0.0
Thomas, John	--	--	3	5	80.0.0
Trussel, John	--	--	--	1	--
Trippet, Joseph	--	--	--	1	8.10.0
Truel, Anthony	--	--	--	1	6.10.0
Weaver, John	--	--	--	1	6.0.0
Welsh, Peter	--	--	--	1	20.0.0
Welty, Jacob	--	--	--	--	135.0.0
Will, Peter	100	--	4	2	55.0.0
Wiker, George	--	--	--	1	10.10.0
Walkman, Henry	15	--	--	2	30.0.0
Wilt, Peter, junior	--	--	--	--	8.10.0
Will, Martin	50	--	--	1	25.0.0
Will, Jacob	--	--	3	3	110.0.0
Will, Nicholas	10	--	--	1	15.0.0
Will, John	100	--	3	3	55.0.0
Wisler, John	--	--	--	--	280.0.0
Welsh, Henry	--	--	1	1	20.0.0
Wine, George	179	--	4	4	115.0.0
Werley, Michael	--	--	--	--	--
Wolf, Jacob	--	--	--	1	12.0.0
Wison, Valentine	--	--	--	--	12.0.0
Walter, Peter	--	--	--	1	18.0.0
Winebrecht, Martin	--	--	--	1	6.10.0
Waltman, John	--	--	1	1	9.10.0
Winter, Eberhard	--	--	--	--	6.10.0
Winebrecht, Michael	150	--	1	2	23.15.0
Walter, Nicholas	5	--	--	1	7.10.0
Wimley, John	--	--	--	1	11.0.0
Winebrenner, George	--	--	--	1	20.0.0
Williams, Jacob	--	--	--	1	15.0.0
Winebrenner, Peter	--	--	1	1	37.10.0
Werner, Balzer	--	--	--	--	6.10.0
White, Robert	--	--	--	1	18.0.0
Zimmer, Michael	--	--	--	2	10.0.0
Ziegler, George	--	--	1	1	10.0.0
Zimmer, Mathias	--	--	--	--	5.0.0
Gayley, Sam'l.	--	--	--	--	4.10.0
House, Mich'l.	--	--	--	--	6.0.0
Hagey, Jacob	--	--	--	--	--
Kitzmiller, John	--	--	--	--	5.0.0
Lilley, Joseph	--	--	--	--	120.0.0
Lostetter, Jacob	--	--	--	--	--
McClean, Arch'd. Esq'r.	--	--	--	--	25.0.0
Millhime, Christian	--	--	--	--	--
Sheffer, Henry	--	--	--	--	6.0.0
Slegel, Jacob	--	--	--	--	4.10.0
Wirking, Philip	--	--	--	--	6.10.0
Shiffler, Casper	--	--	--	--	5.0.0
Smith, Cha's.	--	--	--	--	7.10.0
Byerley, Jacob	--	--	--	--	20.0.0
Giltmyer, Francis	--	--	--	--	29.0.0

Heidelberg Township	Acres	Negroes	Horses	Cattle	Tax
Wine, Henry	--	--	--	--	20.0.0
Furney, Adam	--	--	--	--	20.0.0
Hackman, Henry	--	--	--	--	27.0.0
Sites, Aron	--	--	--	--	20.0.0
Adams, Joseph	--	--	--	--	15.0.0
McAllister, Abdil	84	--	--	--	26.0.0
Bahn, Jacob	--	--	--	--	26.0.0
Hoke, Henry	--	--	--	--	26.0.0
Renecker, George	--	--	--	--	--
Owings, Joshua	--	--	--	--	20.0.0
Boyer, Abraham	--	--	--	--	15.0.0
Boyer, Henry	--	--	--	--	20.0.0
Boyer, Tobias	--	--	--	--	15.0.0
Smith, Andrew	--	--	--	--	7.10.0
John Butch	--	--	--	--	7.10.0
Will, Michael	138	--	--	--	46.0.0
Grate, Nicholas	--	--	--	--	18.0.0
Wine, Adam	--	--	--	--	15.0.0
Bean, Adam	--	--	--	--	--
Lamuth, John	--	--	--	--	26.0.0
Armon, Tho's. Jun'r.	--	--	--	--	15.0.0
Shafer, Henry	--	--	--	--	5.0.0
Hymes, John	--	--	--	--	5.0.0
Hagel, John	--	--	--	--	5.0.0
Wirking, Philip	--	--	--	--	6.0.0
Hull, Isaac	--	--	--	--	5.0.0
Hoffman, Mich'l.	--	--	--	--	15.0.0
Dorliack, John	--	--	--	--	26.0.0

GERMANY TOWNSHIP

	Acres	Negroes	Horses	Cattle	Tax
Angel, Peter	95	--	2	3	25.5.0
Angel, Augustus	125	--	1	1	29.6.0
Alspough, David	--	--	--	--	--
Bard, David	--	--	--	--	3.0.0
Buse, Peter	112	--	2	5	36.8.0
Bich, Adam	80	--	2	2	20.1.6
Bard, Stephen	50	--	--	4	10.0.0
Bard, Francis	125	--	1	2	26.15.0
Beal, Jacob	180	--	5	4	71.19.6
Baker, John	100	--	2	3	27,8.0
Bechtel, Jacob	--	--	--	1	10.0.0
Bard, Bernhard	200	--	3	6	83.0.0
Bare, Peter, Jun'r.	--	--	2	2	7.10.0
Bard, Bernhard, Jr'r.	--	--	--	1	5.0.0
Boughman, Frederick	220	--	2	2	52.17.6
Bishop, Jeremiah	--	--	1	--	5.0.0
Bishop, Henry	150	--	3	2	51.0.0
Beacher, Henry	265	--	2	3	92.0.0
Butt, Jacob	180	--	2	2	40.0.0
Buse, Adam	100	--	2	5	32.16.0
Bittle, Thomas	50	--	4	4	45.8.0

Germany Township	Acres	Negroes	Horses	Cattle	Tax
Bishop, Teeter	--	--	1	1	10.0.0
Behm, Christian	--	--	--	--	--
Bolton, James	--	--	--	1	7.10.0
Bechtel, George	--	--	--	--	10.0.0
Blott, Joseph	--	--	--	--	6.0.0
Blott, John	--	--	--	--	6.0.0
Buffeton, Jacob	--	--	--	--	10.0.0
Beel, Melchior	--	--	--	--	12.10.0
Bard, John	--	--	--	3	9.0.0
Brother, Henry	50	--	2	2	48.16.0
Baumgartner, Jacob	--	--	--	1	19.10.0
Banta, Samuel	--	--	--	1	--
Drayer, Philip	--	--	--	--	5.0.0
Degen, Peter	--	--	--	2	15.5.0
Dill, Nicholas	200	--	4	4	95.17.0
Davison, James	30	--	2	2	12.10.0
Flade, Joseph	184	--	4	3	105.0.0
Flade, Joseph	150	--	--	--	26.4.0
Fisher, Thomas	260	--	3	3	65.0.0
Feezer, Nicholas	30	--	2	2	22.10.0
Feezer, Widow	200	1	4	5	95.0.0
Flinchbach, Philip	140	--	--	6	36.9.6
Furney, Abraham	130	--	2	2	81.0.0
Green, George	--	--	--	1	7.10.0
Gashaw, Peter	--	--	--	1	5.0.0
Garner, George	112	--	2	6	40.0.0
Grogg, Jacob	--	--	--	--	--
Geesler, Adam	--	--	--	1	10.0.0
Gray, John	--	--	--	--	7.10.0
Gray, Jacob	12	--	--	2	25.19.9
Griss, Stephen	50	--	--	2	32.2.0
Garner, George, Jun'r.	--	--	--	3	18.15.0
Guiss, John	--	--	2	1	7.10.0
Gallaugher, James	--	--	2	--	20.0.0
Huckstater, Ulrich	100	--	1	1	27.0.0
Hahn, John	50	--	2	2	62.2.9
Helm, Daniel	--	--	--	2	11.0.0
Hansel, Casper	135	--	2	3	33.0.0
Himble, Christian	24	--	3	4	58.2.0
Hoover, John	300	--	4	7	107.0.0
Harger, Andrew	--	--	--	1	5.0.0
Hockman, Peter	--	--	--	1	--
Houck, George	--	--	--	--	7.10.0
Kint, Christian	150	--	1	1	13.0.0
Krebs, Peter	200	--	2	2	52.0.0
King, Abraham	125	--	2	3	52.0.0
Kitzmiller, Jacob	190	--	2	4	50.0.0
King, George	100	--	3	3	39.0.0
Keller, John	--	--	--	1	10.0.0
Klemmer, George	--	--	--	1	10.0.0
Kerbough, Martin	175	--	4	2	15.0.0
Kooler, Michael	--	--	--	1	5.0.0
Koontz, George	100	--	2	4	55.0.0
Klemmer, Valentine	--	--	--	1	17.6.0
Knous, John	155	--	3	3	55.9.0

Germany Township	Acres	Negroes	Horses	Cattle	Tax
Kiney, John	150	--	2	2	83.4.0
Kiney, Henry	100	--	--	5	48.18.6
Kuntz, Michael	150	--	3	3	50.0.0
Kerbough, Jacob	53	--	1	2	20.0.0
Keefer, Frederick	--	--	--	1	12.10.0
Kline, Ludwig	19	--	2	4	55.0.0
Kline, Ludwig	72	--	--	--	75.0.0
Kline, Henry	65	--	2	4	18.10.0
Kline, Frederick	235	--	2	3	176.13.0
Kountz, Michael	--	--	--	--	18.0.0
Kriffey, Patrick	--	--	--	1	--
Klemmer, Laurence	--	--	--	1	7.10.0
Leitner, Wm.	--	--	--	1	7.10.0
Leitner, George	25	--	1	1	25.0.0
Lash, Henry	100	--	2	3	23.14.9
Latsh, Martin	100	--	2	2	40.0.0
Lebow, Abraham	160	--	2	5	110.0.0
Long, Philip	--	--	--	1	14.15.0
Lowe, David	72	--	2	1	41.0.0
Lore, Andrew	100	--	2	3	40.5.0
Leakner, John	--	--	--	1	10.0.0
Myer, John	--	--	1	1	18.10.0
Miller, Jacob	6	--	1	1	18.10.0
McGuffen, Ja's.	--	--	--	--	28.0.0
Miller, Conrad	--	--	--	1	10.0.0
Moore, Henry	--	--	--	1	8.10.0
Mefford, John	28	--	2	4	48.0.0
McCherry, Patrick	--	--	--	--	20.0.0
Miller, Henry	--	--	1	2	--
Meyer, Adolph	160	--	3	4	45.0.0
Meyer, John	--	--	--	--	18.15.0
Mayrice, George	95	--	4	5	29.0.0
Miller, Ludwig	300	--	3	5	108.1.3
Miller, Nicholas	108	--	2	3	30.5.0
Miller, Nicholas	--	--	--	2	18.15.0
Modare, George	--	--	--	--	18.15.0
McCherry, Edward	240	--	3	3	72.5.0
McElhenny, Robert	--	--	2	2	18.0.0
Otz, Daniel	170	--	2	3	101.1.6
Parr, John	160	--	3	4	94.17.6
Ring, Stephel	--	--	--	2	7.10.0
Reed, Michael	--	--	--	1	9.0.0
Rack, Christian	120	--	2	5	63.7.2
Reblogel, Balzer	7	--	--	1	15.14.2
Rack, Christian, Sen'r.	--	--	--	1	4.10.0
Rigle, John	130	--	3	4	45.0.0
Rigle, John, Jr'r.	--	--	--	--	12.15.0
Rowanzaner, Christian	20	--	--	2	12.10.0
Rode, John	100	--	2	2	30.0.0
Robuck, Michael	90	--	--	4	32.14.0
Rowenzaner, Adam	50	--	2	2	20.0.0
Sower, Wm.	78	--	2	5	28.0.0
Smith, Stophel	40	--	--	3	15.10.0
Stonebach, Adam	80	--	2	2	--
Shilt, Henry	125	--	2	2	29.0.0

Germany Township	Acres	Negroes	Horses	Cattle	Tax
Schreiver, Conrad, Sen'r.	--	--	1	2	7.10.0
Smith, John	--	--	1	1	10.0.0
Sichrist, George	60	--	--	4	15.12.0
Stouver, John	50	--	2	3	20.0.0
Shultz, Joseph	65	--	2	2	32.0.0
Stong, John	80	--	2	1	40.0.0
Shore, John	--	--	--	1	10.0.0
Sell, Isaac	140	--	2	2	27.0.0
Sprenchel, Henry	130	--	--	4	27.0.0
Sell, Jacob	72	--	3	3	43.0.0
Sell, Abraham	40	--	3	3	32.0.0
Sponsyler, Andrew	150	--	2	2	45.0.0
Schneeringer, Laurence	124	--	2	3	35.0.0
Sponsyler, Jacob	--	--	2	2	10.0.0
Sparrow, Henry	80	--	2	2	30.0.0
Sparrow, Valentine	20	--	2	4	20.0.0
Sponsyler, George	250	--	2	3	80.0.0
Sponsyler, Widow	--	--	1	2	7.10.0
Shnider, Henry	75	--	--	3	18.0.0
Stelig, John	--	--	1	1	24.0.0
Shryer, John, in Maryland	60	--	2	2	--
Steley, Stophel	180	--	4	4	58.0.0
Sherman, Jacob	400	--	1	2	160.0.0
Sell, Jacob	--	--	--	--	18.0.0
Steley, Joseph	9	--	--	--	20.0.0
Sell, Adam	--	--	--	1	18.0.0
Stonebraker, Bastian	--	--	1	2	18.15.0
Strong, John, Sen'r.	--	--	--	1	4.0.0
Sealer, Peter	70	--	2	2	28.0.0
Troxel, Daniel	225	--	4	4	95.7.6
Troxel, David	--	--	--	1	7.10.0
Troxel, Jacob	100	--	1	3	33.0.0
Tentlinger, Anthony	--	--	--	2	15.0.0
Unrue, John	200	--	2	2	22.10.0
Vane, Frederick	--	--	--	1	9.0.0
Verner, Jacob	130	--	2	4	42.0.0
Werner, George	30	--	2	2	20.0.0
Will, George	--	--	2	3	15.0.0
Wentz, Michael	--	--	--	1	6.0.0
Winderode, Jacob	150	--	2	4	67.10.10
Weaver, John	--	--	--	1	9.0.0
Walter, Nicholas	--	--	--	1	10.10.0
Yantis, Daniel	--	--	1	2	18.3.0
Yengling, Abraham	80	--	1	2	14.0.0
Zanger, George	--	--	--	1	7.10.0
Zenlop, George	100	--	--	4	26.15.0
Zaucken, Widow	100	--	2	2	20.0.0
Stauffer, Henry	--	--	--	--	18.15.0
Bard, Samuel	--	--	--	--	7.10.0
Kint, Jacob	--	--	--	--	12.0.0
Kuntz, Philip	--	--	--	--	18.0.0
Lukenbach, Henry	--	--	--	--	7.10.0
Rudolph, Peter	--	--	--	--	12.15.0
Stauffer, Henry	--	--	--	--	18.15.0
Schrreyer, John	--	--	--	--	12.10.0

Germany Township	Acres	Negroes	Horses	Cattle	Tax
Sherman, Jacob	--	--	--	--	10.10.0
Winderoth, Adam	--	--	--	--	120.0.0
Zimmerman, Mch'l.	--	--	--	--	10.0.0
Bear, Isaac	--	--	--	--	5.0.0
Greff, Patrick	--	--	--	--	3.0.0

BERWICK TOWNSHIP

	Acres	Negroes	Horses	Cattle	Tax
Adams, Alexander	--	--	1	--	8.0.0
Abbeith, Thomas	235	--	2	3	50.0.0
Abbeith, Edward	235	--	2	1	40.0.0
Abbeith, John	--	--	--	--	16.5.0
Armstrong, Wm.	--	--	--	--	8.15.0
Bittinger, Nicholas	200	2	5	7	95.0.0
Baker, John	--	--	1	1	22.10.0
Betterson, Jacob	--	--	--	--	--
Berlin, Frederick	--	--	--	1	8.0.0
Baugher, George	170	--	3	4	50.0.0
Baugher, Frederick	--	--	--	--	50.0.0
Baugher, Wm.	96	--	2	3	20.0.0
Botter, Philip	156	--	2	2	22.10.0
Berlin, Jacob	195	--	1	2	31.15.0
Berlin, Nicholas	--	--	2	2	8.5.0
Bouser, Noah	100	--	2	2	25.0.0
Backer, George	95	--	2	2	44.9.0
Backer, John	95	--	2	3	45.0.0
Backer, Daniel	95	--	2	2	22.7.6
Beckner, John	--	--	1	2	17.10.0
Beckner, Nicholas	150	--	2	4	65.0.0
Beckner, Abraham	--	--	--	1	5.0.0
Beckner, Jacob	--	--	--	--	24.0.0
Bouser, John	100	--	3	3	87.10.0
Bard, George	136	--	1	3	17.10.0
Bouser, Samuel	--	--	1	2	11.10.0
Brown, Jacob	--	--	--	1	7.10.0
Bower, Peter	--	--	--	--	3.15.0
Bugh, Michael	--	--	--	2	15.0.0
Brown, Jacob, Ju'r.	--	--	--	1	3.15.0
Bicking, Jacob	--	--	--	--	18.10.0
Beckner, Laurence	150	--	3	3	80.0.0
Beckner, Jacob	--	--	--	--	32.0.0
Crawford, James	--	--	2	1	3.15.0
Chester, Robert	--	--	--	2	16.10.0
Carpenter, Daniel	--	--	1	1	22.10.0
Clark, James	266	--	3	6	40.0.0
Carl, Michael	150	1	2	4	46.5.0
Carl, Martin	150	--	2	2	31.17.6
Caldwell, Hugh	200	--	4	7	45.0.0
Clark, John	--	1	2	1	22.10.0
Carrick, Moses	--	--	1	1	--
Campbell, Archibald	--	--	1	--	--
Clapsaddle, Mich'l.	--	--	1	2	11.10.0

Berwick Township	Acres	Negroes	Horses	Cattle	Tax
Conrad, John	21	--	2	2	8.10.0
Crosser, Samuel, Sen'r.	100	--	2	4	26.0.0
Crosser, Adam	--	--	--	--	22.10.0
Carr, John	--	--	2	2	9.0.0
Duncan, Seth	--	1	2	3	45.0.0
Dick, Joseph	--	--	--	1	7.10.0
Derough, Henry	282	--	3	5	50.0.0
Dick, Adam	88	--	1	2	18.15.0
Dick, Christian	118	--	4	5	67.10.0
Diff, Daniel	40	--	2	2	15.0.0
Dorland, Garrett	100	1	5	5	32.10.0
Deardorf, Anthony	50	--	1	2	22.10.0
Dewalt, George	--	--	--	--	1.10.0
Desher, Peter	50	--	3	3	22.10.0
Dalhammer, Nich's.	--	--	--	--	1.10.0
Dalhammer, Nich's, to land, 100	--	--	--	--	12.10.0
Emig, Nicholas	--	--	--	--	12.10.0
Fickes, Yost	--	--	--	1	--
Fisher, Conrad	--	--	--	1	5.10.0
Ferrence, Peter	--	--	--	--	7.10.0
Forman, Andrew	--	--	1	3	7.10.0
Forman, Peter	--	--	--	1	1.10.0
Fronkelberger, Hen'r.	--	--	--	--	18.0.0
Gray, Samuel	--	--	--	--	20.0.0.
Gray, Thomas	150	--	2	3	76.0.0
Gray, Wm.	--	--	--	--	7.10.0
Grosscast, Daniel	180	--	3	2	75.0.0
Grosscast, John	200	--	3	5	70.0.0
Gollicker, Mich'l.	--	--	1	2	3.15.0
Gollicker, Patrick	220	--	3	6	51.5.0
Housil, Peter	260	1	4	7	177.10.0
Hartman, Philip	170	--	2	4	65.10.0
Hartzeal, Jacob	--	--	--	1	1.17.6
Hartzeal, Jacob	100	--	1	--	6.5.0
Hughes, Thomas	100	--	1	--	18.5.0
Hull, Abraham	278	--	4	6	70.0.0
Hull, John	--	--	--	--	16.0.0
Herman, George	--	--	--	2	10.0.0
Houts, Stophel	--	--	1	2	22.10.0
Hutt, Nicholas	90	--	2	3	22.10.0
Hull, Philip	--	--	--	--	14.0.0
Henderson, John	214	--	2	2	50.0.0
Ickes, Henry	200	--	4	4	48.5.0
Ickes, Nicholas	--	--	--	--	18.15.0
Ickes, Peter	--	--	7	1	127.10.0
Kief, David	--	--	--	1	154.10.0
Kuhn, George	250	1	4	3	154.10.0
Klunk, Peter	190	--	2	1	39.0.0
Klunk, Martin	40	--	1	3	42.10.0
Kerbough, George, Sen'r.	100	--	--	2	42.10.0
Kerbough, John	--	--	2	1	10.0.0
Kerbough, Nicholas	--	--	2	2	11.5.0
Kerbough, George, Jun'r.	--	--	3	2	11.5.0
King, Elias	--	--	--	--	6.10.0
Krim, John	40	--	1	1	12.10.0

Berwick Township	Acres	Negroes	Horses	Cattle	Tax
Krabill, John	100	--	2	3	53.8.0
Kline, Gerlach	--	--	--	1	5.0.0
Kepley, Tobias	--	--	--	--	34.0.0
Leonard, John	--	--	2	2	3.15.0
Long, Adam	136	--	3	3	25.0.0
Linefelter, Jacob	200	--	4	4	77.10.0
Larimore, John	266	--	5	7	65.12.0
Lilley, Tho's.	443	2	5	8	116.9.0
Lilley, Joseph	--	--	--	--	26.2.3
Lane, John	--	--	--	1	3.0.0
Lane, Peter	20	--	--	2	81.0.0
Lewis, John	--	--	1	--	3.15.0
Miller, Daniel	--	--	--	--	16.10.0
Mohler, Henry	--	--	--	1	6.10.0
McNichol, Rebecca	--	--	--	1	3.0.0
McTaggart, James	--	--	2	3	12.2.0
McTaggert, John	--	--	--	--	3.0.0
Marshall, Peter	--	--	1	3	7.10.0
Miller, Jacob	--	--	--	1	4.5.0
Mackey, James	--	--	1	1	15.0.0
Miller, George	--	--	--	--	12.10.0
McCurdy, Robert	100	--	2	5	25.12.6
Mullen, John	--	--	--	1	7.10.0
McGihan, Daniel	--	--	2	4	6.0.0
Marshall, Francis	--	--	3	2	11.5.0
Marshall, Francis, Jun'r.	--	--	2	2	7.10.0
Mower, Andrew	--	--	2	2	7.10.0
Moyer, Frederick	100	--	3	6	71.4.0
Mahold, George	--	--	--	--	--
McClure, Tho's.	--	--	1	2	6.5.0
Maginty, Patrick	--	--	--	1	2.0.0
McClenan, Dav'd.	--	--	--	--	16.16.0
Manteeth, John	216	--	3	4	47.10.0
Manteeth, John	--	--	--	--	15.0.0
McIntire, Alexander	200	--	2	4	80.12.0
McMaster, Gilbert	108	--	2	3	22.10.0
McMaster, James	80	1	2	3	37.10.0
McMaster, James, Jun'r.	50	--	2	3	15.12.6
McElwain, Andrew	160	--	2	5	80.10.0
Noll, Yost	150	--	2	2	21.1.0
Noll, George	70	--	1	4	37.10.0
Noll, George, to land	163	--	--	--	--
Noll, George, to land	50	--	--	--	--
Noel, Widow	--	--	--	--	--
Noel, Jacob	--	--	--	1	1.17.6
Oyster, Jacob	--	--	--	1	10.0.0
Owens, Wm.	100	--	2	4	30.0.0
Richards, Peter	460	--	--	--	68.15.0
Persill, John	--	--	2	3	7.10.0
Prisill, Mich'l.	230	--	2	1	43.15.0
Prisill, Valentine	94	--	2	4	33.4.0
Prian, Philip	150	--	3	3	30.0.0
Prisill, David	--	--	--	2	3.0.0
Prubacher, Teeterich	150	--	4	4	100.0.0
Prisill, Widow	--	--	--	--	--

Berwick Township	Acres	Negroes	Horses	Cattle	Tax
Patterson, James	312	--	2	4	53.15.0
Parsil, Richard, Sen'r.	--	--	1	4	--
Parsill, Isaac	100	--	3	5	18.15.0
Parsil, Richard, Ju'r.	150	--	3	7	32.10.0
Polk, Joseph	200	--	2	4	42.10.0
Parsil, Rudolph	104	--	--	1	17.0.0
Parsil, Peter	100	--	3	3	25.0.0
Rode, Herman	--	--	--	2	2.10.0
Roffelsperger, Christian	--	--	--	1	22.10.0
Raudebush, Henry, Jun'r.	--	--	2	2	10.0.0
Raudbush, Henry	300	--	2	2	50.0.0
Roudebush, Mich'l.	--	--	1	2	7.10.0
Roudebush, Jacob	--	--	2	2	12.10.0
Riley, John	--	--	--	--	14.10.0
Sumberland, Wm.	90	--	2	1	14.10.0
Sumberland, John	--	--	--	1	10.0.0
Sumberland, James	--	--	--	1	6.5.0
Sheet, John	--	--	--	1	1.5.0
Sarbach, Jacob	140	1	2	4	105.5.0
Studenbaker, David	--	--	--	--	6.5.0
Skidmore, John	--	--	--	1	10.0.0
Sowers, Adam, Se'r.	180	--	1	2	22.10.0
Sowers, David	--	--	3	2	8.10.0
Sowers, David, to land	175	--	--	--	24.2.6
Sowers, Adam, Ju'r.	--	--	1	1	9.10.0
Sowers, Daniel	--	--	--	--	14.10.0
Spangler, Andy	170	--	3	3	40.0.0
Shoe, Henry	--	--	--	2	5.0.0
Smith, Wm.	--	--	--	1	6.15.0
Sturgeon, Henry	231	--	3	4	47.3.0
Smith, Wm.	80	--	3	5	51.5.0
Sowers, Jacob	90	--	2	4	47.10.0
Simons, Jacob	200	--	4	5	112.14.0
Smith, Godlieb	--	--	--	--	45.0.0
Slagel, Jacob, Se'r.	180	1	5	7	82.10.0
Slagel, Jacob, Ju'r.	212	--	2	2	35.0.0
Slagel, Stophel	120	--	2	4	40.0.0
Steffler, John	--	--	--	1	22.0.0
Shuy, Peter	--	--	--	--	3.15.0
Shultz, Ferdinand	170	--	2	3	57.10.0
Slagel, Henry, Esq'r.	311	--	9	12	105.0.0
Seeley, Henry	--	--	--	1	12.0.0
Studenbaker, Peter	--	--	--	1	7.10.0
Surgert, Abraham	--	--	--	--	45.0.0
Slagel, Daniel	198	--	5	5	62.0.0
Slagel, Daniel, to land	47	--	--	--	--
Smith, Wm.	253	1	3	4	25.0.0
Smith, John	--	--	--	--	18.0.0
Sturgeon, Wm.	80	--	2	2	33.3.0
Timmons, Thomas	45	--	1	4	8.15.0
Ticks, Todley	--	--	--	--	18.15.0
Toffey, Thomas	--	--	--	1	1.5.0
Tickson, James	12	--	--	2	4.0.0
Donaldson, Wm.	--	--	1	1	2.0.0
Thomson, Robert	157	--	2	3	22.10.0

Berwick Township	Acres	Negroes	Horses	Cattle	Tax
Vansdelin, Abraham	--	--	2	3	7.10.0
Vanasdelin, Abraham, to	1a150	--	--	--	18.0.0
Vandike, John	100	--	2	2	21.5.0
Vandike, Peter	--	--	--	1	--
Wuldrich, Michael	--	--	--	--	1.5.0
White, Casper, Ju'r.	100	--	2	3	25.0.0
White, Bastian	100	--	2	3	25.0.0
Wolf, Jonas	188	--	4	2	37.10.0
Wolf, Andrew	--	--	--	--	14.10.0
Wolf, Frederick	155	--	4	4	35.0.0
Winder, Jacob	--	--	1	1	12.0.0
Wheeler, John	--	--	1	1	12.10.0
Waggoner, Wm.	--	--	--	--	3.15.0
Weaver, Reinhard	--	--	--	1	1.5.0
Catler, Widow	--	--	--	1	--
Kepler, Widow	--	--	--	1	3.0.0
Weaver, Leonhard	--	--	--	1	1.5.0
Wishard, Nicholas	--	--	--	2	2.0.0
Kuhn, Widow	--	--	1	2	10.0.0
Weatherspoon, John	--	--	1	1	5.0.0
Weaster, Jacob	170	--	3	3	86.0.0
Williams, Joshua	--	--	1	1	26.5.0
Pryon, Augusta	--	--	--	--	19.10.0
Chamberson, Samuel	--	--	--	--	--
Snider, Mich'l.	--	--	--	--	--
Snider, John	--	--	--	--	--

STRABANN TOWNSHIP

	Acres	Negroes	Horses	Cattle	Tax
Ambrose, Robert	200	1	2	3	30.0.0
Anderson, James	175	--	3	3	29.0.0
Anderson, John	--	--	--	1	5.7
Brown, Joseph	285	--	1	3	30.0.0
Bodine, John	174	--	4	7	50.7.9
Beaty, David	--	--	--	2	14.6
Brinkerhoof, George	480	6	8	9	123.7.6
Bogal, Malcom	220	--	4	7	55.0.0
Broca, George	--	--	7	7	57.19.7
Beaty, David	176	1	3	4	40.14.3
Beaty, John	282	--	3	5	7.10.0
Brewer, Daniel	200	--	3	3	48.5.11
Brewer, Abraham	--	--	--	3	1.7.11
Black, James	180	--	3	4	40.0.0
Brown, Richard	479	3	8	14	177.2.8
Bogal, Joseph	--	--	1	--	1.13.6
Conner, John	--	--	3	1	2.1.10
Colter, Archibald	100	--	2	3	18.11.3
Campbell, Hugh	62	1	2	4	68.10.9
Cox, Laurence	--	1	2	2	32.10.0
Camonger, Henry	50	--	1	3	14.13.1
Camonger, John	50	--	2	2	14.4.9
Crozine, Cornelius, Rev'd.	434	--	5	5	80.0.0

Strabann Township	Acres	Negroes	Horses	Cattle	Tax
Crozine, Cornelius, Ju'r.	100	--	3	3	27.7.2
Crozine, Widow	--	1	--	2	3.0.0
Covert, Isaac	--	--	1	1	3.18.2
Croull, Wm.	239	--	4	3	55.0.0
Croull, Widow	--	--	1	1	--
Camillin, Mathew	--	--	1	1	5.8.2
Cozat, Francis	150	1	4	5	46.6.10
Cozat, David	240	2	5	7	59.14.10
Cozat, Jacob	150	--	3	2	30.0.0
Cowan, Robert	--	--	1	2	2.0.0
Cooper, Wm.	13	--	2	5	53.3.7
Croan, Robert	286	--	3	7	60.0.0
Croan, John	100	--	3	4	26.10.0
Candey, John	--	--	--	2	16.9
Doran, Tera	--	--	2	1	1.16.3
Dimoree, Samuel	111	--	2	5	25.5.3
Detrich, Nicholas	170	--	--	--	35.11.3
Duffield, James	--	--	1	3	3.1.5
Dickson, James, Sen'r.	747	2	7	10	200.0.0
Dickson, James	166	--	3	4	7.10.0
Dickson, Ja's. Ju'r.	--	--	1	2	2.13.0
Douglass, Wm.	300	--	3	6	35.0.0
Decamp, Jacob	--	--	1	2	1.16.3
Dimoree, David	96	1	2	5	18.0.0
Donaldson, Ja's.	--	--	--	1	30.7.0
Ewe, Mich'l.	250	--	2	4	60.0.0
Finley, George	--	--	2	1	--
Flatcher, Abram	--	--	--	1	8.0.0
Fleming, John	240	1	2	8	66.17.7
Galbraith, Rob't. Esq'r.	230	--	3	1	69.15.0
Greams, Hugh	--	--	1	1	1.2.4
Giffen, Stephen	550	--	3	5	90.0.0
Geery, Wm.	--	--	2	3	4.14.11
Greams, Wm.	--	--	--	2	--
Gilbert, Barnet	212	--	4	4	66.3.3
Graft, Philip	268	--	4	5	63.4.8
Hayes, Samuel	250	1	5	2	48.7.3
Hayes, Samuel, Ju'r.	--	--	1	2	1.19.6
Hadan, Samuel	250	2	6	5	77.19.0
Houlsworth, Samuel	203	--	4	5	60.0.0
Harper, Samuel	--	--	2	2	15.0.0
Hayes, George	--	--	2	2	6.11.2
Hamilton, Brethy	--	--	--	2	6.2.10
Hutcheson, James	120	--	3	3	22.12.3
Hamilton, John	--	--	1	1	4.9.4
Jones, Henry	300	1	6	5	77.15.0
James, John	--	--	3	3	5.11.8
Johnson, James	21	--	2	3	9.15.5
Johnson, Wm.	30	--	1	2	6.11.2
Kinkade, Thomas	--	--	3	3	4.12.1
Kayes, John	150	--	2	4	15.0.0
King, Wm.	--	--	--	2	6.11.2
Livingston, John	184	2	3	5	70.0.0
Livingston, Adam	362	1	4	5	77.19.0
Livingston, John, Sen'r.	--	--	1	2	3.0.0

Strabann Township	Acres	Negroes	Horses	Cattle	Tax
Loge, Adam	--	--	--	1	--
Lyon, James	141	--	3	3	35.0.0
Lowery, Wm.	141	--	3	4	35.0.0
McCrery, Wm.	200	--	2	5	45.0.0
Marrow, Samuel	7	--	--	--	4.11.4
McFarlin, John	250	--	2	5	57.15.9
McCush, Ja's.	160	--	3	3	82.1.0
Mancom, Patrick	--	--	--	1	--
McCans, George	--	--	--	2	18.9
Mercer, Peregin	340	3	5	4	70.0.0
McCance, Dav'd, Ju'r.	--	--	2	--	--
McCance, David	150	--	3	4	50.0.0
McCance, Benjamin	--	--	--	2	1.13.6
McMorrison, Hans	858	--	4	5	206.4.6
Manteeth, Daniel	106	--	3	4	25.3.4
McWilliams, James	225	1	2	5	60.10.8
McClure, John	--	--	--	--	50.0.0
McCombs, George	--	--	--	2	19.6
McElhenny, Robert	237	--	5	5	77.14.4
Moody, Samuel	--	--	2	2	3.6.1
McGrew, Robert	240	--	5	5	70.0.0
McGee, Barnet	--	--	--	--	--
Monfort, Laurence	135	--	4	4	35.14.8
Monford, John	135	--	3	3	33.12.9
McCullough, Wm.	--	--	--	1	--
McCush, Widow	--	1	--	2	--
McFarlin, Thomas	100	--	--	--	20.11.9
Peterson, Andrew	100	--	2	6	30.5.9
Peterson, John	270	--	2	5	40.0.0
Potter, David	308	--	4	7	40.0.0
Ramsey, Robert	200	--	1	1	22.6.8
Raney, Alexander	--	--	--	2	2.7.5
Reed, Thomas	184	1	4	5	40.0.0
Reed, John	184	--	3	4	40.12.0
Ross, Wm.	258	--	2	9	61.16.8
Richey, Alexander	--	--	1	--	3.15.4
Scott, David	184	--	2	3	40.13.4
Simson, David	315	--	5	9	60.0.0
Semple, John	269	--	4	5	45.0.0
Smith, James	--	--	--	1	16.9
Stockton, Thomas	211	--	2	3	50.7.10
Sharp, John	82	--	2	4	14.15.11
Sturgeon, Samuel	161	--	--	--	30.9.5
Slit, James	--	--	--	2	2.7.5
Sterling, James	--	--	1	--	20.0.0
Thomson, Wm.	278	--	3	5	79.9.10
Thomson, Samuel, Rev'd.	240	2	1	2	20.0.0
Torbett, John	--	--	--	2	16.9
Thomson, Wm., Jun'r.	280	--	2	1	35.0.0
Vonasdal, Simon, Ju'r.	273	1	5	6	38.0.0
Vanderpelt, James	--	--	2	3	4.3.9
Vandine, David	176	--	3	4	29.0.0
Vonasdal, Garret	206	1	4	7	54.11.6
Vonasdal, Cornelius	188	--	5	3	46.6.10
Vonadel, Garret, Ju'r.	100	--	3	3	25.10.10

Strabann Township	Acres	Negroes	Horses	Cattle	Tax
Vonasdal, Simon	--	--	2	2	--
Vonasdal, John	--	--	2	3	2.13.1
Wear, James	50	--	1	2	11.0.0
Wabler, Ludwig	80	--	2	3	22.15.0
Wilson, Robert	300	--	6	7	70.13.6
Williamson, George	215	--	3	4	41.18.6
Williams, James	--	--	1	1	1.7.11
Wilkeson, John	--	--	--	2	16.9
M'r Steel	272	--	--	--	--

Single Men

Name	Amount of Tax	Name	Amount of Tax
Bogal, Alexander	11.5.0	Martin, Dan'l	11.5.0
Brogar, Abraham	11.5.0	Weer, Andrew	15.0.0
Crowal, Conrad	11.5.0	Ross, David	11.5.0
Crowal, George	11.5.0	Steward, Joseph	11.5.0
Camelin, Charles	7.10.0	Sturgeon, Rob't.	15.5.0
Campbell, Robert	11.5.0	Houlsworth, Joseph	34.15.0
Fleming, George	11.5.0	McClure, John	50.0.0
Griffin, Stephen	11.5.0	Vanderbilt, Dav'd	11.5.0
Gilbert, Jacob	11.5.0	Wilson, Jas.	11.5.0
Hayes, John	11.5.0	Greams, Malcolm	11.5.0
McCherry, John	11.5.0	Mills, Ja's.	3.0.0
McCans, Wm.	11.5.0	Galbreath, Rob't. Esq'r	--
McCans, George	11.5.0	Cox, Laurence	--
McCans, John	11.5.0	Cooper, Wm.	--
McWilliams, John	11.5.0	Steel, Tho's.	--
McGinnes, Patrick	3.0.0	Morrison, Hugh	--
McGraw, Wm.	11.5.0		

READING TOWNSHIP

	Acres	Negroes	Horses	Cattle	Tax
Asper, Isaac	80	--	1	1	3.9.0
Asper, Frederick, Sen'r.	150	--	3	5	54.12.6
Asper, Frederick	--	--	--	--	10.0.0
Asper, George	150	--	2	3	50.12.0
Betty, Samuel	150	--	6	11	47.14.6
Boshea, Christian	100	--	2	3	37.3.8
Brugh, Manus, Se'r.	100	--	2	4	89.0.0
Bashore, Peter	182	--	2	5	30.9.6
Bertenheimer, Wm.	--	--	--	--	132.5.0
Bertenheimer, Simon	--	--	--	--	--
Bettle, Benjamin	100	--	2	5	20.2.6
Boshea, Nicholas	100	--	3	3	49.16.8
Brugh, Manus, Jr'r.	200	--	4	3	91.0.10
Brown, Widow	160	--	2	3	60.0.0
Brown, Daniel	--	--	--	--	10.0.0
Boyd, Thomas	100	--	1	4	43.10.2
Bettie, Walter	142	--	1	--	1.10.0

Reading Township	Acres	Negroes	Horses	Cattle	Tax
Bloomer, Nehemiah	--	--	1	1	2.9.10
Conway, James	150	--	--	--	21.11.3
Conway, Charles	150	--	--	--	21.11.3
Cover, Deetrich	--	--	--	--	19.11.0
Cock, John	--	--	2	1	4.8.2
Chanley, George	50	--	--	--	3.3.9
Chronister, Henry	480	--	2	4	137.0.10
Cratezing, George	--	--	--	--	5.0.0
Clark, John	100	1	2	4	27.10.1
Curswell, Thomas	100	--	2	2	29.12.3
Conner, George	--	--	3	1	2.7.11
Cimple, Jacob	100	--	2	3	--
Cimple, Michael	200	--	2	2	87.4.2
Chamberlain, Robert	--	--	--	--	10.0.0
Coaler, Michael	200	--	2	4	62.5.10
Chamberlain, John	196	1	3	4	37.1.9
Chamberlain, Ja's.	240	1	3	4	53.7.7
Chamberlain, Nenian	169 1/4	--	2	4	--
Davison, Widow	--	1	2	--	30.0.0
Laurence, Detter	292	--	3	6	37.13.3
Deardorf, Anthony, Se'r.	200	--	5	5	88.3.4
Dorra, Wm.	--	--	--	--	10.0.0
Develin, Roger	28	--	1	3	4.16.8
Deardorf, Anthony, Ju'r.	180	--	3	6	81.12.6
Etchison, Thomas	--	--	1	2	1.4.11
Ehrhard, Philip	100	--	2	1	59.18.4
Fox, Henry	100	--	2	1	29.18.0
Fox, Peter	125	--	2	2	40.12.6
Fullerton, Robert	--	--	--	--	10.0.0
Fickes, Valentine	100	--	2	3	37.3.8
Fanestock, Peter	30	--	--	--	2.7.11
Garner, James	--	--	1	--	5.0.0
Gun, John	--	--	--	--	5.0.0
Gilmore, Henry	100	--	2	2	26,1.4
Gross, Henry	50	--	2	3	14.15.2
Hineman, John	--	--	1	--	10.0.0
Hineman, Philip	150	--	3	5	108.11.4
Hevisey, Philip	150	--	3	3	68.0.10
Hevisey, John	--	--	--	--	10.0.0
Hannah, Wm.	25	--	3	2	9.4.0
Hemphill, James	--	--	4	4	5.18.0
Hempton, John	--	--	--	--	--
Hockelberger, Jacob	3	--	--	2	1.1.1
Hodge, Samuel	130	--	3	5	25.0.0
Hodge, Wm.	--	--	--	--	5.0.0
Hazelit, Robert	--	--	1	--	19.2
Hunt, Samuel	50	--	1	2	8.0.0
Hunt, Edward	5	--	--	--	34.10.0
Herman, Frederick	--	--	1	1	2.9.18
Herman, Adam	50	--	--	--	7.3.9
Hull, Henry	132	--	1	5	18.13.9
Jameson, Widow	90	--	2	4	16.5.10
Irwin, John	200	--	2	4	32.15.6
Johnson, Wm., Sen'r.	--	--	2	--	--
Johnson, Wm., Ju'r.	222	1	3	4	40.18.5

Reading Township	Acres	Negroes	Horses	Cattle	Tax
John, Thomas	--	--	1	1	2.5.0
King, Esaiah	50	--	2	2	21.5.6
King, Thomas	--	--	--	--	10.0.0
King, Michael	200	--	3	3	98.14.2
King, Nicholas	--	--	--	--	10.0.0
Knop, Valentine	200	--	2	7	65.3.4
Kinsor, George	--	--	3	2	31.8.8
Kunckel, Adam	50	--	2	3	22.16.2
Leas, Stephen	100	--	2	2	34.10.0
Leas, John	--	--	--	--	10.0.0
Leas, Samuel	--	--	2	2	6.18.0
Leas, John, Sen'r.	58	--	1	1	65.3.4
Lichey, John	200	--	1	3	76.13.4
Lowick, Philip	--	--	--	--	94.13.8
Leas, Leonard, Ju'r.	--	--	--	--	107.14.4
Leas, Leonard, Sen'r.	60	--	2	2	53.13.4
Leas, Daniel	--	--	--	1	5.11.6
Latshaw, Isaac	180	--	2	3	87.4.2
Meyer, David	100	--	2	3	46.0.0
Myers, Nicholas	200	--	6	5	35.18.9
McCorckel, Rob't.	180	--	3	7	28.4.7
McCurdy, John	--	--	2	2	5.18.10
McFarland, James	292 1/2	--	5	10	51.15.0
McFarland, Wm.	--	--	--	--	--
Morrison, James	--	--	1	1	1.2.6
McCorckel, James	100	--	2	4	16.9.8
Myers, John	100	--	4	3	62.5.10
Myers, Ludwig	100	--	--	--	10.3.4
Myer, John	200	6	3	5	68.0.0
Myers, Christian	--	--	--	--	10.0.0
Minehart, Peter	140	--	2	4	43.2.6
Melaun, John	--	--	--	--	99.13.4
Malaun, Mathias	100	--	2	3	49.16.8
Modan, John	--	--	--	1	5.9
McFarland, Thomas	--	--	3	4	4.10.7
Myers, Nicholas	140	--	--	--	9.3.4
Myers, Nicholas, Sen'r.	100	--	2	2	38.6.8
McCalley, Andrew	100	--	2	2	39.9.8
McCalley, John	--	--	--	--	5.0.0
Miley, John	350	--	3	7	65.0.0
Miley, Jacob	--	--	--	--	10.0.0
Neely, John	300	--	3	7	61.1.8
Neely, Thomas	--	--	1	--	10.0.0
Neely, Jonathan	--	--	--	--	4.19.8
Nell, Henry	120	--	3	4	47.18.4
Nichman, John	80	--	--	1	24.10.8
Ohimbough, Antony	170	--	3	4	39.15.5
Oblenus, John	349	2	4	6	65.0.0
Orsan, Wm.	--	--	1	2	2.10.6
Orsan, George	200	--	4	4	43.6.4
Ohimbough, John	180	--	3	3	62.2.0
Ohimbough, John, Sen'r.	50	--	--	--	7.13.4
Overhulser, John	180	--	2	4	68.8.6
Picken, John	15	--	1	3	48.17.6
Pecker, John	--	--	--	--	164.16.8

Reading Township	Acres	Negroes	Horses	Cattle	Tax
Polke, James, Sen'r.	512	--	5	12	81.9.2
Polke, John	--	--	1	--	1.8.9
Polke, David	--	--	1	--	10.0.0
Polke, Robert	--	--	--	--	10.0.0
Polke, James	--	--	--	--	10.0.0
Polke, John, Se'r.	--	--	--	--	10.0.0
Polke, Joseph	--	--	1	--	5.0.0
Painter, Peter	--	--	--	1	4.8.2
Pupp, George	--	--	2	4	7.1.10
Pupp, Peter	--	--	--	--	--
Posterman, Mich'l.	250	--	2	5	16.0.0
Reed, Thomas	--	--	--	1	16.13.6
Rumble, George	120	--	3	5	24.8.9
Rumble, Jacob	--	--	--	--	10.0.0
Slegel, Daniel	150	--	--	--	19.3.4
Slegel, Jacob	214	--	--	--	33.10.10
Stagg, James	--	1	2	3	7.5.8
Sorbough, David	30	--	1	2	14.11.4
Snyder, Mich'l.	60	--	2	2	21.5.6
Snyder, Mich'l., Ju'r.	--	--	1	1	2.9.10
Spring, Laurence	--	--	--	--	10.0.0
Shriber, Philip	48 3/4	--	1	3	7.3.4
Troub, Henry	--	--	--	2	1.3.0
Troub, Paul	--	--	--	--	104.5.4
Troub, Peter	--	--	--	--	20.0.0
Thomas, Peter	--	--	--	1	11.6
Trimmer, Andrew	150	--	2	5	78.11.8
Trimmer, Andrew	150	--	--	--	14.7.6
Vance, John	50	--	2	2	25.0.3
Vance, Nicholas	100	--	3	2	34.17.8
Twinam, James	165	--	4	8	27.15.0
Twinam, Wm.	--	--	--	--	5.0.0
Werner, Daniel	--	--	2	3	--
Werts, Peter	200	--	4	4	90.9.4
Weaver, David	--	--	--	--	--
Walker, Ezael	--	--	--	--	291.6.8
Webster, Richard	--	--	1	1	2.17.6
Wetherspoon, James	150	--	--	--	15.6.8
White, Joshua	--	--	2	2	--
White, James	--	--	1	1	--
Weakley, Wm.	246	2	4	9	62.15.3
Wilson, Marmaduke	216	--	4	5	44.11.3
White, James	--	--	--	--	199.6.8
White, James, Ju'r.	--	--	1	4	6.2.8
White, Peter	--	--	--	--	20.0.0
White, Andrew	--	--	--	--	20.0.0
Yoder, Daniel	200	--	1	3	64.11.10
Clax, Christian	--	--	--	--	--
Fisher, Peter	--	--	--	1	11.6
Larew, Francis	120	--	3	5	--
Thomson, John	--	--	1	1	1.18.4
McCurdy, Robert	--	--	--	--	--
Huzzy, Jediah	--	--	--	--	--
Barney, James	--	--	--	2	--
Cooper, Wm.	72	--	--	--	--

Reading Township	Acres	Negroes	Horses	Cattle	Tax
Riley, Barnet	--	--	--	--	--
Biken, Henry	--	--	--	--	--
Boudenhimer, Simon	--	--	--	--	20.0.0
Boshea, Mich'l.	--	--	--	--	10.0.0
Close, Christian	--	--	--	--	362.15.0
Cooper, Wm.	--	--	--	--	7.13.4
Crannister, Henry	--	--	--	--	--
Huzzey, Jediah	--	--	--	--	106.11.4
Leru, Francis	--	--	--	--	18.13.9
McCurdy, Rob't.	--	--	--	--	14.17.6
Picken, Henry	--	--	--	--	10.0.0
Ryley, Barney	--	--	--	--	10.0.0

MANAHAN TOWNSHIP

	Acres	Negroes	Horses	Cattle	Tax
Adams, James	156	--	2	2	30.0.0
Anderson, John, Cumberland	50	--	--	--	6.6.0
Anderson, William	--	--	1	2	20.18.0
Arnold, Peter	140	--	2	3	36.16.0
Adams, Elijah	--	--	--	--	--
Braley, James	40	--	--	1	10.4.0
Beans, Thomas	557	--	3	5	100.0.0
Beans, Francis	118	--	1	3	18.15.0
Beans, Hugh	--	--	2	1	1.8.0
Buchanon, Andrew	58	--	1	1	7.10.0
Bealy, Daniel	50	--	2	5	12.0.0
Boil, John	50	--	--	--	--
Bash, Joseph	--	--	--	3	1.19.0
Bennet, Joseph	--	--	--	1	8.0
Blatchford, Richard	100	--	2	1	45.0.0
Bayers, Charles	90	--	2	2	15.0.0
Cooper, Wm.	--	--	1	1	1.3.6
Clinger, Philip	--	--	--	1	13.6
Kennedy, John	50	--	2	2	11.8.0
Camron, Finley	--	--	2	2	1.8.0
Comfort, Andrew	300	--	3	7	70.0.0
Crothers, John	192	--	3	4	65.0.0
Croop, Casper	50	--	1	1	8.0.0
Cannady, Bailiff	50	--	2	4	27.0.0
Coiner, Criften	35	--	--	1	8.12.0
Craford, Robert	--	--	--	2	16.0
Cooper, John	--	--	--	--	7.6
Condry, Wm.	100	--	--	--	15.0.0
Archibald, Campbell	200	--	--	--	20.0.0
Cook, Jesse	145	--	3	5	37.10.0
Camlin, Wm.	160	--	--	--	80.0.0
Cooper, Mathias	--	--	1	1	2.7.0
Cabel, Benjamin	150	--	2	3	28.0.0
Coulston, Charles	350	--	3	4	80.0.0
Coulston, Wm.	--	--	3	2	1.18.0
Cunningham, Rob't.	--	--	2	2	2.12.0
Cline, Casper	60	--	--	--	15.0.0

Manahan Township	Acres	Negroes	Horses	Cattle	Tax
Cook, Joseph	--	--	--	--	40.8.0
Dill, James	400	4	6	8	162.14.0
Dougherty, George	50	--	1	2	11.10.0
Dill, Thomas	100	--	1	2	21.8.0
Dickson, Joseph	250	--	1	2	1.7.6
Elliot, Andrew	--	--	--	--	30.12.0
Deardorf, Henry	100	--	2	3	58.12.0
Dill, Mathew, Colonel	353	1	6	8	56.10.0
D'o, in Westmoreland county	356	--	--	--	--
D'o, in Westmoreland county	366	--	--	--	--
D'o, in Westmoreland county	374	--	--	--	--
D'o, in Westmoreland county	280	--	--	--	--
D'o, in Northumberland county	300	--	--	--	--
D'o, in Nrthumberland county	30	--	--	--	--
Deardorf, Jacob	200	--	2	4	60.0.0
Deardorf, Isaac	150	--	3	5	160.0.0
Develin, John	--	--	1	2	1.7.6
Elliot, Benjamin	100	--	3	3	44.16.0
Elliot, Isaac	--	--	--	1	1.7.0
Eikener, John	6	--	1	2	4.5.0
Ernst, James	--	--	--	--	--
Elliot, Robert	100	--	1	1	20.0.0
Elliot, Joseph	165	--	4	4	40.0.0
Fisher, James	60	--	2	2	41.12.0
Fisher, Isaac	--	--	--	--	41.12.0
Finley, Henry	--	--	--	2	19.6
Freezer, Joshua	60	--	1	2	13.0.0
Frederick, Abram	--	--	--	--	12.0
Godfrey, Wm.	400	1	2	6	200.16.0
Grist, Wm.	--	--	--	--	84.0.0
Hanna, Alexander	--	--	--	2	1.5.0
Hanna, James	--	--	2	1	1.12.0
Haller, Christian	60	--	2	2	18.4.0
Hoppel, George	50	--	2	2	7.10.0
Hoffman, Stophel	80	--	2	3	13.16.0
Swartz, Herman	--	--	--	--	--
Hover, John	150	--	--	--	90.0.0
Hykess, George	100	--	2	3	28.12.0
Harrison, John	50	--	--	1	6.0.0
Hykess, George	97	--	2	3	18.10.0
Hail, Hugh	1123	--	2	2	15.10.0
Henderson, Samuel	--	--	3	5	3.3.6
Ipe, Jacob	--	--	--	1	2.7.0
Johnston, Thomas	--	--	2	--	30.0.0
Kelley, James	100	--	2	2	33.4.0
King, Christopher	250	--	2	9	40.6.0
Kerr, John	100	--	2	2	16.12.0
Kyser, Teeter	160	--	1	3	22.10.0
Kerr, John	200	--	2	2	35.0.0

Manahan Township	Acres	Negroes	Horses	Cattle	Tax
Lewis, David	30	--	1	1	5.12.0
Livingston, James	--	--	1	2	18.0
Leech, Henry	--	--	2	3	3.12.0
Logan, John	140	--	4	4	40.0.0
Leamer, John	50	--	--	--	19.0.0
Leamer, Wm.	100	--	4	5	96.16.0
Lobach, Abraham	80	--	1	2	60.0.0
Moore, Hugh	--	--	1	1	1.8.0
McNichol, James	100	--	2	4	54.0.0
Mills, Wm.		--			
Moore, James	--	--	--	1	4.0
Mitchel, Wm.	308	--	5	4	40.0.0
McMullen, Hugh	50	--	2	5	12.4.0
McCurdy, Daniel	60	--	3	4	16.0.0
Morgan, Isaac	--	--	2	3	1.12.0
Minch, Daniel	--	--	1	2	3.19.0
McMullen, George	80	--	--	--	24.0.0
Miller, Philip	100	--	2	2	33.4.0
McClure, Samuel	--	--	--	2	15.6
Miller, George	130	--	2	2	18.0.0
Mumper, Mich'l.	250	2	3	8	182.16.0
Moudy, Balzer	100	--	--	2	7.10.0
Messersmith, George	40	--	--	3	8.12.0
Nessley, Samuel	100	--	--	--	40.0.0
Nelson, Samuel	166	--	3	5	36.5.0
Nessly, John	--	--	--	--	12.15.0
Lobach, Daniel	--	--	--	--	56.0.0
Olshose, John	150	--	2	3	33.12.0
Ots. Laurence	--	--	1	2	--
Olvert, Andrew	96	--	--	--	40.0.0
Orendorf, Henry	100	--	2	2	18.15.0
Person, Henry	100	--	2	2	--
Park, Wm.	192	3	3	4	40.0.0
Peater, Andrew	100	--	--	--	20.0.0
Peden, Samuel	180	--	2	4	58.0.0
Peters, Richard	1,347	--	--	--	202.0.0
Porter, Wm.	100	--	3	5	16.0.0
Prince, John	--	--	2	2	81.12.0
Potter, Wm.	131	--	2	3	16.0.0
Quigley, James	--	--	2	3	1.12.0
Ross, George	50	--	1	3	2.4.0
Robison, Samuel	--	--	--	1	2.4.0
Reed, James	30	--	2	2	7.8.0
Robison, Thomas	155	--	3	4	42.4.0
Richardson, Jacob	130	--	3	2	42.4.0
Rees, George	45	--	1	2	15.10.0
Stanton, Daniel	--	--	--	3	12.0
Santz, Andrew	15	--	--	1	1.14.0
Schnell, John	100	--	2	1	14.0.0
Shannon, Patrick	--	--	2	3	1.16.0
Smith, Jacob, Ju'r.	150	--	2	4	20.0.0
Smith, Jacob		--			
Smith, John	300	--	--	--	135.0.0
Steel, Godfrey	--	--	1	2	2.15.0
Stees, Rudy	--	--	2	--	10.0.0

Manahan Township	Acres	Negroes	Horses	Cattle	Tax
Steel, George	50	--	1	1	5.16.0
Shepherd, Henry	93	--	2	5	18.0.0
Shoman, David	60	--	--	1	5.0.0
Steel, Isaac	--	--	--	1	1.3.0
Stouffer, Abram	400	--	3	4	247.12.0
Swisher, Laurence	--	--	2	2	21.12.0
Squibb, Wm.	--	--	1	1	1.12.0
Sever, Henry	50	--	1	1	7.5.0
Steel, George, Ju'r.	50	--	3	4	8.11.0
Simmerman, Ludwig	247	--	4	9	75.0.0
Torbert, Allen	200	--	2	4	37.10.0
Thomson, John	60	--	1	2	13.0.0
Troup, John	--	--	--	2	8.0
Triplet, Francis	--	--	2	3	3.4.0
Thaeser, Henry	--	--	--	--	--
Wilson, Daniel	--	--	2	3	1.12.0
Wilson, Andrew	187	--	2	3	18.15.0
Williams, Andrew	75	--	1	2	21.0.0
Williams, Daniel	300	--	3	5	50.0.0
Williams, John	100	--	3	3	17.8.0
Wilson, James	50	--	2	4	7.8.0
Wilson, John	200	--	3	6	55.0.0
Wilson, John	--	--	1	2	2.15.0
Williams, John	150	--	--	--	150.0.0
Williams, Amos	100	--	--	2	4.10.0
White, William	105	--	--	2	16.2.0
Wilson, John	--	--	2	2	1.19.6
Williams, Abraham	100	--	5	6	48.14.0
Wilson, John	--	--	--	--	--
Weaver, Conrad	100	--	2	2	33.4.0
Wilson, William	--	--	1	1	--
Wilson, Andrew	300	--	4	5	120.0.0
Wilhelm, Michael	--	--	1	2	--
Williams, Lewis	241	--	3	3	25.0.0
Young, Mathew	--	--	2	2	1.8.0

Single Men

	Amount of Tax		Amount of Tax
Potter, John	15.0.0	McGomery, Thomas	10.0.0
Griffith, John	20.7.6	Wilson, Alexander	10.0.0
Gallacher, Alexander	20.7.6	Shannon, Patrick	10.0.0
Wagoner, Jacob	15.0.0	Ohail, John	10.0.0
Philips, Joseph	20.0.0	Ohail, Edward	15.0.0
Seidel, Godfrey	20.0.0	Canady, John	5.0.0
Colston, David	10.0.0	Boyle, Robert	5.0.0.
Colston, Ripley	--	Beans, William	5.0.0
Torbit, Robert	15.0.0	Beans, Thomas	--
Torbit, David	15.0.0	Kirk, David	20.0.0
Ross, James	10.0.0	Robison, John	10.0.0
Ross, Robert	10.0.0	Arnold, John	20.7.6
Pearson, Vintz	15.0.0	Wessler, William	20.7.6
Fulton, John	5.0.0	Gregory, John	20.7.6

Manahan Township   Single Men

Shannon, John	15.0.0	Shreiper, Philip	20.7.6
Seidel, George	20.7.6	Shannon, John	--
Morrow, James	20.0.0	Adams the weaver, at James'	10.0.0
Williams, Jonathan	1.12.0	Grist, Daniel	75.0.0

HUNTINGTON TOWNSHIP

	Acres	Negroes	Horses	Cattle	Tax
Brandon, Alexander	--	--	2	1	--
Brandon, Richard	--	--	2	1	7.10.0
Brandon, John	200	--	4	8	60.0.0
Branard, Barney	100	--	--	1	14.0.0
Burckholder, Henry	188	--	3	3	30.0.0
Baldridge, James	--	--	1	2	1.5.0
Brandon, Thams	300	--	4	8	75.0.0
Black, Thomas	50	--	1	1	5.0.0
Boner, John	--	--	1	1	5.0.0
Bayles, Abraham	--	--	1	1	3.0.0
Boner, Charles	96	--	2	4	20.0.0
Bradey, James	200	--	2	6	37.10.0
Carrathers, Thomas	--	--	1	2	3.0.0
Cooly, John	75	--	2	2	12.10.0
Deal, Felix	64	--	2	3	15.0.0
Donald, William	--	--	--	--	3.0.0
Dodds, Joseph	380	--	4	5	71.0.0
Dawson, Richard	--	--	1	--	2.0.0
Figel, Gabriel	50	--	1	4	7.10.0
Fleck, Felty	100	--	2	3	15.0.0
Glen, Joseph	50	--	2	2	7.10.0
Gribble, Widow	100	--	4	5	11.5.0
Garret, Luke	100	--	3	5	22.10.0
Hickes, George	169	--	2	7	40.0.0
Hamilton, William	--	--	2	3	6.0.0
Land belonging to Wm. Moor	150	--	--	--	35.0.0
Canady, John	140	--	2	4	35.0.0
Lewis, Lewis	--	--	3	3	17.10.0
Laughlin, William	100	--	2	2	17.10.0
Lightner, James	--	--	--	--	2.0.0
Lukens, Heres	250	--	--	--	--
Mathews, Samuel	--	--	2	3	--
Moorehead, James	100	--	2	2	35.0.0
Miller, Michael	250	--	3	6	60.0.0
Moll, Henry	30	--	1	1	5.0.0
McGrew, John	200	--	3	3	45.0.0
Myers, Frederick	100	--	3	3	20.0.0
Neely, John	260	--	2	4	42.10.0
Neely, Thomas	260	1	3	3	45.0.0
Orr, Arthur	100	--	3	3	27.10.0
Robinet, George	90	--	3	7	25.0.0
To land by him and Canady	100	--	--	--	17.10.0
Rubbert, John	64	--	1	4	17.10.0
Reamer, Henry	200	--	2	3	35.0.0
Richey, David	300	--	3	4	58.10.0

Huntington Township	Acres	Negroes	Horses	Cattle	Tax
Richey, Andrew	--	--	2	3	10.0.0
Rothenheiser, Peter	--	--	1	2	10.0.0
Smith, John	140	--	2	3	10.0.0
Sanderson, Alexander	100	--	3	4	27.10.0
Stephens, Thomas	--	--	2	3	13.0.0
To rent	--	--	--	--	15.0.0
Stirling, Joseph	50	--	3	6	20.0.0
Stewart, William	130 1/4	--	2	2	20.0.0
Shroth, John	300	--	1	1	25.0.0
Smith, John	--	--	--	1	--
Stevenson, George	300	--	4	5	40.0.0
Thomson, Andrew, Esq'r.	200	--	3	7	50.0.0
Thomson, William	--	--	1	2	5.0.0
Thomson, John	--	--	2	1	2.0.0
Thomson, John, school m'r.	5	--	--	--	2.10.0
Wander, Stephen	100	--	3	5	25.0.0
Waggoner, Casper	46	--	--	5	2.0.0
Wisley, Edward	--	--	--	--	5.0.0
Waltimyer, David	20	--	1	1	1.0.0
Wolf, Henry	--	--	2	4	7.10.0
Wylich, John	--	--	3	3	--
Ziegler, John	150	--	--	5	52.10.0
Ziegler, Henry	150	--	2	3	35.0.0
Ziegler, George	190	--	2	4	25.0.0
Ziegler, Philip, near York	150	--	--	--	27.10.0

Single Men Who Have Sworn

	Acres	Negroes	Horses	Cattle	Tax
Brandon, Walter	200	--	2	1	47.10.10
Boner, Francis	--	--	--	--	10.0.0
Boner, Robert	--	--	1	--	7.10.0
Boner, Thomas	100	--	2	4	22.10.0
Balden, John	--	--	--	2	7.10.0
Chambers, James	--	--	--	--	7.10.0
Carlisle, John	--	--	--	--	7.10.0
Dodds, Wm.	--	--	--	--	7.10.0
Gallespy, Wm.	--	--	1	--	10.0.0
Hext, Christian	86	--	--	4	15.0.0
Wilson, Samuel	200	--	5	4	52.10.0
Wyley, Robert	200	--	5	4	52.10.0
Williamson, John	--	--	--	--	5.0.0
Smith, James	150	--	2	2	65.0.0
Smith, Wm.	--	--	--	2	15.0.0
Shay, Edward	--	--	1	--	7.10.0

Young Men Who Have Not Sworn

	Acres	Negroes	Horses	Cattle	Tax
Robinson, John	--	--	--	--	15.0.0
Shikemer, Ebenezer	--	--	--	--	10.0.0
Wessler, Henry	--	--	--	--	15.0.0
Wiseley, Wm.	--	--	2	--	15.0.0
Simons, James	--	--	--	--	15.0.0
Albert, Andrew	--	--	--	--	--

Young Men Who Have Not Sworn

Name					
Brandon, Jonathan	--	--	--	--	--
Bails, Jesse	--	--	--	--	15.0.0
Bails, Moses	--	--	--	--	15.0.0
Bails, Calep	--	--	--	--	15.0.0
Bails, Elisha	--	--	1	--	15.0.0
Bails, Jacob	--	--	--	--	--
Calehin, Thomas	--	--	--	--	15.0.0
Cox, Wm.	150	--	2	2	110.0.0
Carson, John	--	--	1	1	--
Camel, James	--	--	1	--	7.10.0
Dodds, Joseph	--	--	--	--	7.10.0
Donally, John	200	--	--	--	70.0.0
Donally, James	--	--	--	--	15.0.0
Flood, Timothy	--	--	--	--	15.0.0
Hunt, Edward	--	--	--	--	15.0.0
Hess, Valentine	--	--	--	--	10.0.0
Hess, Isaac	--	--	--	--	15.0.0
Hens, Jacob	--	--	--	--	4.0.0
Hickes, Peter	--	--	--	--	15.0.0
John, John	--	--	--	--	4.0.0
Folk, Moses	--	--	--	--	15.0.0
Myers, Ludwig	--	--	--	--	--
Myers, Jacob	--	--	--	--	15.0.0
Myers, Henry	--	--	--	--	15.0.0
Mitchel, Andrew	--	--	1	--	10.0.0
Morrison, John	--	--	--	--	--
Person, Isaac	--	--	--	--	15.0.0
Petty, John	--	--	--	--	10.0.0
Rittenhouse, Gerard	--	--	1	--	15.0.0
Richeson, Edward	--	--	--	--	15.0.0
Roberts, John	--	--	1	--	15.0.0
Robinet, Allen	--	--	--	--	15.0.0
Robinet, James	--	--	--	--	--
Wilson, James	--	--	--	--	15.0.0
Wessler, John	--	--	1	--	25.0.0

Taxables Not Sworn

Name	Acres	Negroes	Horses	Cattle	Tax
Albert, Laurence	100	--	3	3	82.10.0
Armor, Thomas	--	--	--	1	--
Albert, John	100	--	1	2	40.13.0
Albert, John	--	--	--	2	15.0.0
Bower, Jacob	--	--	--	--	3.0.0
Brinley, Mathias	100	--	1	3	20.0.0
Bower, John	200	--	3	4	110.0.0
Bower, Abraham	150	--	3	3	83.0.0
Bails, William	150	--	2	2	63.10.0
Bails, David	--	--	1	--	15.0.0
Brady, John	--	--	1	--	4.0.0
Brakin, Wm.	--	--	2	3	--
Bower, Widow	--	--	--	1	2.0.0
Bold, Wm.	--	--	--	1	6.0.0
Bails, John	150	--	1	2	90.0.0

Taxables Not Sworn	Acres	Negroes	Horses	Cattle	Tax
Bails, John, Ju'r.	60	--	2	2	40.0.0
Bails, Jacob, Ju'r.	50	--	2	2	34.0.0
Bails, Jacob, Se'r.	165	--	2	3	30.0.0
Bails, Solomon	--	--	1	3	15.0.0
Bails, Isaac	--	--	1	2	12.0.0
Bails, Caleb	200	--	4	5	190.0.0
Brakin, Elizabeth	80	--	2	2	50.0.0
Buckholder, John	110	--	3	5	60.0.0
Butt, William	--	--	2	2	18.0.0
Brown, Alexander	300	--	--	--	30.0.0
Cox, Solomon	--	--	--	--	--
Comer, John	150	--	3	4	70.0.0
Crine, Casper	100	--	3	4	40.0.0
Crup, Peter	100	--	3	5	52.10.0
Crup, Philip	100	--	2	3	52.0.0
Collins, John	94	--	2	2	51.16.0
Cimberly, Mich'l.	--	--	1	2	15.0.0
Censor, Jacob	150	--	3	5	90.0.0
Cronister, John	100	--	2	4	40.0.0
Cronister, John, Ju'r.	--	--	--	--	8.0.0
Cox, John	100	--	2	2	51.16.0
Coulston, Cha's. ex'r of the Widow Kenworthy	100	--	--	--	40.0.0
Clark, William	--	--	2	2	10.0.0
Dennis, John	--	--	--	1	3.0.0
Dumb, Andrew	200	--	1	2	43.10.0
Dansil, George	--	--	1	2	--
Dill, John	--	--	1	1	10.0.0
Day, Salvenius	--	--	1	2	18.0.0
Elker, Henry	200	--	3	6	70.0.0
Everit, Isaac	150	--	3	3	70.0.0
Fickes, Valentine	100	--	1	4	40.0.0
Fickes, Abraham	100	--	3	3	60.0.0
Fickes, Jacob	150	--	2	3	62.0.0
Fickes, Isaac	100	--	3	2	60.0.0
Fickes, John	62	--	2	2	61.0.0
Fickes, Valentine, Ju'r.	--	--	1	1	8.0.0
Folk, Stephen	300	2	4	5	262.0.0
Fleck, Peter	100	--	2	2	40.0.0
Funk, Daniuel	100	--	2	2	40.0.0
Grist, Thomas	100	--	2	2	80.0.0
Hutton, James	100	--	3	3	31.5.0
Hutton, Elizabeth	100	--	1	2	22.10.0
Hutton, Leonard	150	1	3	4	87.10.0
Hooker, John	--	--	--	1	11.10.0
Horsman, Abram	100	--	--	--	7.10.0
Herman, Adam	100	--	3	4	70.0.0
Howe, John	--	--	--	1	8.0.0
Herman, John	--	--	--	1	8.0.0
Hunt, John	200	--	2	2	83.0.0
Hess, Felty	167	--	3	2	73.6.0
Hostetter, Christian	100	--	2	2	40.0.0
Howel, Jehemiah	--	--	1	--	7.10.0
Holtzinger, Jacob	--	--	--	1	10.0.0
Jones, Jacob	100	--	2	2	22.0.0

Taxables Not Sworn	Acres	Negroes	Horses	Cattle	Tax
Jones, Elijah	--	--	1	--	--
Loback, Andrew	80	--	2	1	23.6.0
Lukens, Jesse	--	--	--	--	7.10.0
Lerew, Jacob	--	--	1	1	9.0.0
Lerew, George	6	--	1	1	13.0.0
Lightner, Wm.	200	--	--	--	42.10.0
Mull, Henry	--	--	--	1	3.0.0
Mandorf, John	100	--	3	2	63.6.0
Mails, Samuel	--	--	1	2	15.0.0
Myers, Nicholas	440	--	8	10	145.10.0
May, Jacob	--	--	1	1	15.0.0
McGrew, James	--	--	3	2	--
McGrew, Archbald	--	--	1	1	15.0.0
Mitchell, John	--	--	--	1	--
Meneigh, Philip	--	--	--	1	--
Nickle, James	100	--	2	2	40.0.0
Zigler, Jacob	--	--	--	1	--
Ocker, Henry	--	--	2	2	15.0.0
Oldshoe, John	100	--	--	--	15.0.0
Patterson, Robert	--	--	1	1	10.0.0
Person, Elias	84	--	2	2	43.0.0
Pilketon, Vinson	100	--	2	3	65.0.0
Robeson, Thomas	200	--	3	4	80.0.0
Robinet, James	100	--	3	3	60.16.0
Richeson, Hannah	10	--	--	1	3.0.0
Rosemiller, Ludwig	145	--	2	3	51.10.0
Rosemiller, Ludwig, Geo'e	145	--	--	--	57.10.0
Ringler, Jacob	--	--	--	1	4.0.0
Shitz, Anthony	--	--	--	2	6.0.0
Sadler, Isaac	150	--	2	4	32.5.0
Singhorse, Abraham	--	--	2	1	40.0.0
Steward, Wm.	--	--	2	1	--
Shipton, Thomas	--	--	1	--	7.0.0
Spikeman, Joshua	150	--	2	4	60.0.0
Simmons, Adams	100	--	2	3	60.10.0
Snider, Peter	--	--	1	2	15.0.0
Tachenbach, Mathias	--	--	1	2	15.0.0
Vanscofe, Aron	100	--	1	2	35.0.0
Vanscofe, Moses	100	--	--	--	40.0.0
Watson, John	--	--	--	--	--
Weaver, Nicholas	60	--	2	4	35.0.0
Weaver, Jacob	--	--	--	--	4.0.0
Wierman, Nicholas	200	1	2	6	130.0.0
Wierman, Benjamin	100	--	2	2	55.0.0
Wierman, Wm.	120	--	2	3	63.0.0
Wierman, John	100	--	3	8	100.0.0
Wierman, Nicholas, Ju'r.	--	--	2	2	19.0.0
Wierman, Henry, Se'r.	400	--	4	6	207.0.0
Wierman, Henry, Ju'r.	--	--	3	4	28.10.0
Wessler, Henry	200	--	3	4	86.0.0
Wisely, John	--	--	1	--	10.0.0
Montgomery, Rob't.	--	--	--	--	25.0.0
Smatz, John	--	--	--	--	1.0.0
Densyl, Rich'd.	--	--	--	--	11.0.0
Apple, Leonard	--	--	--	--	3.15.0
Stewart, Rob't.	--	--	--	--	7.10.0

HAMILTON'S BANN TOWNSHIP

	Acres	Negroes	Horses	Cattle	Tax
Agnew, James, Colonel	100	2	5	9	91.4.2
Agnew, John	212	1	5	6	60.0.0
Agnew, James	200	1	3	5	60.16.3
Agnew, David	504	1	1	13	122.1.6
Adams, John	104	--	4	4	29.14.9
Agnew, Samuel	100	--	5	6	38.0.6
Agnew, Samuel	250	--	--	--	--
Adams, Samuel	--	--	--	--	1.8.6
Annan, Rob't., Rev'd.	188	--	--	--	30.10.0
Adair, John	104	--	2	3	7.7.7
Agnew, Widow	--	--	1	2	--
Achert, Christopher	--	--	--	1	6.0
Brice, James	200	--	3	7	57.11.0
Bigham, Robert, Se'r.	120	--	2	5	24.7.6
Bingham, Samuel	240	1	3	3	28.5.6
Brown, Joseph	180	--	3	3	56.11.3
Biers, Samuel, Se'r.	--	--	1	2	1.19.0
Biers, David	225	--	2	4	66.17.9
Biers, Samuel, Ju'r.	--	--	1	2	1.11.3
Brown, Wm.	250	--	3	5	63.2.2
Beard, John	--	--	--	2	14.0
Blyth, David	150	--	2	4	28.5.6
Boston, George	30	--	2	1	2.14.0
Bigam, Thomas	200	--	4	5	48.6.9
Bigham, Wm.	180	--	3	3	37.9.0
Bigham, Hugh	80	--	1	3	14.12.6
Bigham, Rob't.	46	3	4	3	36.0.0
Barkman, John	80	--	1	2	9.15.6
Buttrim, Benjamin	--	--	1	2	1.12.0
Cunningham, Rob't.	158	--	5	7	42.8.9
Craig, Thomas	--	--	3	2	3.18.0
Carnachan, Alex'r.	120	1	2	1	23.19.9
Caldwell, James	172	--	5	10	34.5.0
Clugston, Joseph	100	--	4	5	22.8.6
Cochran, Andrew	376	4	5	14	125.9.2
Clugston, Joseph	300	--	--	--	--
Cochran, James	400	2	4	8	117.4.0
Cochran, Wm.	400	4	5	7	127.5.6
Cochran, John	376	--	4	5	98.18.6
Cotton, Henry	221	--	7	7	58.0.0
Carrick, John	--	--	2	--	4.4.0
Carrick, James	236	--	2	3	58.2.9
Clark, John	50	--	2	2	5.0.0
Clinger, Thomas	353	--	6	9	107.19.4
Cochran, John	35	--	3	4	8.15.6
Campbell, Joseph	72	--	2	2	--
Cummings, James	180	--	3	6	29.5.0
Castles, Alexander	83	--	2	2	7.8.3
Carnachan, David	--	--	2	2	3.7.8
Craig, Rob't.	92	--	2	3	20.7.0
Cook, Andrew	--	--	2	1	--
Cook, Andrew	300	--	--	--	--
Craig, Robert	--	--	--	1	8.0
Duncan, Henry	50	--	1	1	--

Hamilton's Bann Township	Acres	Negroes	Horses	Cattle	Tax
Dickson's land	530	--	--	--	77.0.0
Dunwiddy, Widow	273	1	4	8	90.1.8
Dunwiddy, Widow, Cumb'd t'w'p	400	--	--	--	--
Duff, Peter	--	--	2	2	2.12.8
Douglass, Timothy	245	--	3	2	44.13.8
Depounds, Adoniah	--	--	2	3	6.12.4
Diver, John	--	--	1	3	2.8.9
Davidson, Phineas	--	--	1	2	1.4.0
Eliss, James	104	--	1	1	1.16.0
Eliss, James, in Bedford	200	--	--	--	--
Elder, James	155	--	4	8	45.2.9
Elliot, George	--	--	3	4	5.6.3
Emite, Samuel	30	--	--	--	7.6.3
Emite, Widow	200	2	2	2	10.5.9
Elder, Benjamin	--	--	2	2	4.2.0
Fuderell, Laurence	--	--	--	1	6.0
Findley, Wm., Se'r.	179	--	3	5	48.13.1
Findley, Mich'l., Se'r.	179	--	4	7	55.7.8
Findley, Wm.	243	--	4	5	58.10.0
Findley, Mich'l.	130	--	2	4	5.7.3
Fleming, Rob't.	--	--	2	2	43.17.6
Galbraith, John	--	--	1	2	1.10.0
Galbraith, Joseph	--	--	1	2	1.12.0
Guinn, Patrick	--	--	2	1	2.8.0
Guest, Benjamin	250	--	2	1	3.0.0
Gibson, Widow	--	--	1	2	--
Gill, Thomas	--	--	1	1	1.6.0
Grossman, Benjamin	125	--	1	2	50.10.6
Gettys, Samuel	100	--	--	--	8.5.9
Honnan, John	--	--	2	2	4.2.0
Hughes, Barnabas	--	--	2	3	2.10.0
Henney, Patrick, Se'r.	23	--	2	1	4.2.0
Henney, Patrick	--	--	2	2	1.16.0
Hill, Wm.	385	--	6	11	65.6.6
Heart, David	200	--	4	5	43.18.6
Heart, Andrew	100	--	3	5	26.6.6
Heart, Wm.	200	--	4	--	26.6.6
Hamilton, Joseph	243	--	4	3	75.14.3
Hudson, Mathew	--	--	2	2	1.10.0
Heart, Widow	--	--	1	5	--
Jack, James	190	--	3	5	20.0.0
Jack, Andrew	--	2	3	5	18.12.0
Johnson, Thomas	--	--	--	1	8.0
Kennedy, David	400	2	6	7	149.8.4
Kerr, George	170	2	5	6	50.0.0
Kerr, Wm.	130	1	3	4	46.18.0
Kerr, John	200	--	3	4	29.12.8
Kerr, Wm.	83	--	2	2	24.3.4.
Kerr, Thomas	--	--	2	3	3.12.0
Knox, Samuel	220	1	4	6	59.9.9
Kirkpatrick, Wm.	125	--	2	1	11.2.4
Kincaid, Michael	93	--	2	5	24.19.3
Kincaid, Robert	--	--	1	1	1.8.0
Latta, Thomas	106	--	--	--	5.0.0

Hamilton's Bann Township	Acres	Negroes	Horses	Cattle	Tax
Lingheart, Bernhard	100	--	2	2	5.16.10
Little, David	--	--	--	4	1.6.0
Law, Thomas	175	--	3	3	38.6.0
Love, James	100	--	2	3	17.11.0
Lazier, Nicholas	--	--	2	2	1.4.0
Loag, Hugh	--	--	--	1	1.5.6
McMachan, James	--	--	1	--	1.12.6
McElroy, James	--	--	3	5	3.18.0
McGaughey, James	200	--	--	--	23.18.6
McGaughey, Thomas	200	--	2	3	40.7.8
McGaughey, Alex'r.	200	--	3	4	40.2.2
Moore, John	100	--	5	8	28.12.4
Moore, Samuel	475	--	3	5	79.2.10
McClellan, Dav'd	413	--	3	4	92.7.2
McClellan, Tho's.	150	--	3	7	40.12.3
McNea, John, Sen'r.	100	--	3	5	19.4.2
Marshall, James	55	--	2	3	8.3.10
McKindly, Wm.	150	--	2	5	29.15.6
McMillian, Wm.	180	--	4	8	29.15.6
Marshal, James	420	1	4	8	110.0.0
McNea, John	--	--	2	2	2.12.8
Montgomery, Nathan	97	--	2	5	18.12.0
McKisson, James	--	--	1	1	1.5.9
McKee, Joseph	150	--	4	5	28.19.5
McKission, Alexander	200	--	4	6	61.8.0
McKisson, Wm.	200	--	3	6	55.3.8
McGinley, Widow	200	1	5	6	78.0.0
McAllister, James	276	--	5	11	79.3.5
McGinley, John	200	1	7	8	74.2.0
McGimsy, Rob't.	200	--	5	7	41.18.6
McColough, Widow	150	1	3	6	40.0.0
Meredith, Francis	276	--	3	6	46.8.2
McClean, Wm. Esq'r.	200	--	6	7	58.10.0
Martin, Robert	--	--	2	2	2.12.6
Martin, Robert, in Bedford	100	--	--	--	--
Miller, John	247	--	1	3	58.3.2
Murray, John, Rev'd.	230	--	4	3	18.0.0
Murray, John	222	1	3	8	46.10.0
McKindley, Benjamin	100	--	--	--	10.14.6
Moor, John	--	--	2	2	--
Murray, Duncan	--	--	1	1	16.0
McNare, Alex'r.	260	--	4	6	102.0.0
McAdams, Gilbert	140	--	5	5	37.2.6
McCherry, Barnabas	--	--	1	--	1.10.0
Mays, Charles	--	--	2	4	4.0.0
McKisson, James	130	--	5	5	68.14.7
McVay, Wm.	--	--	--	1	6.0
Moore, Samuel	--	--	2	3	3.0.0
McClean, Alexander	--	--	1	1	1.6.0
McTiney, Thomas	--	--	2	2	2.0.6
McCay, Wm.	--	--	6	7	2.3.0
Martin, Robert	100	--	1	2	2.3.0
McNare, Samuel	--	--	--	2	--
McCall, John	--	--	--	--	1.8.5
Orr, James	100	--	1	2	14.12.6

Hamilton's Bann Township	Acres	Negroes	Horses	Cattle	Tax
Orr, Wm.	--	--	1	1	1.17.6
Orr, Wm.	--	--	1	1	--
Patton, John	--	--	2	4	--
Patton, Joh, in West'm co.	300	--	--	--	
Porter, Samuel	150	--	4	7	34.3.0
Patton, Robert	245	--	2	4	46.6.3
Peden, Samuel	245	--	6	10	95.3.3
Peden, Samuel, in Lanc. co.	104	--	--	--	
Porter, Wm.	392	1	5	7	90.13.6
Patterson, Nathaniel	80	--	--	--	9.15.0
Paxton, Joseph	--	--	3	4	4.5.8
Paxton, Joseph, in Bed. co.	100	--	--	--	
Pinchin, John	--	--	--	1	6.0.0
Patterson, Thomas	--	--	3	6	5.5.4
Ralson, Widow	169	--	--	--	45.5.8
Rowan, Henry	175	--	4	4	42.19.6
Risk, Robert	--	--	2	6	3.18.0
Reid, Samuel	200	--	2	1	47.5.9
Reid, James	100	--	1	2	7.0.6
Reid, Benjamin	175	--	3	4	40.7.3
Reid, John	175	--	3	5	35.2.0
Reid, Wm.	175	--	2	4	30.6.6
Reid, Thomas	175	--	1	1	--
Ramsey, Reynold	259	2	5	7	113.11.9
Robison, Thomas	--	--	4	2	5.19.0
Robison, Isaac	200	--	4	5	42.12.2
Roberts, George, Ju'r.	--	--	2	3	3.10.3
Riddle, John	272	--	3	--	20.15.5
Russel, Andrew	--	--	5	4	6.14.7
Roberts, George	30	--	1	2	1.7.5
Robinson, John	188	--	2	5	50.0.0
Redy, Peter	--	--	--	1	10.0.0
Rider, John	25	--	--	2	3.18.0
Rineberger, Wm.	--	--	--	1	--
Rea, Samuel	--	--	2	2	2.12.0
Rea, Samuel, in Bed. co.	240	--	--	--	--
Russel, Wm.	--	--	--	2	14.0
Stevenson, John	--	--	1	1	--
Stevenson, Wm.	100	--	3	4	31.3.1
Slemons, John, Rev'd.	214	3	3	5	55.0.0
Smith, Robert	205	--	5	7	65.0.0
Spear, Robert	186	--	4	7	38.3.4
Scott, Sam'l.	242	--	5	8	55.1.9
Scott, John	150	--	3	1	32.2.6
Shannon, Thomas	154	--	2	2	28.8.4
Shannon, Joseph	300	--	1	4	45.17.6
Slemonds, James	200	--	3	4	36.11.3
Scott, William	200	--	2	5	24.12.6
D'o in Cumberland county	120	--	--	--	--
Stuart, Samuel	--	--	1	--	1.0.3
Stockton, Robert	--	--	2	1	1.13.2
Smith, John	--	--	2	2	2.7.10

Hamilton's Bann Township	Acres	Negroes	Horses	Cattle	Tax
Stivers, Lewis	8	--	2	2	30.12.5
Stewart, James	100	--	3	5	22.14.5
Stevenson, Wm.	150	--	3	3	19.0.3
Stevenson, James	--	--	1	--	12.10.0
Smith, Abraham	--	--	--	2	8.0
Stuart, Joseph	--	--	1	2	1.7.5
Steel, John	--	--	1	2	1.19.0
Sims, John	--	--	1	2	1.7.5
Thomson, James	255	--	3	5	48.1.5
Thomson, John	194	--	4	9	45.17.6
Taylor, John	--	--	1	2	10.4.9
Walker, John	--	--	2	2	2.1.0
Waugh, Wm.	175	2	3	8	72.0.10
Waugh, Widow	100	--	3	3	15.0.0
Waugh, David	175	1	4	9	39.19.6
Wilson, Hugh	221	--	2	3	39.15.8
Wilson, Widow	233	1	3	3	30.0.0
Wilson, David	245	1	5	6	75.11.3
Wilson, Wm.	150	--	3	3	19.10.8
Wilson, James	--	--	2	--	16.0
D'o in Bedford	240	--	--	--	--
Witherow, Wm.	268	1	2	6	78.0.0
Wilson, Widow	--	1	--	3	--
White, Wm.	--	--	1	2	1.9.3
D'o in Westsmoreland co.	200	--	--	--	--
Welsh, John	--	--	--	1	--
Witsel, Peter	280	--	--	--	15.10.0
Young, James	30	2	4	7	27.4.1

		Young Men			
	Acres	Negroes	Horses	Cattle	Tax
Bigham, John	--	--	--	--	7.10.0
Burns, James	--	--	1	--	15.0.0
Burns, Wm.	--	--	1	--	10.0.0
Brandan, Wm.	--	--	2	--	13.0.0
Brown, Henry	--	--	--	1	15.4.0
Clark, Wm.	--	--	--	--	15.0.0
Christopher, Hugh	--	--	1	2	12.10.0
Cotton, Hugh	--	--	--	--	12.10.0
Cowley, Henry	--	--	1	--	12.10.0
Cotton, John	--	--	--	--	12.10.0
Collins, David	--	--	1	--	12.10.0
Cherridon, John	--	--	--	--	10.0.0
Clark, Ja's.	--	--	--	--	12.10.0
Crookshanks, George	--	--	1	--	12.10.0
Corbit, John	--	--	1	--	12.10.0
Deniston, John	--	--	3	--	14.0.0
Devany, Daniel	--	--	--	--	10.0.0
Dunsmore, Robert	--	--	--	--	12.10.0
Fegan, James	--	--	--	--	10.0.0
Gilley, James	--	--	--	--	--
Gibson, John	--	--	--	--	13.0.0
Hesslet, James	--	--	--	--	7.10.0

Young Men	Acres	Negroes	Horses	Cattle	Tax
Hutchinson, John	--	--	--	--	7.10.0
Howlay, Wm.	--	--	--	--	10.0.0
Herbison, Francis	--	--	1	--	16.10.0
Jack, Wm.	--	--	1	--	15.0.0
Kirkpatrick, Andrew	--	--	2	2	14.12.0
Kerr, Andrew	--	--	--	--	15.0.0
Lucky, James	--	--	1	--	12.10.0
Lintill, William	--	--	--	--	12.10.0
McBride, Wm.	--	--	1	--	14.0.0
McBrier, James	--	--	1	--	12.10.0
McOrr, John	--	--	--	--	15.0.0
D'o in Westmoreland	--	--	--	--	--
McKindly, James	--	--	3	--	15.0.0
Miller, James	--	--	1	--	15.0.0
Miller, William	--	--	1	--	12.10.0
McGurhan, John	--	--	1	--	14.0.0
McAdam, David	--	--	--	--	12.10.0
McKee, Thomas	--	--	2	--	12.10.0
Miller, Richard	--	--	--	--	14.0.0
McClintack, Daniel	--	--	1	--	15.0.0
Do. in Cumberland	--	--	16	8	--
Montgomery, David	--	--	--	--	--
Marshall, Paul	--	--	1	--	15.0.0
Nelly, Joseph	--	--	2	--	15.0.0
Orr, John	--	--	--	--	12.10.0
Porter, James	--	--	--	--	10.0.0
Patton, Alex'r.	--	--	2	1	15.0.0
Ried, Patrick	--	--	1	--	15.0.0
Rowan, James	--	--	--	--	12.10.0
Ross, Joseph	--	--	1	--	12.10.0
Russel, Alexander	--	--	--	--	12.10.0
Scott, Joseph	--	--	--	--	10.0.0
Stitt, Isaac	--	--	1	--	12.10.0
Scott, Robert	--	--	1	--	7.10.0
Stuart, Thomas	--	--	1	2	12.10.0
Stitt, David	--	--	--	--	5.0.0
Todd, Andrew	--	--	--	--	14.0.0
Thomson, James	--	--	--	--	15.0.0
Woods, James	--	--	--	--	12.10.0
McCree, Widow	--	--	--	--	--
Marshal, James	--	--	--	--	--
Kelly, James	--	--	1	--	12.10.0
Kirkpatrick, Wm.	--	--	1	--	23.6.0
Kenny, Christopher	--	--	1	--	--
Russel, John	--	--	--	--	12.10.0
Conelly, Jenkins	--	--	--	--	1.4.0
Campbell, Joseph	--	--	--	--	8.8.0
Ferguson, John, and Finley	--	--	--	--	4.17.6
Kurtz, Nicholas, Rev'd.	--	--	--	--	1.4.0

YORK TOWNSHIP

	Acres	Negroes	Horses	Cattle	Tax
Alt, Henry	132	--	3	3	20.10.0
Anstine, George	--	--	2	2	9.10.6
Altenfield, Jacob	--	--	--	--	4.9.3
Albright, Felix	100	--	1	1	15.19.6
Bard, George	100	--	1	2	25.11.3
Bence, George	158	--	4	4	100.14.9
Boly, Laurence	--	--	--	--	3.15.0
Brown, George	1 1/2	--	--	1	5.0.6
Bence, Wyrick	150	--	2	3	80.0.0
Betz, Christian	--	--	--	1	--
Bush, John	70	--	2	3	16.0.0
Blymyer, Martin	130	--	--	1	11.5.0
Blymyer, Jacob	200	--	1	2	8.10.6
Bittner, Mich'l.	--	--	--	--	49.2.0
Bock, Patrick	50	--	--	1	5.0.0
Bergdoll, Peter	--	--	--	2	5.0.0
Berminger, Henry	100	--	2	6	14.0.6
Byer, Jacob	150	--	2	2	40.0.0
Eichinger, Jacob	20	--	--	--	10.10.0
Eichelberger, Jacob	100	--	--	--	9.0.6
Detwiler, Samuel	--	--	1	1	1.15.3
Deel, Nicholas	230	--	--	2	90.14.9
Deel, George	--	--	3	3	18.0.0
Deel, Peter	160	--	4	4	275.1.6
Dice, Mich'l.	50	--	2	2	14.0.6
Dollman, Henry	150	--	2	2	9.0.0
Drexler, Peter	--	--	--	4	5.5.0
Dome, Benedick	--	--	--	--	12.0.0
Dome, John	50	--	2	1	15.0.0
Danner, Abram	7	--	--	--	11.0.0
Dinckel, Peter	225	--	--	--	35.0.6
Fink, George	--	--	--	1	4.0.3
Funk, Benedick	300	--	2	4	130.0.0
Ford, Peter	--	--	--	1	11.0.0
Fry, George	50	--	--	--	13.10.0
Fenus, Frederick	--	--	--	1	7.10.0
Fisher, Frederick	100	--	2	3	15.0.0
Fry, Godfrey, Se'r.	150	--	2	5	77.0.0
Feeser, Peter	95	--	--	4	11.5.0
Flinchbach, Martin	30	--	1	1	15.0.0
Flinchbach, Adam	150	--	2	4	16.0.0
Foust, Peter	--	--	1	2	5.0.0
Fry, Godfrey	50	--	--	--	14.0.3
Freed, Jacob	147	--	2	2	50.0.0
Fischel, Mich'l.	140	--	2	3	55.10.0
Gilbert, Wm.	--	--	--	1	2.5.0
Getz, Yost	--	--	2	2	6.10.0
Geezy, Jacob	150	--	1	2	8.10.6
Geezy, Conrad	50	--	1	1	9.10.6
Geezy, Conrad, Se'r.	100	--	1	1	15.0.3
Geezy, John	--	--	1	1	7.10.0
Gossler, John	250	--	2	2	40.0.0
Gartner, Adam	7	--	--	--	5.5.3
Harnish, John	89	--	2	3	9.0.0

York Township	Acres	Negroes	Horses	Cattle	Tax
Hower, Wm.	--	--	--	--	4.0.0
Hetman, Bastian	--	--	2	1	7.0.0
Hertlein, George	300	--	2	4	35.0.0
Hose, Philip	82	--	2	2	9.0.0
Hengst, Michael	200	--	3	5	40.0.0
Henigo, Michael	144	--	1	--	7.10.0
Housil, Frederick	--	--	--	1	1.10.0
Hell, Jacob	30	--	--	2	5.0.0
Hay, John	66	--	--	--	23.0.0
Herbach, John	200	--	3	4	118.15.0
Hackman, Abram	200	--	--	--	10.0.0
Jameson, David	110	--	--	--	15.0.0
Jones, James	--	--	1	2	7.10.0
Jefferys, Joseph	200	--	4	5	118.15.0
Johnston, Wm.	--	2	1	3	61.0.0
Immel, John	200	--	2	3	80.0.6
Irich, Bastian	100	--	2	--	36.0.0
Yost, Nicholas	150	--	2	3	40.0.0
Yost, Nicholas	100	--	--	--	7.10.0
Inners, Jacob	100	--	1	1	12.0.0
Koch, Jacob	100	--	2	1	40.15.0
Kissinger, Conrad	7	--	1	2	12.0.0
Kuntz, Wm.	--	--	--	--	--
Keller, Jacob	293	--	4	9	105.0.0
Kurtz, Michael	240	--	4	8	60.0.0
Keefer, Henry	50	--	1	--	16.3
Kerhard, Yost	--	--	1	--	5.0.0
Krim, Philip	100	--	2	3	16.3
Krim, Philip, weaver	--	--	--	--	7.10.0
Krim, Peter	--	--	--	--	3.10.6
Kern, Widow	100	--	--	--	4.0.0
Kayler, Daniel	100	--	1	2	8.0.0
Keiner, George	--	--	--	1	5.0.0
Kousler, Bernhart	--	--	1	1	7.0.0
Korell, Jacob	--	--	--	--	30.15.0
Kauffman, Henry	150	--	1	2	10.0.0
Kauffman, Solomon	150	--	2	2	62.0.3
Klein, Henry	60	--	1	--	12.0.0
Kousler, John	--	--	--	1	--
Kuntz, Francis	5	--	--	--	4.0.3
Collins, John	75	--	--	--	15.0.0
Krantz, Valentine	7	--	--	--	5.5.3
Lefever, Jacob	185	--	4	4	80.0.0
Kegereis, Christian	100	--	2	2	20.0.0
Leh, George	--	--	--	1	3.7.6
Lehman, Joachim	--	--	2	2	--
Long, Mich'l.	130	--	--	2	23.0.3
Long, John	136	--	2	4	16.0.0
Long, George	150	--	2	3	15.0.3
Landis, Stephen	150	--	2	3	17.0.3
Leisner, Conrad	80	--	2	1	4.0.0
Lehman, Jacob	125	--	3	3	43.10.0
Meyer, Jacob	50	--	4	--	6.0.0
Muggrove, Edward	--	--	--	--	3.3.4
Miller, Wm.	200	--	3	4	19.2.6

York Township	Acres	Negroes	Horses	Cattle	Tax
Meyer, Henry	200	--	3	5	47.0.0
Mosser, Mich'l.	50	--	2	2	9.0.0
Mosser, Samuel	100	--	2	4	55.0.0
Mosser, Samuel	--	--	--	--	8.0.6
Miller, Jacob	--	--	--	1	3.10.6
Marks, Jacob	50	--	2	1	5.0.0
Mosser, Mich'l., Se'r.	100	--	1	1	20.0.0
Mosser, Jacob	--	--	2	2	9.0.0
Michael, Jacob	150	--	1	2	12.0.0
Michael, Jacob, Se'r.	50	--	1	2	13.0.0
Murray, James	175	--	--	1	13.0.0
Miller, Francis Jacob	250	--	--	1	24.0.0
Neaf, John	--	--	1	2	7.10.0
Neaf, Ulrich	110	--	1	2	10.0.0
Nebbinger, Geo'r.	8	--	--	--	15.0.0
Oberdler, Philip	50	--	--	1	5.0.0
Pflieger, Jacob	260	--	4	6	45.0.0
Pflieger, Frederick	--	--	--	--	50.0.0
Peter, Peter	200	--	2	3	52.1.3
Peter, Mich'l Geo'r.	40	--	--	1	7.0.0
Rang, Philip	86	--	2	2	12.0.0
Rose, George	150	--	--	--	18.0.0
Rudrauf, Jonas	--	--	--	1	7.10.0
Raus, Lucas, Parson	100	--	--	--	5.0.0
Reigert, John	140	--	2	3	12.0.0
Reigert, Wm.	120	--	2	2	20.5.0
Roth, John	80	--	2	2	15.0.0
Ritz, Antony	14	--	--	--	4.0.3
Ritz, John	50	--	--	3	9.0.0
Sech, Henry	--	--	--	1	12.0.0
Shuy, Daniel	180	--	4	3	78.0.0
Spengler, Philip Casper	300	--	2	8	140.0.0
Stuart, John	160	--	2	4	85.0.0
Speck, Martin	--	--	1	2	15.0.0
Sumwald, Balzer	--	--	1	1	10.0.0
Spengler, George	160	--	3	6	50.0.0
Striebig, Jacob	40	--	--	4	5.0.0
Shank, Joseph	100	--	3	1	14.0.0
Stauffer, Henry	163	--	7	3	117.10.6
Stauffer, Daniel	--	--	--	--	30.0.0
Smith, Jacob	50	--	1	2	3.0.0
Stebler, Henry	100	--	2	3	8.0.0
Sherer, Jacob	100	--	2	2	120.0.0
Sense, Nicholas	120	--	2	3	52.1.3
Spitler, Jacob	120	--	--	--	16.0.3
Shindler, Conrad	169	--	2	3	14.0.3
Smith, John	--	--	1	1	20.0.0
Swoope, Mich'l. Esq'r.	75	--	--	3	31.10.0
Sprenckel, Peter	100	--	--	2	9.0.0
Swartz, Henry	80	--	1	3	8.0.0
Sheffer, John	80	--	2	2	11.5.0
Sebald, Jacob	60	--	2	2	9.0.0
Shoemaker, John	100	--	2	1	8.0.0
Spangler, George, Se'r.	100	--	2	3	45.0.0
Shetler, Mary	200	--	2	1	12.0.0

York Township	Acres	Negroes	Horses	Cattle	Tax
Spangler, Bernard	300	--	4	6	70.0.6
Spangler, Rudolph	--	--	--	3	13.0.0
Spangler, Jonas	--	--	--	2	7.10.0
Spangler, Balzer	10	--	--	--	8.0.0
Spangler, Balzer	40	--	--	--	8.0.0
Spangler, Rudolph, Y. town	5	--	--	--	6.0.0
Small, William	30	--	--	--	12.15.0
Smith, James	177	--	--	3	129.0.3
Shultz, John, ex'r. for Corad Holtzbaum	--	--	--	--	10.0.0
Spangler, John	200	2	4	6	110.15.0
Treichler, John	200	--	2	5	100.0.0
Updegraff, Jacob	9	--	--	--	8.0.0
Wolf, Peter	1 1/2	--	--	1	6.0.0
Welshantz, Abram	--	--	1	1	7.10.0
Welshantz, Joseph	--	--	--	--	3.0.0
Weller, Martin	200	--	4	3	70.0.0
Welshantz, Abram, Se'r.	50	--	2	1	13.10.0
William, George	--	--	2	1	7.10.0
Wohlfart, Stophel	126	--	2	4	14.0.0
William, John	90	--	2	2	14.0.0
Wisendahl, Henry	--	--	--	--	5.0.0
Waltman, Ludwig	171	--	2	4	12.0.0
Welshantz, Jacob	--	--	--	--	2.10.3
Walter, Henry	--	--	--	--	6.10.0
Young, Frederick	80	--	2	2	9.0.0
Youce, Frederick	6	--	--	--	5.5.3
Yessler, Henry	100	--	1	2	60.0.3
Ziegel, Widow	200	--	2	3	40.0.0
Zech, Jacob	--	--	3	3	8.10.0
Miller, John	--	--	--	1	7.10.0
Eckhart, Jacob	--	--	2	1	5.0.0
Wierman, Jacob	30	--	--	--	3.0.0
Kauffman, Conrad	--	--	--	--	--
Stuck, Martin	100	--	2	4	25.0.0
Albright, Mich'l.	--	--	1	2	6.0.0
Ganshorn, Mathias	87	--	--	1	1.10.0
Myer, Martin	30	--	2	1	--
Drorbach, Wm.	200	--	2	2	14.0.6
Michael, Wendel	100	--	1	4	6.0.0
Messersmith, Widow	50	--	1	2	4.10.0
Henigo, Widow	50	--	1	2	--
Kirchhard, Widow	50	--	--	1	3.0.0
Smith, Widow	100	--	1	1	7.10.0
Keffer, John	--	--	1	2	10.5.0
Kaufman, Widow	2	--	--	2	4.0.3
Cooper, Joseph	--	--	--	--	5.0.0
Johnson, Widow	--	--	--	--	--
Leatherman, Conrad	200	--	--	--	84.14.9
Hartley, Thomas	12	--	--	--	14.0.0
Spangler, Widow	5	--	--	--	--
Sultzberger, George	--	--	--	--	3.0.0

York Township   Single Men

	Amount of Tax		Amount of Tax
Kirchhard, John	18.0.0	Waltman, Henry	8.0.0
Lehman, Peter	7.10.0	Bittner, Jacob	--
Miller, John	11.5.0	Neff, George	15.0.0
Spangler, Henry	11.5.0	Sumwald, Godfrey	15.0.0
Spangler, Michael	11.5.0	Zech, George	11.5.0
Spangler, Charles	20.0.0	Sence, Peter	15.0.0
Life, Christian	20.0.0	Meyer, John	11.5.0
Koch, Jacob	11.5.0	Smith, Samuel	11.5.0
Stuart, John	11.5.0	Stuart, Mathias	11.5.0
Pfleiger, George	11.5.0	Krebs, George	15.0.0
Pfleiger, Jacob	11.5.0	Weaver, Frederick	16.0.0
Weishantz, Wm.	15.0.0	Rump, George	1.2.6
Waggoner, John	15.0.0	Weller, George & Rothrock	16.0.3
Kaufman,	20.0.0	Waggoner, Mich'l	3.0.0
Swartz, George	15.0.0	Wintersmith, Ch's	6.0.0
Mosser, Daniel	5.0.0	Boley, George	3.6.0
Stetler, Jacob	11.5.0	Sites, Mich'l	8.0.6
Michael, Jacob	--		

CHANCEFORD TOWNSHIP

	Acres	Negroes	Horses	Cattle	Tax
Adams, Henry	--	--	2	1	5.9.6
Andrew, John	150	--	3	5	27.7.6
Adams, Hugh	50	--	1	2	7.6.0
Andrew, Francis	--	--	2	2	9.2.6
Allison, Thomas	--	--	2	2	7.6.0
Adams, William	500	--	3	4	25.0.0
Adams, Wm., Ju'r.	--	--	--	--	21.18.0
Adams, Mathew	176	--	1	3	--
Armstrong, Andrew	100	--	2	2	29.4.0
Arnold, John	50	--	1	1	6.7.9
Adams, Wm., Sen'r.	80	--	1	1	--
Barr, Wm.	--	--	--	1	1.16.6
Buchanon, Wm.	233	--	1	7	20.0.0
Boker, Christian	121	--	2	2	9.2.6
Burkholder, Abram	112	--	2	4	19.16.4
Buchanon, John, Se'r.	200	--	3	5	27.7.6
Bradshaw, Charles	150	--	4	4	19.3.3
Blain, Robert	300	--	3	5	35.11.9
Buchanon, Wm.	100	--	2	4	15.19.4
Bunges, Joseph	207	--	3	2	40.0.3
Buchanon, John	--	--	2	2	5.9.6
Cunningham, Adam	134	--	2	3	16.3.4
Craigmiles, James	173	--	3	6	21.18.0
Cunning, Samuel	22	--	--	--	1.2.0
Coss, George	80	--	2	3	13.13.9
Clist, George	200	--	1	2	10.19.0
Campbell, Widow	130	--	1	2	9.11.7
Collins, Wm.	--	--	2	4	10.10.0
Coon, John	80	--	2	2	11.17.3
Caldwell, John	113	--	2	2	14.12.0

Chanceford Township	Acres	Negroes	Horses	Cattle	Tax
Curly, Wm.	208	--	3	6	36.6.8
Cown, Michael	80	--	2	3	20.0.0
Clarkson, James, Rev'd.	169	--	3	7	9.2.6
Cown, Adam	60	--	1	2	4.11.0
Cown, Jacob	88	--	1	2	7.6.0
Cooster, John	20	--	1	1	10.19.0
Cown, Andrew	100	--	2	2	25.0.0
Crowl, Henry	160	--	2	2	16.8.6
Downing, Alexander	255	--	4	3	31.0.6
Downing, John	--	--	1	1	--
Douglass, Wm.	300	--	2	4	27.7.6
Downing, James	200	--	--	1	10.0.9
Dougherty, Wm.	360	--	2	5	36.10.0
Duncan, James	60	--	2	2	51.2.0
Donley, John	--	--	1	2	11.17.2
Duncan, John	132	--	3	3	17.18.0
Elder, James	100	--	3	3	20.1.0
Elder, Samuel	267	--	2	1	13.13.99
Elias, George	80	--	--	2	18.5.0
Elias, Philip	--	--	9	9	5.9.6
Forsythe, Robert	180	--	2	3	20.1.6
Fellows, James	160	--	1	1	9.2.6
Fullerton, John, Sen'r.	100	--	3	3	10.0.0
Fullerton, Samuel	--	--	--	2	2.14.9
French, John	200	--	1	4	25.0.0
Fullerton, Robert	100	--	3	1	15.0.0
Fulton, James	264	2	3	5	27.7.6
Fullerton, John	381	--	4	6	41.1.3
Fullerton, Wm.	144	--	2	3	32.17.0
Finley, John	582	4	4	9	175.0.0
Garin, Widow	100	--	3	3	18.5.0
Groves, Thomas	50	--	2	3	9.11.1
Grahams, Thomas	--	--	2	2	9.2.6
Grove, Jacob	50	--	1	3	8.13.4
Hoge, John	--	--	2	2	7.6.0
Hums, Charles	350	--	4	4	34.13.4
Henry, George	--	--	3	2	9.2.6
Henry, Wm.	224	--	3	6	36.10.0
Henderson, James	140	--	3	3	10.19.0
Holton, Wm.	370	--	3	4	41.1.3
Henderson, John	--	--	2	2	6.6.0
Hill, James	300	--	2	4	29.4.0
Hering, James	--	--	2	1	--
Hill, John	220	--	3	4	55.12.6
Hughs, Widow	380	--	3	4	35.11.9
Henry, George, Se'r.	275	--	1	3	15.0.0
Jackson, Joseph	420	--	5	2	60.0.0
Jolly, James	--	--	3	4	14.12.0
Johnston, Thomas	104	--	3	3	20.1.6
Johnston, Wm.	158	--	2	5	18.5.0
Killgrove, Mathew	351	1	3	3	40.3.0
Kirkwood, John	65	--	2	2	7.15.7
Kirkwood, Thomas	30	--	2	--	10.0.0
Kirks, John	50	--	2	2	11.0.0
Kirks, James	258	--	2	3	20.10.0

Chanceford Township	Acres	Negroes	Horses	Cattle	Tax
Killpatrick, Wm.	135	--	3	4	18.5.0
Keith, Ludwig	--	--	--	2	5.9.6
Kelley, Thomas	650	2	2	11	186.0.0
Kiner, Adam	100	--	1	1	7.6.0
King, Patrick	--	--	1	2	3.13.0
Log, James	237	--	2	4	21.18.0
Leaper, James	170	--	1	4	18.15.0
Long, Wm.	150	--	3	--	18.5.0
Lehman, William	130	--	2	3	9.9.3
Little, Widow	100	--	3	2	17.6.9
Leaper, Alexander	--	--	2	--	5.9.6
Leaper, Samuel	--	--	2	3	40.3.0
List, George	30	--	2	4	15.10.0
Lusk, John	280	--	3	3	32.17.0
Land of James Melhorn, Lancaster county	100	--	--	--	9.2.6
Land of Francis Groves	40	--	--	--	--
Land of Walter Robinson, Hartford county	148	--	--	--	9.2.6
Land of Conrad Lookup	150	--	--	--	6.16.10
Land of Stoner's, in Lancaster county	100	--	--	--	6.7.6
Land of Richard Cords	80	--	--	--	3.13.0
Land of Jacob Hiles, Hartford county	150	--	--	--	9.2.6
Land of Wm. Mathews	200	--	--	--	10.19.0
Land of James Craigmiles	57	--	--	--	2.5.7
Land of John McCalls	44	--	--	--	2.5.7
Land of James Laird	300	--	--	--	13.13.9
Land in the tenor of George Henry Ju'r	191	--	--	--	9.2.6
Land in the tenor of Wm. Collins	150	--	--	--	8.4.3
Land of John Burgholder	120	--	--	--	4.11.3
Land of Isaac Buckholder, Lancaster county	40	--	--	--	6.7.9
Land of Abraham Newcomer, Lancaster county	30	--	--	--	1.16.6
Land of George Burgholder	100	--	--	--	13.13.9
Land in the tenor of Arch'd Shaw	150	--	--	--	6.7.9
Land of Mathew Hartford	120	--	--	--	4.11.3
Land of Keith's	45	--	--	--	3.13.0
McClorge, Widow	100	--	2	4	10.15.0
McGowan, Thomas	--	--	1	1	4.11.3
McLaughlin, Wm.	376	--	3	4	47.18.6
Martin, Robert	200	--	4	6	47.9.0
McCall, John	100	--	1	2	20.1.6
McCollough, Alex'r.	110	--	2	2	14.2.3
Martin, Samuel	150	--	2	2	22.0.0
McElvay, Wm.	--	--	1	2	5.9.6
McFee, Michael	69	--	2	2	9.2.6
McClorge, Wm.	--	--	2	3	9.2.6
Morrison, Wm., Sen'r.	300	1	2	4	69.7.0
Morrison, Wm., Ju'r.	101	--	2	5	35.0.0

Chanceford Township	Acres	Negroes	Horses	Cattle	Tax
McCall, Mathew	114	2	2	4	81.11.0
Land at the Hill Head	513	--	--	--	45.12.6
McNay, Thomas	270	--	3	6	25.11.0
McGee, Patrick	300	--	2	4	30.0.0
McCollough, Wm.	--	--	2	2	9.2.6
McWilliams, Alex'r.	--	--	2	2	--
McNeary, John	150	--	3	4	18.5.0
McNeary, David	100	--	2	3	11.17.3
Morrison, John	250	--	2	3	15.0.0
McKinley, Stephen	360	--	3	8	35.11.9
McGuffy, William	--	--	2	2	7.6.0
McPherson, Frederick	50	--	1	2	7.15.0
McElhannon, John	--	--	--	2	1.16.6
McHarter, Moses	300	--	4	4	51.15.0
Marlain, William	355	--	3	5	40.9.0
Marlain, John	344	1	1	4	50.17.6
McKissock, Widow	--	--	--	2	3.13.0
McCall, William	170	--	3	3	20.16.3
Maxwell, Patrick	--	--	1	2	2.14.9
McMichael, Samuel	--	--	1	2	5.9.6
McQuay, Thomas	--	--	1	3	6.7.9
Maxwell, William	30	--	2	--	5.0.0
Murphy, John	--	--	--	1	18.3
Nelson, Samuel	205	1	4	4	36.10.0
Oason, George	92	--	--	2	58.12.6
Odewalt, Jacob	--	--	--	2	18.3
Owens, William	2	--	2	2	7.6.0
Peden, Benjamin, Esq'r.	307	--	4	3	39.4.4
Peden, James	151	--	2	2	18.5.0
Paxton, Andrew	150	--	2	3	14.8.6
Parker, James	240	--	3	3	22.16.3
Porter, James	66	--	1	3	20.0.0
Parks, James	--	--	4	3	17.6.9
Pendry, Robert	--	--	--	--	--
Patterson, Widow	100	--	3	3	27.7.6
Purdey, Arch'd.	--	--	--	--	11.17.3
Quiggle, Hanichel	--	--	2	2	9.2.6
Robison, James	240	--	3	5	27.7.6
Reed, William	282	--	1	4	26.9.3
Robb, Joseph	341	--	3	5	33.15.3
Reid, William, Se'r.	40	--	2	1	12.0.0
Reid, Joseph	147	1	3	6	80.6.0
Reid, John	300	--	1	2	21.18.0
Rippey, John	329	--	3	3	27.7.6
Robb, John	170	--	3	4	18.15.0
Reid, John	160	--	2	3	18.5.0
Ross, William, Colo'l.	611	2	4	9	116.2.0
Reed, Joseph, Esq'r.	320	--	5	3	81.10.0
Ramsey, Thomas	230	--	3	4	40.2.3
Robison, John	--	--	2	2	9.2.6
Reed, John, collier	150	--	2	3	32.0.0
Stilley, Stephen	80	--	--	1	3.3.10
Stilley, Jacob	360	--	2	4	46.1.7
Stilley, Andrew	317	--	2	3	32.0.0
Sengury, Peter	180	--	3	4	18.5.0

Chanceford Township	Acres	Negroes	Horses	Cattle	Tax
Shaw, Widow	--	--	1	2	3.0.0
Smith, Patrick	100	--	2	3	9.2.6
Speer, James	200	--	2	3	18.5.0
Snider, Peter	50	--	--	1	3.3.10
Stuart, John, Ju'r.	100	--	2	--	10.0.0
Stuart, Robert, Sen'r.	--	1	1	2	23.14.6
Shaw, Archibald	--	--	--	2	1.16.6
Shaw, Robert	150	--	3	3	20.19.9
Smith, Robert	335	--	3	4	20.19.9
Scott, Thomas	150	--	2	1	10.0.0
Scott, Allen	150	--	2	3	16.3.3
Scott, Gain	150	1	3	7	50.3.9
Sprout, Hugh	300	--	4	5	50.0.0
Stewart, James	243	--	3	3	29.0.9
Steward, Widow	70	--	3	3	12.6.5
Stewart, John	50	--	2	3	12.15.6
Sealer, Casper	--	--	--	--	36.10.0
Spots, Jacob	100	--	2	3	10.19.0
Smith, Widow	60	--	--	1	7.6.0
St. Clair, Daniel	140	--	1	3	25.0.0
Strair, Nicholas	450	--	4	5	33.15.3
Stuart, Robert	250	--	2	3	28.5.9
Smith, Joseph	--	1	2	2	--
Thomson, John	320	2	3	4	120.15.0
Thomson, George	150	--	2	3	14.12.0
Williams, Isaac	204	--	2	2	23.4.7
Warm, Michael	--	--	--	1	8.4.3
Willey, John	--	--	1	1	4.11.3
Wallace, John	150	--	2	2	18.14.1
Wason, James	--	--	2	3	10.0.9
Winter, Philip	60	--	1	2	52.0.2
Wallace, John, Se'r.	--	--	2	1	8.4.3
Wulrich, John	50	--	1	2	6.16.10
Wilson, Thomas	370	--	2	8	55.0.0
Wallace, Moses	--	--	1	2	20.1.6
Wallace, Mathew	150	--	2	2	20.1.6
To land in tenor of John Wallace	200	--	--	--	18.5.0
Wilson, William	136	--	2	2	15.0.0
To land of Andrew Stilley's	133	--	--	--	--
In the tenor of,	16	--	--	--	--
Land of William Reid's, in Lancaster County	200	--	--	--	--
Land of Joseph Brown in Caecil county	250	--	--	--	11.8.6
Land of James Cooper's heirs	205	--	--	--	11.8.6
Land in the tenor of Samuel Leeper	200	--	--	--	--
Lands late Matsons Hugh's	--	--	--	--	18.15.0

Single Men

	Amount of Tax		
Adams, William	7.10.0	Hair, Daniel	15.0.0
Duncan, Thomas	15.0.0	Pedey, William	
McGowan, Samuel	7.10.0	Gordon, John	10.0.0
McCoy, Nathaniel	10.0.0	Gordon, Christian	7.10.0
Downing, William	25.0.0	Donelly, William	10.0.0
Kelley, John	15.0.0	Porter, George	15.0.0
McKissock, John	10.0.0	Grove, Francis	2.5.7
Armstrong, John	7.0.0	Stiley, Andrew	1.9.6
Adams, Matthew	7.10.0	Quiggel, Hannichel	2.18.6
Robison, Henry	15.0.0	D'o of the heirs of	
Evans, Thomas	--	Jn'o McDowl	11.0.0
Sprout, Samuel	--	Allison, Joseph	16.8.6
Patton, John	7.10.0	Coon, Adam	--
Harvey, Thomas	10.0.0	McCandless, John	9.2.6
Wilson, Benjamin	25.0.0	McClure, Andrew	40.2.0
Reed, Joseph	20.0.0	Reed, John	--
Shaw, Daniel	25.0.0	Rippey, John	--
Buchanon, Ebenezer	25.0.0	Weister, Jacob	12.15.6
Collins, Samuel	15.0.0	McGee, James	--
Douglass, David	15.0.0	Dedy, Thomas	20.0.0
Wallace, William	15.0.0	Dorough, John	7.10.0
McGee, Robert	20.0.0	Patterson, David	7.10.0
Spots, Joseph	7.10.0	St. Clair, John	10.0.0
McGown, Isaac		Conner, John	5.0.0
Stewart, Andrew	7.10.0	Stuart, Samuel	3.0.0
Reid, Hugh	7.10.0	Keener, Geo'r.	6.0.0
Wilson, William	15.0.0	Douglass, James	3.0.0
Sprout, Hugh		Reed, William	5.9.6
Hill, John		Coopers, James	--
Hill, Robert	7.10.0	Adam, William	45.12.6
Wallace, Aron	20.0.0	James, Alexander	18.3.0
McNullen, Robert		Cowan, William	4.11.3
Gill, Robert	10.0.0	Scott, Gavin & Semple	9.2.6
McCullough, George		Adams, Matthew	16.8.6
Ramsey, John			

CUMBERLAND TOWNSHIP

	Acres	Negroes	Horses	Cattle	Tax
Armstrong, Quintain	352	--	6	9	96.15.0
Armstrong, Archibald	--	--	--	--	10.0.0
Armstrong, Isaac	--	--	--	--	10.0.0
Anderson, Thomas	--	--	2	1	26.12.0
Armstrong, John	130	--	3	5	38.16.0
Arthur, Hugh	--	--	--	1	9.0
Armstrong, Quintain	--	--	--	--	3.15.0
Byers, John	50	--	1	1	4.19.0
Black, James	--	--	2	--	15.0.0
Bigham, Robert	128	--	--	--	19.4.0
Black, Robert, Se'r.	365	1	4	7	105.18.0
Black, James	--	--	--	--	10.10.0
Black, Henry	200	--	4	5	42.0.0

Cumberland	Acres	Negroes	Horses	Cattle	Tax
Browster, Widow	--	--	1	3	--
Bredan, William	121	--	3	5	27.0.0
Boyd, William, Se'r.	200	--	5	6	87.0.0
Bickly, William	--	--	1	--	11.10.0
Boyd, William	--	1	2	2	12.6.0
Black, Robert	150	--	2	3	38.2.6
Black, James	240	--	4	2	71.8.0
Buchanon, William	100	--	2	3	26.17.0
Boyd, Widow	100	--	1	2	15.0.0
Brown, Wm.	--	--	--	--	10.0.0
Bittinger, Mich'l.	150	--	2	2	18.0.0
Black, Adam	200	--	2	3	35.17.0
Blair, John	150	--	5	7	44.14.0
D'o in Sinking Valley	100	--	--	--	--
Blair, John	--	--	--	--	10.0.0
Branwood, Andrew	150	--	3	3	76.4.0
Buchanon, Walter	280	--	3	6	69.9.0
Buchanon, Robert	--	--	--	--	10.0.0
Boyd, William	--	--	--	--	10.0.0
Boyd, Andrew	300	--	--	--	60.0.0
Black, Mathew	--	--	--	--	10.0.0
Buchanon, John	100	--	1	3	26.9.0
Clark, Thomas	--	--	--	--	10.0.0
Coffee, Michael	--	--	--	--	10.0.0
Cox, Joseph	--	--	1	3	--
Caban, John	--	--	2	2	10.16.0
Craig, Henry	--	--	--	1	9.0
Craig, John	100	--	3	3	31.4.4
Campbell, John	300	--	1	--	22.19.0
Cutbertson, Samuel	--	--	--	2	18.0
Cobin, Samuel	250	1	5	5	128.5.0
Cox, Joseph	--	--	1	3	2.17.0
Carson, David	--	--	--	--	--
Cross, William	143	--	2	2	43.10.0
Cross, Thomas	203	--	2	5	60.15.0
Corbock, Christian	136	--	2	3	60.17.0
D'o to 40 acres	--	--	--	--	1.10.0
Douglass, Archibald	--	--	1	8	5.17.0
Douglass, Thomas	470	--	6	9	143.17.0
Douglass, Robert	--	--	--	--	10.0.0
Dunwoody, Dav'd, Ju'r.	--	--	2	3	5.17.0
Dunwoody, David	504	1	6	8	138.0.0
Donaldson, Wm.	323	--	2	3	84.3.0
Davison, William	--	--	2	3	40.13.0
Douglass, Thomas	263	--	--	--	50.2.0
Dunwoody, Jane, Widow	--	--	--	--	90.0.0
Eckels, Francis	--	--	--	1	9.0
Elder, Robert	--	--	2	1	9.18.0
Ewing, James	650	1	5	7	180.0.0
Entricken, James	--	--	3	3	6.12.0
Edy, Samuel	205	--	6	6	67.13.0
Ferguson, James	200	--	4	6	56.0.0
Ferguson, Robert	--	--	--	--	10.0.0
Fletcher, Robert	250	--	3	6	60.0.0
Fletcher, Dav'd.	--	--	1	2	2.14.0

Cumberland	Acres	Negroes	Horses	Cattle	Tax
Fergus, Hugh	100	--	4	6	31.4.0
Fergus, John	--	1	--	1	10.0.10
Fergus, Thomas	--	--	--	--	10.0.0
Finley, Archibald	250	--	4	5	56.11.0
Flemming, John	50	2	2	4	71.14.0
Fletcher, Charles	150	--	3	6	49.10.0
Finly, Michael	150	--	--	--	18.0.0
Ferguson, Hugh	--	--	1	2	2.8.0
Ferguson, John	--	--	1	--	10.0.0
Ferguson, Wm.	--	--	3	3	--
Ferguson, James	--	--	1	--	10.0.0
Fass, George	115	--	--	--	25.10.0
Fletcher, John	263	--	5	5	83.17.0
Gettys, Samuel	500	3	10	12	184.13.0
D'o in Cumberland county	100	--	--	--	--
Galloway, James	150	--	3	5	42.15.0
Goudy, John, Se'r.	200	--	3	4	52.1.0
Gurly, Thomas	--	--	1	--	10.0.0
Gettys, Wm.	--	--	3	3	8.2.0
Gilgrist, James	102	--	2	4	29.0.0
Gilgrist, Thomas	--	--	2	4	4.16.0
Gilgeson, James	--	--	2	5	5.5.0
Gallagher, Hugh	--	--	1	1	10.0.0
D'o in Bedford county	300	--	--	--	--
Gondy, Wm.	150	--	2	2	37.13.0
Grass, Jacob	150	--	1	2	20.0.0
Goudy, John, Ju'r.	150	--	2	4	3.6.0
Getty, Samuel, in trust	600	--	--	--	150.0.0
Hosack, Henry	300	--	2	3	84.12.0
Hughs, Francis	60	--	1	4	7.16.0
Hughs, John	170	--	3	3	32.2.0
Henderson, Andrew	100	--	3	5	21.15.0
Hughs, David	--	--	3	2	6.18.0
Hall, Edward	300	--	2	1	76.4.0
Hall, Wm.	--	--	2	1	10.0.0
Hosack, Michael	--	--	4	5	8.5.0
Hutchinson, Joseph	260	--	5	7	70.0.0
Hosack, John	18	--	4	5	66.0.0
Hamilton, John	--	--	2	4	14.14.0
Hart, John	200	--	2	3	50.17.0
Hope, Adam	80	--	2	4	33.11.0
Hamilton, Hugh	200	--	3	2	28.13.4
Hosack, John	200	--	--	--	45.0.0
Johnston, Wm.	--	--	2	4	6.6.0
Johnson, Andrew	--	--	4	6	73.0.0
Johnson, Thomas	--	--	1	2	2.6.0
Jenkins, Moses	192	--	2	4	50.8.0
Jenkins, Walter	--	--	1	2	2.10.0
Johnson, Bernard	--	--	1	--	10.0.0
Irwin, Widow	200	--	--	3	25.0.0
Johnson, John	200	--	2	3	28.0.0
Johnson, James	200	2	6	8	83.0.0
Keshoner, David	--	--	--	--	7.10.0
King, Jane, widow	145	2	4	6	26.0.0
Keshoner, John	140	--	2	6	53.4.0

Cumberland	Acres	Negroes	Horses	Cattle	Tax
Kellough, John	--	--	--	--	--
Kar, James	145	--	2	3	30.0.0
Linn, John, Sen'r.	206	--	2	4	44.14.0
Linn, David	100	--	1	--	15.15.0
Lessly, Samuel	140	--	1	3	28.7.0
Lessly, Hannah, widow	140	--	1	--	15.0.0
Lessly, John	--	--	2	3	14.7.0
Linn, Andrew	--	--	4	3	8.17.0
Long, Robert	140	--	3	5	35.0.0
Long, Jonathan	--	--	--	--	10.0.0
Lyon, Hugh	--	--	1	--	10.0.0
Latta, Thomas	380	1	7	14	138.6.0
Linn, Adam	--	--	--	1	10.0.0
Laird, William	134	--	4	5	38.8.0
D'o in trust	134	--	--	--	20.0.0
Laird, Hannah, widow	160	--	2	2	10.0.0
Lindsay, William	185	--	3	4	45.0.0
Latta, Thomas	--	--	--	--	--
Murphy, John	183	--	2	4	41.5.0
Moore, David	335	--	4	7	75.18.0
McFarlen, Thomas	350	--	4	5	70.0.0
McPeak, Daniel	300	--	4	4	76.16.0
McPeak, Daniel	90	--	--	--	16.16.0
McPeak, John	--	--	--	--	10.0.0
McPeak, Wm.	--	--	--	--	10.0.0
McMun, Wm.	--	--	4	4	12.16.0
McCormick, John	--	--	1	2	3.13.0
McFerrin, John, Se'r.	300	--	2	2	50.0.0
Moore, William	--	--	2	2	5.8.0
McFerrin, John	--	--	3	5	5.3.0
Marshall, William	200	--	2	4	87.12.0
Morrow, Wm.	--	--	1	--	10.0.0
McKinley, Benjamin	537	--	3	6	109.0.0
McKinley, John	--	--	1	--	10.0.0
McKinney, Wm.	80	--	2	3	15.0.0
McGlaughlin, John	--	--	2	3	5.17.0
Murphy, Hugh	--	--	3	2	5.8.0
McKinstry, James	--	--	--	--	--
McFerrin, William	150	--	4	5	38.5.0
McCreary, William	305	--	4	7	85.19.0
McConaughy, John	200	--	2	3	13.1.0
McWilliams, John	--	--	--	--	10.0.0
Murray, Robert	--	2	2	4	37.12.0
McNutt, Mathew	360	--	2	--	99.0.0
McNutt, Robert	--	--	2	4	6.6.0
McClellan, William, Ju'r.	364	--	7	14	100.0.0
McCleary, Thomas	200	--	6	6	66.9.0
McClellan, John	150	--	2	2	20.0.0
McClellan, Jacob	142	--	4	8	45.12.0
McDowel, Wm. Se'r.	100	--	2	2	12.0.0
McDowel, William	--	--	1	2	1.13.0
McGaughey, James	60	--	4	10	65.15.0
McBride, John	145	--	3	5	46.19.0
McBride, John	--	--	1	--	10.0.0
McCleary, Michael	--	--	--	--	10.0.0

Cumberland	Acres	Negroes	Horses	Cattle	Tax
McClellan, Wm., Se'r.	--	--	3	3	--
McClure, James	200	--	5	4	49.1.0
McBroom, William	--	--	--	2	15.0
McNight, James	135	--	3	2	37.10.0
Morrison, Robert	42	--	2	6	14.2.0
McCush, Samuel	120	--	--	--	23.8.0
McAffet, John	--	--	2	2	3.0.0
McPherson, Wm.	--	1	4	2	16.16.0
Maxwell, Alexander	122	--	2	4	27.12.0
McCommick, John	--	--	1	1	1.19.0
McMullen, Samuel	--	--	1	1	2.14.0
McKain, Robert	100	--	1	1	60.9.0
McPherson, Robert	222	4	6	8	119.2.0
D'o in Bedford	200	--	--	--	--
D'o in Bedford	436	--	--	--	121.19.0
D'o in Bedford	170	--	--	--	31.16.0
D'o in partnership with Grier	218	--	--	--	49.1.0
D'o with Wm. McPherson	341	--	--	--	80.7.0
McPherson, Rob't.	--	--	4	--	9.0.0
Morrison, Joseph	213	1	5	4	74.17.0
Martin, Thomas	100	--	4	8	38.17.0
McKain, Hugh	80	--	--	--	4.19.0
Martin, Thomas	--	--	--	--	10.0.0
McCarley, John	150	--	3	3	45.0.0
McClure, Wm.	125	--	2	3	33.18.0
McClure, Martin	50	--	--	--	10.0.0
McCoy, Robert	--	--	3	1	10.0.0
Marshall, Samuel	200	--	2	3	50.0.0
Murphy, Hugh	140	--	3	3	53.14.0
Masters, George	100	--	--	--	22.10.10
Milligan, Mark	40	--	--	--	1.10.0
McCurdy, Hugh	100	--	2	2	18.0.0
McGone, Wm.	--	--	2	1	1.16.0
McNutt, Thomas	--	--	--	2	15.0
McClean, Moses	430	1	4	9	125.0.0
Millekan, Mark	140	--	2	1	49.14.0
McPeak, James	--	--	--	--	10.0.0
McCurdy, Robert	319	--	--	--	71.14.0
Reid, Wm.	--	--	2	1	22.19.0
Reid, Daniel	--	--	1	--	4.10.0
Reid, John	150	--	1	1	27.9.0
Renfrew, John	--	--	1	--	--
Ryan, Wm.	40	--	--	1	1.19.0
Rose, John	--	--	1	--	10.0.0
Riddle, James	340	3	5	7	119.8.1
Riddle, David	--	--	1	--	10.0.0
D'o in Bedford county	250	--	--	--	--
Russel, Robert	--	--	1	2	2.10.0
Russel, James	342	--	7	8	118.19.0
Russel, Samuel	--	--	--	--	10.0.0
Russel, Joshua	200	1	3	6	64.4.0
Ross, John	250	1	5	6	84.0.0
Ramsey, David	155	--	4	3	38.17.0
Rightsell, George	--	--	--	--	10.0.0

Cumberland	Acres	Negroes	Horses	Cattle	Tax
Nichol, Joseph	--	--	1	2	2.2.0
Newel, John	--	--	--	--	--
Newel, Andrew, lives in Manallen Township	100	--	--	--	3.15.0
Noil, Daniel	--	--	1	1	1.1.0
Oyler, Jacob	142	--	2	3	41.11.0
Oar, Robert	200	--	2	1	11.14.0
Oar, Alexander	--	--	2	--	10.0.0
Poe, Alexander	182	--	4	6	189.19.0
Paxton, Joseph	--	--	2	2	3.18.0
Paxton, Samuel	120	--	2	4	63.10.0
Paxton, John, cooper	140	--	--	--	--
Prigoner, Godlieb	100	--	--	--	3.15.0
Patterson, Hugh	--	--	--	--	--
Parkhill, David	--	--	2	4	--
D'o in Bedford county	264	--	--	--	--
Porter, Alexander	225	--	5	8	83.2.0
Porter, William	--	--	1	--	10.0.0
Porter, Samuel	177	--	4	9	58.4.0
Porter, Andrew	200	1	5	7	78.18.0
Porter, John	--	--	1	--	10.0.0
Paxton, Nathaniel	200	2	5	--	51.15.0
Piper, Peter	121	--	4	6	43.7.0
Paxton, John	150	--	3	6	22.10.0
Scott, John	180	--	--	--	46.16.0
Scott, David	--	--	--	--	5.0.0
St. Clair, James	--	--	2	5	4.10.0
Scott, Robert	180	1	3	3	45.0.0
Shakely, John	250	--	3	4	45.6.0
Sutter, John	--	--	2	4	--
Sipes, George	120	--	3	4	65.1.0
Stewart, Wm.	160	--	5	10	51.0.0
D'o in Mount Joy t'w'p	120	--	--	--	--
Stewart, Robert	56	--	2	3	10.0.0
Stratton, Abraham	300	--	1	1	1.19.0
Stanley, John	200	--	1	2	60.0.0
Stanley, Wm.	--	--	1	--	24.10.0
Swisher, Peter	100	--	--	1	4.11.0
Stillinger, Michael	--	--	1	1	1.10.0
Shepherd, George	30	--	2	2	2.5.0
Stevenson, James	180	--	4	6	61.4.0
Stewart, Robert	100	--	2	4	23.11.0
St. Myer, Bernard	--	--	2	10	9.0.0
Swaney, James	--	--	2	--	10.0.0
Swaney, John	227	--	7	9	86.8.0
Swaney, Alex'r.	--	--	1	--	10.0.0
Swaney, Miles	500	--	4	4	124.16.0
Swaney, Thomas	--	--	--	--	10.0.0
Slemons, Robert	165	1	3	8	59.11.0
Simpson, James	49	--	2	2	14.5.0
Stockslagey, Widow	159	--	2	2	30.0.0
Stockslagey, John	159	--	2	4	46.10.0
St. Myer, Christopher	250	--	1	2	59.8.0
Shelleberger, Henry	60	--	2	2	15.3.0
Smith, Andrew	--	--	2	2	2.5.0

Cumberland	Acres	Negroes	Horses	Cattle	Tax
Stewart, Alexander	100	--	1	1	1.19.0
Speer, James	420	1	5	8	156.12.0
Speer, James	120	--	--	--	--
Speer, Alexander	--	--	--	--	10.0.0
Speer, John	--	--	--	--	10.0.0
Taylor, Robert	140	2	4	6	58.10.0
D'o in Westmoreland co.	360	--	--	--	--
Tater, Archibald	150	--	4	9	40.0.0
Tate, Wm.	--	--	--	--	10.0.0
Thomson, John	--	--	--	--	--
Thomson, John	--	--	--	1	20.0.0
Vantz, George	--	1	2	--	24.6.0
Work, Robert	400	--	7	3	80.0.0
Wilson, Hugh	--	--	6	5	15.15.0
Walker, Gabriel	315	--	4	4	81.12.0
Walker, James	272	--	4	5	67.4.0
Watson, Andrew	--	--	--	1	9.18.0
Watt, George	192	--	3	4	40.0.0
Wade, Ebenezer	--	--	1	--	1.10.0
Wilson, Robert	--	--	1	2	3.3.0
Wilson, John	--	--	--	--	10.0.0
Wilson, Joseph	100	--	4	7	42.18.0
White, John	50	--	2	2	6.18.0
White, John, miller	170	--	5	7	92.8.0
White, John	100	--	--	--	--
Williams, John	50	--	--	--	--
Wilson, John	--	--	--	--	10.0.0
Walker, John	--	--	--	--	--
Myers, John	200	--	--	--	40.0.0
Black, Henry, Se'r.	--	--	2	2	5.8.0
Gregg, John	--	--	--	--	10.0.0
Crawford, James	--	--	1	2	--
Fletcher, John	--	--	2	2	5.8.0
Murphy, John	--	--	2	1	3.9.0
Marshall, James	--	--	1	--	10.0.0
Marshall, Wm.	--	--	1	--	2.5.0
Whiteman, Sam'l.	--	--	1	1	1.19.0
Paxton, George	--	--	1	1	1.19.0
Walker, Joseph	--	--	--	--	10.0.0
Marshall, John	--	--	1	1	--
Kill, Samuel	--	--	2	3	--
Mahollen, Wm.	--	--	--	--	10.0.0
Russel, Thomas	--	--	1	--	15.0
Smith, John	--	--	1	1	--
Finley, James	--	--	2	2	3.18.0
Hamilton, Arch'd.	--	--	--	--	10.0.0
Buchanon, Walter	--	--	--	--	10.0.0
St. Mire, Barnabas	--	--	--	--	33.6.0
Ornt, Jacob	--	--	--	--	33.15.0
McClure, John	--	--	--	--	4.19.0
Oar, Patrick	--	--	--	--	11.14.0
Borland, John	--	--	--	--	31.10.0
Steel, Wm.	--	--	--	--	31.13.0
Thomson, John	--	--	--	--	3.10.0
McMullen, John	--	--	--	--	2.14.0

Cumberland	Acres	Negroes	Horses	Cattle	Tax
McMullen, Thomas	--	--	--	--	10.0.0
McMullen, John	--	--	--	--	10.0.0
Moore, James	--	--	--	--	10.0.0
Black, John, Rev'd.	--	--	--	--	10.0.0
Murdy, The Rev'd. Mr.	--	--	--	--	15.0.0
Dobbins, The Rev'd.	--	--	--	--	12.0.0

INDEX

---, Willard 7
ABBEITH, Edward 82
  John 82
ABBEITH, Thomas 82
ABERCROMEY, John 50
ABLE, George 26
  John 26
ACHERT, Christopher 102
ADAIR, John 48, 102
  Robert 37
  William 48
ADAM, William 117
ADAMS, weaver 97
  Alexander 82
  Elijah 93
  Henry 112
  Hugh 50, 112
  James 93
  John 34, 102
  Joseph 78
  Matthew 112, 117(2)
  Samuel 102
  Widow 74
  William 112(3), 117
  Williams 37
ADLUM, Joseph 1
AGNEW, David 102
  James 102(2)
  John 102
  Samuel 102(2)
  Widow 102
AKER, Michael 65
ALBERT, Andrew 98
  Charles 44
  John 99(2)
ALBERT, Laurence 99
ALBRIGHT, Bernard 14
  Felix 108
  Henry 26, 58
  John 70
  Michael 111
  Philip 1
ALCOCK, Francis 65
  John 65
ALEXANDER, Andrew 41
  Henry 37
  Isaac 37
  James 37
  John 37
  Thomas 37
  William 1, 41
ALLEBACH, Frederich 41
ALLEN, Thomas 37
ALLENDER, William 19

ALLISON, Alexander 33
  Joseph 117
  Mathew 70
  Thomas 112
  William 26
ALLOWAYS, Stephen 37
ALMEROTH, George 58
ALSOP, John 19
ALSPOUGH, David 78
ALT, Henry 108
  Jacob 35
  Valentine 58
ALTENFIELD, Jacob 108
ALTLAND, Philip 54
AMBROSE, Robert 86
AMENT, Dice 13
  John 41
  Philip 8
AMMERMAN, Henry 62
AMMON, Jacob 54
AMSPOKER, George 58
ANDERSON & LOWREY 41
ANDERSON, David 34
  James 19, 35(2), 86
  John 35(2), 50, 86, 93
  Robert 36
  Thomas 117
  William 37, 70, 93
ANDREW, Francis 112
  John 62, 112
  Reverend 2
ANDREWS, Humphrey 37
  John 8, 37
ANGEL, Augustus 78
  Peter 78
ANNAN, Robert 102
ANSTINE, George 108
ANTHONY, Nicholas 1
APFEL, George 14
APPLE, Leonard 101
  Vendel 50
APPLEMAN, John 54
APPLEY, George 20
APPLY, Jacob 19
ARB, Jacob 31
ARCHIBALD, Campbell 93
ARGENTANT, John 19
ARMON, Thomas 78
ARMOR, Thomas 1(2), 19, 99
ARMSTRONG, Andrew 112
  Archibald 117
  David 40
  Henry 19

Isaac 117
  John 117(2)
  Quintain 117(2)
  Robert 37
  Thomas 50
  William 82
ARNOLD, John 96, 112
  Peter 93
  Samuel 54
ARTHUR, Hugh 117
  Thomas 19
ASBY, William 1
ASDIL, Aaron 26
ASHLIMAN, David 57
ASPER, Frederick 89(2)
  George 89
  Isaac 89
ASPOUGH, Andrew 48
ASTON, John 19
  William 20
ATHERTON, Henry 65
  Richard's widow 65
  Thomas 65(2)
ATKINS, Robert 36
ATKINSON, Caiphas 19
  John 19
  Richard 36
ATTICK, George 26
ATTICKS, John 19
AULEBACH, Nicholas 74
AUMOR, Daniel 54(2)
AYRES, David 65

BACHMAN, Christian 14
  Christopher 14
  Widow 14
BACHNER, Daniel 14
BACKER, Daniel 82
  George 82
  John 82
BACLER, Jacob 58
BADERS, George 37
BAHN, Jacob 78
  John 41
BAILEY, Daniel 20, 70
  George 70
  Jacob 58, 70
  James 64
  William 1, 8
BAILS, Caleb 100
  Calep 99
  David 99
  Elisha 99
  Isaac 100
  Jacob 99, 100(2)

INDEX

Jesse 99
John 99, 100
Moses 99
Solomon 100
William 99
BAINTER, Valentine 48
BAIR, Henry 31
John 1, 26(2)
BAKER, Henry 58
John 78, 82
Mathias 62
William 58(2)
BALDEN, John 98
BALDRIDGE, James 97
BALDWIN, Joseph 37
Thomas 51
BALLANCE, James 74
BALLENDINE, William 40
BALSLEY, Henry 54
Joseph 54
BALZER, Jacob 41
BANTA, Peter 62
Samuel 79
BARBER, Samuel 20
BARD, Bernhard 78(2)
David 78
Francis 78
George 82, 108
John 79
Samuel 81
Stephen 78
BARE, Peter 78
BARKMAN, John 102
BARNET, Charles 20
John 51
BARNEY, James 92
BARNITZ, Charles 1
Charles 1
Daniel 74
BARNS, William 8
BARR, Charles 65
Henry 8
Jacob 14
James 48(2)
Michael 14
William 12, 112
BARTEN, James 44
BARTLEY, Widow 26
BARTON, Edward 20
BASH, Joseph 93
BASHORE, Peter 89
BATTENFELT, Philip 14
BAUGHER, Frederick 82
George 82
William 82

BAUM, Adam 41
Jacob 19
Peter 14(2)
BAUMAN, Henry 14(2)
Jacob 14(2), 65
John 14, 58, 74
BAUMGARTNER, Henry 70
Jacob 19, 79
John 20
BAUSER, Christian 19
Daniel 19
BAXTER, John 20
Joseph 20
William 20
BAYERS, Charles 93
BAYLES, Abraham 97
BAYMILLER, Michael 26
BEACHER, Henry 78
BEAKER, Peter 70
Philip 51
BEAL, Jacob 78
BEALER, Jacob 58
Michael 58
BEALEY, William 62
BEALY, Daniel 93
BEAM, Henry 65
BEAN, Adam 78
James 20
BEANER, Fite 26
BEANOR, George 26
BEANS, Francis 93
Hugh 93
Thomas 93, 96
William 96
BEAR, Christian 74
Isaac 82
Jacob 20, 58, 62
Jeremiah 44
Ludwig 44
BEARD, John 37, 70, 102
BEATEMAN, Henry 74
BEATMAN, Andrew 20
BEATY, David 86(2)
James 48
John 86
William 40
BEAVER, Jacob 26
BECHER, David 54
Frederick 8
Jacob 54, 55
John 54
BECHTEL, Christian 14
George 79
Jacob 62, 78

BECK, George 55
Jacob 74
BECKER, Adam 14
Christian 14
Conrad 8
Frederick 26
Nicholas 26
Philip 44
William 1, 12
BECKLEY, Henry 14
BECKNER, Abraham 82
Jacob 82(2)
John 82
Laurence 82
Nicholas 82
BEEL, Melchior 79
BEER, Michael 74
BEHLER, Jacob 14
BEHM, Christian 79
BEHMER, Jacob 20
John 20
BELLET, Craft 41
Thomas 44
BELSHUBER, Widow 1
BELTZ, Jacob 74
Michael 62
BELTZHUBER --- 1
Conrad 44
BELTZNER, John 7
BENCE, George 108
Wyrick 108
BENDER, Conrad 51
Henry 1
Jacob 50(2)
BENEDICK, Melchior 44
BENEDICT, Philip 8
BENGEL, Leonard 26
BENMER, Henry 74
BENNET, Enoch 1
Henry 20
Isaac 20
Joseph 93
Thomas 20
BENNINGTON, Ephraim 1
BENSON, James 37
BENTZ, Andrew 57
Henry 1
Michael 8
Philip 1
Wyrich 1
BENTZEL, Henry 44
Philip 44
BERBOWER, Casper 44
Philip 44
BERCKER, Valentine 14

INDEX

BERGDOLL, Peter 108
BERGER, Peter 1
BERKGOLD, Michael 74
BERKHEIMER, Martin 57
  Valentin 55, 58
BERLIN, Frederick 82
  Jacob 82
  Nicholas 82
BERMINGER, Henry 108
BERNARD, Ulrich 54
BERNHARD, Nicholas 1
BERNHART, John 41
BERTENHEIMER, Simon 89
  William 89
BESENOUR, Anthony 44
BEST, John 37
  Sarah, widow 37
BETTERSON, Jacob 82
BETTIE, Walter 89
BETTLE, Benjamin 89
BETTY, Samuel 89
BETZ, Christian 108
BEYER, John 14, 58
  Peter 41
BICH, Adam 78
BICK, John 1
BICKING, Jacob 82
BICKLY, William 118
BIDLER, Barbara 41
  Peter 41
BIEGLER, John 20
BIERS, David 102
  John 1
  Samuel 102(2)
BIGAM, Thomas 102
BIGGAR, William 51
BIGHAM, Hugh 48, 102
  John 106
  Patrick 48
  Robert 102(2), 117
  William 102
BIGLER, Jacob 44
  Joseph 44
BIKE, Abraham 1
BIKEN, Henry 93
BILLMEYER, Andrew 1
  Helena 1
  Jacob 1
  Michael 1
BINDER, Martin 65
BINGHAM, Samuel 102
BIRCKER, Andrew 14
BISHOP, Henry 78
  Jeremiah 78
  Teeter 79

BITTINGER, Michael 118
  Nicholas 14, 54, 82
BITTLE, Thomas 78
BITTNER, Jacob 112
  Michael. 108
BITZEL, John 44, 48
  Jonathan 44
  Laurence 44
BIXLER, Christian 8
  Jacob 14, 19
  John 8, 14
  Joseph 8
  Samuel 74
  Adam 118
  Henry 117, 123
  James 86, 117(2), 118
  John 50, 124
  Mathew 118
  Robert 117, 118
  Thomas 97
BLACKBURN, James 31
  John 31
  Moses 53
  Thomas 50
BLACKFORD, Mary 65
BLAIN, Robert 112
BLAIR, Brice 65, 70
  John 65, 70, 118(2)
BLASSER, Abraham 33
  John 34
BLATCHFORD, Richard 93
BLECKLEY, James 50
  William 50
BLESSINGER, Michael 41
BLILLHART, Peter,
  Jun'r 62
BLINMYER, Christopher 33
BLINTZINGER, George 74
BLOCKER, Mathias 14
BLOOMER, Nehemiah 90
BLOTT, John 79
  Joseph 79
BLOUSE, John 26
BLYER, Adam 54
BLYMEYER, Bernard 70
BLYMYER, Abraham 1
  Jacob 108
  Martin 108
BLYTH, David 102
BOB, Jacob 44
BOBLITZ, Michael 44
BOCK, Patrick 108
BODINE, John 26, 86

BOGAL, Alexander 89
  Joseph 86
  Malcom 86
BOHN, Jacob 13
  Nicholas 8
  Valentine 8
BOIL, John 93
BOKER, Christian 112
BOLD, William 99
BOLEY, George 112
BOLLINGER, Abraham 58
  Henry 14
  Jacob 14(2)
  Joseph 14
BOLTEN, Robert 62
BOLTON, James 79
BOLY, Laurence 108
BOMBACH, George 1, 8
BONER, Charles 97
  Francis 98
  John 97
  Robert 98
  Thomas 98
BONINE, James 20
  Thomas 20
BONIX, George 44
BOPE, Mathias 58
BORG, George 1
BORGER, Michael 20
BORLAND, John 123
BORTNER, George 58
BOSE, John 14
BOSHEA, Christian 89
  Michael 93
  Nicholas 89
BOSTON, George 102
BOTT, George 13
  Jacob 13
  Jonas 8
  Reinhard 8
BOTTER, Philip 82
BOUDENHIMER, Simon 93
BOUGHMAN, Frederick 78
BOURSAX, Valentine 55
BOUSER, Abraham 54
  Daniel 14, 55(2)
  Jacob 55
  John 74, 82
  Noah 82
  Samuel 82
  Widow 1
BOWAN, Jonathan 50
  Thomas 50, 51

INDEX

BOWER, Abraham 99
  Andrew 70
  Daniel 1
  George 20
  Jacob 14, 99
  John 99
  Martin 13
  Michael 31, 65
  Peter 65, 82
  Widow 99
BOWMAN, John 41
BOWSMAN, Laurence 51
BOYD, Andrew 118
  George 65
  Thomas 89
  Widow 118
  William 36, 118(3)
BOYER, Abraham 78
  Henry 78
  Jacob 26
  Philip 26
  Tobias 70, 78
BOYL, Widow 48
BOYLE, Robert 96
BRACKEN, Thomas 51
  Widow 51
BRADEY, James 97
BRADLEY, Hannah 37
  William 26, 74
BRADSHAW, Charles 112
BRADY, John 99
  Nicholas 64
BRAIM, Henry 31
BRAKIN, Elizabeth 100
  William 99
BRALEY, James 93
BRANARD, Barney 97
BRAND, Nicholas 1
BRANDAN, William 106
BRANDON, Alexander 97
  John 97
  Jonathan 99
  Richard 97
  Thams 97
  Walter 98
  William 51
BRANNAM, William 58
BRANWOOD, Andrew 118
BRATON, William 20
BRAUSER, John 14
BRECKENRIDGE, Robert 48
  William 37, 48
BREDAN, William 118
BRENNAN, Thomas 37
BRENNEISEN, Martin 1

BRENNEMAN, Isaac 8
  Peter 8
BRENNER, Adam 55
BREWER, Abraham 86
  Daniel 86
BREWEY, George 20
BRICE, James 102
BRICKER, Anthony 19
  Nicholas 14
  Stophel 14
BRIDE, John 1
BRIGHNER, Godlieb 54
  Peter 54
BRILLHARD, Peter 58
BRILLHART, Jacob 61
  John 74
  Joseph 62
  Peter 70
BRINDLEY, Jacob 65
  Jacob 65
BRINGMAN, Frederick 1(2)
BRINKERHOOF, George 86
  Gilbert 62
  Jacob 62
  James 62
  Raliff 62
BRINLEY, Mathias 99
BRITTON, James 8
BROBAND, Ann,
  Christian's widow 20
  Ann, Jacob's widow 20
BROBST, Jacob 1
  John 7
BROCA, George 86
BRODBECK, John 58
BROGAR, Abraham 89
BROOKS, Charles 7
  John 1
BROSS, Frederick 34
BROTHER, Henry 79
BROUSTER, Charles 65
BROWL, William 44
BROWN Alexander 13, 31, 100
  Andrew 33
  Daniel 89
  George 108
  Henry 106
  Hugh 51
  Jacob 8, 82(2)
  James 57
  Joseph 86, 102, 116
  Joshua 37

  Richard 86
  Thomas 37
  Widow 89
  William 102, 118
BROWSTER, Widow 118
BRUBACHER, Conrad 26
BRUCHARD, Julius 8
BRUCKHARD, Abram 13
  Adam 14
  David 13
  Martin 14
BRUCKHART, Jacob 41
BRUGH, Jacob 65
  John 65
  Manus 89(2)
BRUMAGIM, John 65
BRUNNEMAN, Benjamin 58
  Samuel 58
BRUNNER, Peter 44
BRUNTON, John 65
  Thomas 65
BRYAN, Jeremiah 65
BRYERLY, John 8
BRYSON, Andrew 31
BUCHANNON, John 35
BUCHANON, Andrew 93
  Ebenezer 117
  Henry 62
  James 37
  John 112(2), 118
  Robert 118
  Samuel 37
  Thomas 37
  Walter 118, 123
  William 118, 112(2)
BUCHER, John 19
  Nicholas 14(2)
BUCKHOLDER, Isaac 114
  John 100
BUFFETON, Jacob 79
BUGH, Michael 82
BUNGES, Joseph 112
BURCKHOLDER, Henry 97
BURGAN, Peter 62
BURGHOLDER, George 114
  John 114
BURKHARD, Jacob 14
BURKHOLDER, Abram 112
BURNET, George 62
BURNS, James 106
  William 106
BURNTREGGER, Andrew 51
BUSE, Adam 78
  Peter 78

INDEX

BUSH, John 108
  Michael 19
BUSHONG, Jacob 8
BUSHY, Henry 14
BUTT, Jacob 78
  William 70, 100
BUTTRIM, Benjamin 102
BUYER, Henry 19
BUZZARD, Jacob 70
BYARD, George 20
BYER, Henry 73
  Jacob 108
  John 8
  Martin 74
BYERLEY, Jacob 77
BYERS, John 117

CABAN, John 118
CABEL, Benjamin 93
CADWALLADER, James 65
CAFFELT, Jacob 70
CAFFMAN, Solomon 71
CAGE, John 26
CALDWELL, Hugh 82
  James 102
  John 112
  Robert 38
CALEHIN, Thomas 99
CAMEL, James 99
CAMELIN, Charles 89
CAMILLIN, Mathew 87
CAMLIN, William 93
CAMONGER, Henry 86
  John 86
CAMP, George 62
CAMPBELL, Archibald 82
  Hugh 86
  John 118
  Joseph 102, 107
  Robert 89
  Widow 112
  William 19
CAMPBLE, John 38
CAMPER, Michael 64
CAMRON, Finley 93
CANADY, John 96, 97
CANDLER, David 1
CANEDY, John 87
CANN, Henry 41
CANNADY, Bailiff 93
CANNINE, Peter 62
CANNON, Thomas 62
CARBERRY, Michael 71
CARL, Martin 82
  Michael 82

CARLISLE, Henry 51
  John 98
CARMAN, Mathias 41
  Philip 27
CARNACHAN, Alexander 102
  David 102
CARPENTER, Daniel 82
CARR, John 83
CARRATHERS, Thomas 97
CARRICK, James 102
  John 102
  Moses 82
CARSON, David 118
  John 99
CARSON, William 38, 51
CARSTIMAN, Christian 51
CARSWELL, James 35
  Robert 36
CASHADY, Nicholas 66
CASSELMAN, George 70
  Michael 71
CASTLES, Alexander 102
CATLER, Widow 86
CATTERWOOD, John 38
CAUFELT, Michael 26
CAUFFMAN, Jacob 41
  Michael 43
CAYLOR, Martin 26
CELLER, Henry 74
  Jacob 70
  John 70
  Samuel 71
CELLOR, Anthony 26
CEMERLY, Jacob 26
CENSOR, Jacob 100
CERSEY, Jacob 71
CERVER, Casper 8
CHAMBERLAIN, James 90
  John 90
  Nenian 90
  Niviath 62
  Robert 90
CHAMBERS, Arthur 74
  James 51, 98
  John 62
  Joseph 1, 31
  Robert 51(2)
CHAMBERSON, Samuel 86
CHANLEY, George 90
CHANNEL, Nathan 1
CHERRIDON, John 106
CHESNEY, William 20(3)
CHESTER, Robert 82

CHRIST, Adam 55
CHRISTOPHER, Hugh 106
CHRISTY, Samuel 26
CHRONISTER, Henry 90
CHRYST, Andrew 70
CIMBERLY, Michael 100
CIMPLE, Jacob 90
  Michael 90
  Nicholas 66
CITTERMAN, Andrew 20
CLANFELTER, Laurence 71
  Michael 71
  Peter 71
CLAPSADDLE, Daniel 64
  Francis 64
  Michael 62, 82
CLARK, Henry 51
  James 82, 106
  John 82, 90, 102
  Thomas 118
  William 100, 106
CLARKSON, James 113
CLATFELDER, Casper 74
CLATFELTER, Jacob 71
CLAX, Christian 92
CLAYTON, Daniel 41
CLEAVER, Peter 66
CLEINFELTER, George 70
  John 70
CLEMENS, Patrick 38
CLERK, James 38
CLIMSON, John 20
CLINE, Andrew 20
  Casper 93
  Conrad 8
  John 62
  Peter 26
CLINGER, Philip 93
  Thomas 102
CLIST, George 112
CLOPER, George 41
CLOSE, Christian 93
CLOUDY, Martin 65
CLOUGH, Charles 31
CLOYD, John 3
CLUGSTON, Joseph 102(2)
CLYNE, Adam 31
COALER, Michael 90
COARMAN, Michael 26
COBEL, Abraham 41
  Christopher 20
COBIN, Samuel 118
COBLER, Adam 41

INDEX

COCHENAUER, Garret 65
  John 62
COCHRAN, Andrew 102
  James 102
  John 102(2)
  William 51, 102
COCK, John 90
COFFEE, Michael 118
COINER, Criften 93
COLE, Philip 1
COLLER, Balzar 70
  Christian 70
  Jacob 70
  John 71
COLLINGWOOD, Richard 27
COLLINS, David 106
  John 1, 100, 109
  Samuel 117
  William 114, 112
COLMERY, John 51
  William 51
COLSTON, David 96
  Ripley 96
COLTER, Archibald 86
COLTRIDER, Henry 41
COLVIN, William 38
COMER, John 100
COMFORT, Andrew 93
  Jacob 41
COMMONS, John 38
CONDRY, William 100 93
CONELLY, Hugh 25
  James 66
  Jenkins 107
CONGELL, Michael 71
CONN, John 43
CONNER, George 90
  John 70, 86, 117
  Thomas 27
CONRAD, Corpman 73
  John 83
CONSER, Henry 20
CONWAY, Charles 90
  James 90
COOK, Andrew 102(2)
  Jacob 65
  Jesse 93
  Joseph 20, 94
  Peter 65
  Samuel 65
COOKIS, Adam 65
COOLY, John 97
COON, Adam 117
  John 112

COOPER, Alexander 37
  Archibald 37
  James 62, 116
  John 41, 93
  Joseph 111
  Mathias 93
  Nicholas 37
  Samuel 66
  Thomas 37
  William 31, 37, 62, 87, 89, 92, 93(2)
COOPERS, James 117
COOSTER, John 113
COPELAND, Davis 20
COPLAND, Thomas 20
COPP, John 62
CORBIT, John 106
CORBOCK, Christian 118
CORD, John 51
CORDS, Richard 114
CORNELIUS, James 1
  John 34
  Justa 34
  Stephen 36
CORPMAN, Daniel 70
  Henry 70
  Jacob 71
CORRELL, Abraham 20
CORRETHERS, James 48
COSS, George 112
COTTON, Henry 102
  Hugh 106
  John 106
COUGH, George 66
  Widow 66
COULSTON, Charles 93, 100
  William 93
COURTS, Martin 71
COVER, Deetrich 90
COVERT, Isaac 87
COWAN, Robert 87
  William 117
COWLEY, Henry 106
COWN, Adam 113
  Andrew 113
  Jacob 113
  Michael 113
COX, Abraham 66
  Jacob 20, 44
  John 100
  Joseph 118(2)
  Laurence 86, 89
  Nathaniel 66
  Richard 66

  Solomon 100
  William 66(2), 99
COXAN, William 65
COZAT, David 87
  Francis 87
  Jacob 87
CRAFFORD, John 66
  Robert 93
CRAFT, Conrad 41
  Widow 2
CRAIG, Henry 118
  John 118
  Robert 102(2)
  Thomas 102
CRAIGHTEN, Alexander 33
CRAIGMILES, James 112, 114
CRAMER, Adam 66(2)
  Henry 66
  John 66
CRANNISTER, Henry 93
CRATEZING, George 90
CRAWFORD, James 82, 123
CRAYMER, Adam 20
CRINE, Casper 100
CROAN, John 26, 87
  Robert 87
CRONE, Simon 20
CRONEMILLER, Widow 1
CRONISTER, John 100(2)
CROOKSHANKS, George 106
CROOP, Casper 93
CROSS, James 27
  John 27, 35
  Randle 27
  Thomas 118
  Widow 27
  William 118
CROSSER, Adam 83
  Samuel 83
CROSSES, --- 33
CROTHERS, John 93
CROUD, Anna 70
CROULL, Widow 87
  William 87
CROUSE, Christian 70
  Michael 13
CROUSS, Daniel 66
CROW, Alexander 41
  Michael 41
  Samuel 38
CROWAL, Conrad 89
  George 89
CROWL, Henry 113

130

INDEX

CROZINE, Cornelius 86, 87
  Widow 87
CRULL, John 20
CRUP, Peter 100
  Philip 100
CUMMINGS, James 102
CUNNING, Samuel 38, 112
CUNNINGHAM, Adam 112
  Benjamin 41
  Henry 34
  Robert 36, 93, 102
CUNNINGS, James 74
CUNTRY, William 66
CURLY, William 113
CURRY, Joseph 40
CURSWELL, Thomas 90
CUTBERTSON, Samuel 118

DAHLMAN, John 2
DAHOFE, George 58
  Henry 58
  Nicholas 58
DALHAMMER, Nicholas 83(2)
DAMAREE, David 62
DAMBACH, Frederick 2
DAME, Joseph 40
DAMY, Jacob 15
DANNER, Abraham 1
  Abram 108
  Casper 44
  Henry 15
  Martin 2
  Michael 15
DANSIL, George 100
DARBOROUGH, Isaac 51
DARON, Adam 42
DAVIDSON, Phineas 103
DAVIS, Benjamin 20
  Daniel 66
  David 20
  Henry 44
  Hugh 27
  John 44, 66(2)
  Joseph 51
  Joshua 66
  Lewis 66
  Richard 15
  Thomas 8
  William 20
DAVISON, James 79
  John 41
  Widow 90
  William 118

DAVYDAL, John 48
DAWNEY, Patrick 40
DAWSON, Richard 97
DAY, Jacob 27
  John 38
  Nicholas 27
  Salvenius 100
DEAL, Felix 97
DEAN, Nehemiah 66
DEARDORF, Anthony 44, 83, 90(2)
  Henry 94
  Isaac 94
  Jacob 94
DECAMP, Jacob 87
DECKER, Frederick 55
  John 62
  Joseph 74
  Philip 41
DEDY, Thomas 117
DEEDS, George 41
  Jacob 61
DEEL, Adam 71
  Charles 71
  George 108
  Nicholas 108
  Peter 108
DEELMAN, Jacob 71
DEER, Ulrich 44
DEERDORF, Paul 48
DEGEN, Peter 79
DEGRAFF, Abraham 62
  Michael 62
  Samuel 65
  William 62
DEIDENHEFER, George 71
DEIFINGER, Killian 71
DEITSH, Bartholomew 7
DELAP, John 31
  Robert 31
  William 31
DELLINGER, Jacob 27
  John 27
  Joseph 27, 41
DELLO, Nicholas 55
DELONG, George 34
DEMAND, Frederick 15
DEMINT, John 44
DEMUTH, Widow 42
DENISTON, John 106
DENNIS, John 100
DENNISON, James 66
DENSYL, Richard 101
DENTLINGER, Adam 58
DEPOUNDS, Adoniah 103

DEROUGH, Henry 83
DERR, Gabriel 13
DERWECHTER, John 15
DESHER, Peter 83
DESHNER, George 8
DESTEIN, Michael 41
DETRICH, Nicholas 87
DETTER, Mathias 13, 48
DETTERER, Conrad 74
DETWILER, Samuel 108
DEVANY, Daniel 106
DEVELIN, John 94
  Roger 90
DEVISE, Joseph 44
DEWALT, George 83
  Henry 15
  Peter 55
  Valentine 15
DIAR, John 48
DIAS, Thomas 71
DICE, Mich'l. 108
DICK, Adam 83
  Christian 83
  Joseph 83
DICKENS, John 71
DICKESON, Joshua 66
  Robert 36
DICKONSON, Samuel 36
DICKS, John 55
  Peter 55
DICKSON --- 103
  James 87(3)
  Joseph 94
  Thomas 36
DIDDY, Peter 41
DIEL, Charles 58
  George 58
DIERDORF, John 55
  Peter 55
DIFF, Daniel 83
DIGGS, William 74
DILL, James 94
  John 100
  Mathew 94
  Nicholas 79
  Thomas 94
DILLOW, John 48
DIMOREE, David 87
  Samuel 87
DINCKEL, Peter 108
DINKEL, Oster 1
DINKLE, Peter 8
DIVER, John 103
DIVINE, Daniel 34

INDEX

DOBBINS, James 8
  Rev'd. 124
DODDS, John 31
  Joseph 97, 99
  William 98
DOLL, Conrad 55
  Daniel 14
  John 55
DOLLMAN, Henry 108
DOME, Benedick 108
  John 108
DOMI, George 51
DONALD, William 97
DONALDSON, James 87
  John 44
  Joseph 2, 8, 58
  William 85, 118
DONALLY, James 99
  John 99
DONELLY, William 117
DONET, George 20
DONLEY, John 113
DONOUGHAH, John 27
DOOB, Joseph 39
DORAN, John 38, 48
  Tera 87
DORLAND, Garrett 83
DORLIACK, John 78
DORMAN, John 41
DORNY, Henry 19
DOROUGH, John 117
DORRA, William 90
DOTTER, Conrad 62
DOUDLE, Jacob 1, 8, 20
  Mary, widow 1
  Michael 2, 8
  Widow 47
DOUGHERTY, George 94
  John 38
  Richard 66
  William 20, 113
DOUGLASS, Archibald 118
  David 117
  James 117
  Patrick 36
  Robert 118
  Thomas 118(2)
  Timothy 103
  William 31, 36, 87, 113
DOWNING, Alexander 113
  James 113
  John 113
  William 117
DOWNS, Henry 71

DRACK, William 66
DRAYER, Philip 79
DREXLER, Peter 108
DRIVER, James 66
  John
DROHRBACH, Jacob 20
DRONNON, David 41
DRORBACH, William 111
DRUMP, Abram 15
DUBBS, John 15
  Oswald 15
DUFF, James 65
  John 62, 65
  Peter 103
DUFFIELD, George 31
  James 87
DULL, Joseph 38
DUMB, Andrew 100
DUMEREE, Garret 65
DUNCAN, Andrew 33
  Henry 102
  Jacob 38
  James 113
  John 35, 113
  Robert 38
  Seth 83
  Thomas 117
DUNDORE, Henry 44
DUNLAP, James 38
  Robert 38
DUNN, Robert 1
  Thomas 13
  William 66
DUNSMORE, Robert 106
DUNWIDDY, Widow 103(2)
DUNWOODY, David 118(2)
  Jane, Widow 118
DUPS, Daniel 15
DUVAL, Samuel 38

EABY, John 27
EADY, Bastian 27
  Frederich 27
EAGER, James 38
EALY, George 66
EASON, Archibald 27
EASTING, Jacob 34
EBERHARD, Henry 13
  Vendle 71
EBERSOLT, Jacob 15
EBERT, Martin 8(2)
  Michael 2, 8
  Philip 13
ECKART, Conrad 75
  John 75

ECKELS, Francis 118
ECKHART, Jacob 111
EDGAR, William 37
EDMONDSON, Thomas 66
EDMUNDSON, --- 21
  John 66
EDWARDS, Jonathan 7
  Michael 7
EDY, Samuel 118
  William 37
EGY, Michael 58(2)
EHRHARD, Michael 15
  Philip 90
EHRMAN, John 2
  Joseph 74
  Michael 58
EICHELBERGER, Adam 15, 71
  Frederick 12, 13, 58
  George 8
  Jacob 2, 75, 108
  Lenard 15
  Leonard 75
  Ludwig 62
  Martin 2, 8
  Widow 2
EICHHOLTZ, Frederick 44
EICHINGER, Jacob 108
EICHOLTZ, Frederick 44
  Mathias 44
EICKART, Peter 48
EIGER, Joseph 44
EIGHINGER, Jacob 2
EIKENER, John 94
EILER, Peter 27
EINGHELL, Henry 73
EIRICH, Michael 2
EISENHARD, Conrad 8
EISENHART, George 74
ELDER, Benjamin 103
  James 103, 113
  Robert 118
  Samuel 113
ELENBERGER, Peter 8
ELGENFRITZ, George 44(2)
ELIAS, George 113
  Philip 113
ELISS, James 103(2)
ELKER, Henry 100
ELLENBERGER, Ulrich 27
ELLIOT, Alexander 21
  Andrew 94
  Benjamin 94
  George 103
  Isaac 94

INDEX

James 21, 31
John 21, 31
Joseph 94
Oliver 31
Robert 51, 94
Samuel 36
Widow 31, 66
William 31
ELSEROTH, Nicholas 19
EMENHEISER, Adam 27
John 27
EMICH, George 58
John 8(2), 19
Philip 58
Valentine 8
EMIG, Nicholas 83
Paul 57
EMITE, Samuel 103
Widow 103
EMLET, Michael 13, 75
ENDLER, Jacob 2
Philip 2, 7
ENGLAND, Joseph 66
ENGLISH, David 62
William 31
ENSMENGER, Conrad 8
David 21
George 21
Henry 21
ENTRAS, Nicholas 55
ENTRICKEN, James 118
EPELY, Christopher 2
EPPLEY, John 15
Mathias 15
Peter 15
EPPLY, Jacob 58
ERISMAN, Frederick 13
Jacob 8
ERNST, James 94
John 15
ERP, Joseph 43
ERWIN, Robert 74
ESHBAUGH, Eve 21
ESHELMAN, Peter 21
ETCHISON, Thomas 90
ETTER, George 2
Lawrence 2
ETTING, Widow 2
ETTINGER, Michael 13
Philip 8
ETZLER, Andrew 74
George 74
EUREY, Michael 66
Widow 66

EVANS, Able 44
Azariah 66
Cadwalleder 66
Evan 21
Jonathan 44
Thomas 36, 44, 117
EVERHART, John 58
EVERIT, Isaac 100
EVEY, Christian 33
EVY, John 8
EWE, Mich'l. 87
EWING, Isaac 62
James 42, 118
John 43, 62
Mathew 35
Robert 62
Samuel, Esq'r 62
EWINGS, Alexander 38
EYERS, Henry 21
EYLER, Frederick 75
John 15
EYRES, John 21
EYSTER, Elias 8
George 8

FACKLER, Godlieb 9
Jacob 2
Widow 2
FANDIKE, Henry 63
FANESTOCK, Peter 90
FARIS, George 63
FARNSLER, George 58
FARRA, William 66
FASS, Christian 15
George 119
FASTER, Henry 66
FEAGON, James 66
FEDDERO, John 21
Philip 21(2)
FEESER, Peter 108
FEEZER, Nicholas 79
Widow 79
FEGAN, James 106
FEGLEY, Paul 55
FEHL, George 15
Nicholas 15
FEIGELY, Martin 74
FELGER, Frederick 9
Henry 15
FELIX, John 15
FELLOWS, James 113
FELTEN, Conrad 15
FELTON, John 15
FENUS, Frederick 108

FERGUS, Hugh 119
John 119
Thomas 119
FERGUSON, Finley 107
Hugh 119
James 118,119
John 107, 119
Robert 118
Widow 51
William 119
FERREE, Conrad 71
Henry 71
FERRENCE, Peter 83
FERRIS, William 37
FERSITH, John 27
FERSITHE, Alexander 75
FETTER, John 8
FETTERRO, Joseph 21
FICKES, Abraham 100
Isaac 100
Jacob 100
John 100
Martin 15
Valentine 90, 100(2)
Yost 83
FIDLER, Philip 31
FIERNSHIELD, William 2
FIESER, John 44
FIFFER, George 71
FIESER, George 71
FIGEL, Gabriel 97
FIGELY, Mathias 2
FINDLEY, Michael 103(2)
William 103(2)
FINFROCK, Michael 8
Stephen 8
FINK, Bastian 44
Casper 51
George 44, 108
FINKS, Michael 55
FINLEY, Andrew 33
Archibald 119
George 87
Henry 94
James 123
John 113
FINLY, Michael 119
FINZENTZ, Imfeld 2
FIRST, Adam 57
FISCHEL, Adam 44
Frederick 71
Henry 58, 61
John 44, 55
Michael 55, 108
Wendel 55

INDEX

FISHEL, Henry 55
  John 2
FISHER, Adam 15
  Conrad 83
  Frederick 108
  Godlieb 21
  Isaac 94
  James 21, 94
  John 2, 71
  Peter 92
  Samuel 2
  Thomas 79
  Valentine 15
FISSEL, Adam 57
FISTER, Jacob 27
FISTERLAND, Jacob 34
FITS, Balzer 42
  Frederick 27
  John 43
FITZGERALD, James 41
FLADE, Joseph 79(2)
FLANAGAN, James 38
FLATCHER, Abram 87
FLECK, Felty 97
  Peter 100
FLEMING, Archibald 51
  George 89
  James 48
  John 87
  Robert 103
FLEMMING, John 119
FLEMON, Robert 63
FLENDER, John 2
FLESHMAN, Martin 75
FLETCHER, Charles 119
Fletcher, David 118
  John 119, 123
  Robert 118
FLETTER, George 75
FLICKINGER, Jacob 15
  Peter 75
  Samuel 15
FLINCHBACH, Adam 108
  Martin 108
  Philip 79
FLIND, Michael 44
FLOHR, Leonard 44
  Valentine 44
FLLOD, Timothy 99
FLORY, Abraham 42
  Daniel 43
  Henry 66
  Isaac 42
  Jacob 42

FLOWERS, Catharine 71
  John 38
FLOYD, Samuel, old 21
FOERST, Adam 55
  Martin 55
FOGELGESONG, Philip 66
  Stophel 66
FOLK, Moses 99
  Stephen 100
FOLLER, Adam 62
FOLTZ, Adam 58
FONASDELIN, Lukens 63
  Simon 62, 63
  Simon 63
FONASTOCK, Benjamin 66
  Boras 66
  Daniel 66
FONCANORA, Michael 42
FONHOVER, Jacob 62
FORD, Peter 108
FORMAN, Andrew 83
  Peter 83
FORNEY, Adam 19
  Christian 19
  Henry 63
  Philip 75
FORREY, Christian 21
  John 21
FORRY, --- 9
FORSYTHE, Nathaniel 27
  Robert 113
FOSTER, Fidelis 27
FOUST, Peter 108
FOWBLE, John 15
FOX, Henry 90
  John 42
  Peter 90
FRANK, David 15
FRANKENBERGER, John 55
  Philip 55
  William 55
FRASER, Frederick 58
FRAZIER, Ezechiel 66
FREDERICK, Abram 94
  Andrew 54, 55
  Michael 55
FREED, Christian 63
  Jacob 108
  Peter 63
FREELEIN, John 71
FREEMAN, John 21
  Nathaniel 21(2)
FREES, David 42
  George 42
  Jacob 42

FREEZER, Joshua 94
FRENCH, John 113
FREW, Alexander 38
FREYTER, John 61
FRITZ, Philip 42
FRITZLEY, George 2
FRONKELBERGER, Henry 83
FRY, Barnet 27
  Conrad 27
  Frederick 27
  George 2, 8, 108
  Godfrey 2, 108(2)
  John 27, 71
  Martin 2
  Peter 27
  Philip 27
  Tobias 44
FRYER, George 9
FUCKS, George 15
FUDERELL, Laurence 103
FUGET, Edward, Maryland 34
FUHRMAN, Jacob 15, 19
  Michael 19
  Stephen 15
  Valentine 19
FULFORD, Henry 15
FULKNER, Jacob 58
FULLER, John 75
FULLERTON, John 113(2)
  Robert 31(2), 90, 113
  Samuel 113
  William 113
FULTON, Andrew 33
  David 33
  James 113
  John 96
  Samuel 36
  William 38
FULWILER, John 66
  Michael 66
FUNDREWS, Adam 38
FUNK, Adam 15
  Benedick 108
  Daniuel 100
  Jacob 2
FURNACE, Mary 19
FURNEY, Abraham 79
  Adam 78
  Philip 15
FURNY, Mark 15
  Nicholas 15

INDEX

GALAGHER, Hugh 34
  James 38
GALBRAITH, John 103
  Joseph 103
  Robert 63, 87
GALBREATH, Robert 89
GALHOON, John 15
GALLACHER, Alexander 96
GALLAGHER, Barney 32
  Charles 32
  Hugh 119
  James 32
  Thomas 32
  William 32
GALLAUGHER, James 79
GALLENTINE, John 75
GALLESBY, John 67
GALLESPY, William 98
GALLOWAY, James 119
GALLY, Moses 19
GANSHORN, Mathias 111
GANTLEY, George 44
  William 48
GANTZ, Francis 58
GARDMAN, Isaac 2, 3
GARDNER, Adam 2
  Jacob 2
  Peter 67
GARIN, Widow 113
GARNER, George 27, 79
  James 90
GARNOR, George 79
GARRET, Luke 97
GARRETSON, Cornelius 21
  John 21
  Joseph 2, 21
  Samuel 21
GARREY, James 63
  John 63
GARRISON, John 67(2)
  William 66
GARTNER, Adam 108
  Henry 45
  Martin 42
  Philip 42
GARWOOD, Mideon 67
GASHAW, Peter 79
GASPER, Clemer 34
GASTNER, Jacob 9
GAUFF, George 45
GAYER, George 45
GAYLEY, Samuel 77
GEERY, William 87
GEESLER, Adam 79

GEEZY, Conrad 108(2)
  Jacob 108
  John 108
GEIP, Peter 57
GEISEY, Christian 70
GEISS, Elias 43
  Peter 55
GEITZEL, Leonhart 75
GELWIX, Charles 75
  Daniel 63
  Frederick 15(2)
  George 19
  Nicholas 19
  Peter 16
GEMMIL, David 34
  John 35
  William 36
GENSWILER, Andrew 75
GENTZLER, Philip 59
GEORGE, William 21
GERBER, George 2
  John 15
  Michael 3
GERBERICH, Peter 58
GERDAN, Jonas 71
GERHARD, John 9
GERRARD, Christian 19
  William 15
GETTIS, William 63
GETTY, Samuel, in
  trust 119
GETTYS, Samuel 103
  Samuel 119
  William 119
GETZ, Martin 58
  Yost 108
GEYER, George 2
GEYGER, Wendle 55
GIBBON, Patrick 21
GIBBONS, William 21
GIBSON, James 38
  John 35, 106
  Robert 38
  Widow 48, 103
  William 48
GICH, Balzer 15
GICK, Balzer 31
GIESS, George 9
GIFFEN, Stephen 87
GILBERT, Andrew 27
  Barnet 87
  George 51
  Jacob 89
  William 108

GILBREATH, Bertram 9
  John 51
GILCRIST, Agnes 38
GILES, James 38
GILGESON, James 119
GILGRIST, James 119
  Thomas 119
GILL, Robert 117
  Thomas 103
GILLEY, James 106
GILLILAND, John 51
  Samuel 51
  William 51
GILLMEYER, Francis 19
GILMORE, Henry 90
GILTMYER, Francis 77
GINDER, Michael 9
GIPE, George 43
  Henry 42
  Peter 42
GITSON, William 21
GITT, Peter 16
  William 75
GLANCEY, Jesse 21
  Joseph 21
  Torrence 21
GLASGOW, James 51
  Nathaniel 51
GLASICK, Samuel 59
GLASS, Mathias 51
GLEN, Joseph 97
GLESY, George 2
GMINTER, Martin 16
GOBBLE, John 71
GODFREY, William 37, 94
GOHN, Adam 27
  Philip 27(2)
  Widow 27
GOHO, John 2
GOLD, Thomas 21
GOLL, Baltzer 2
GOLLICKER, Michael 83
  Patrick 83
GOLLOUGHER, Abraham 27
GONDY, William 119
GONSTON, Robert 27
GOOD, Charles 51
  David 27(2)
  Jacob 9
  John 27
  William 37
GOODWIN, Seth 48
GOODYEAR, George 2

INDEX

GORDON, Christian 117
  James 38
  John 35, 38, 117
  Robert
  Thomas 40
  Widow 38
GORGUS, Benjamin 2
GORMAN, James 21
GOSS, George 27
  John 27
GOSSLER, John 108
  Philip 2
GOTTWALT, Jacob 9, 13, 21
GOTTY, George 15
GOUDY, John 119(2)
GOUL, William 13
GRAFF, Henry's widow 55
  Matthias 55
  Michael 55
GRAFIUS, Abraham 2
  Martin 2
GRAFT, George 2
  John 66
  Philip 87
  Widow 3
GRAHAM, Henry 38
  James 51, 65
  John 74
  Nathan 63
  Robert 51
  William 51(2)
GRAHAMS, Thomas 113
GRAMER, Adam 15
  Andrew 15
  Helfrey 62
  Laurence 71
  Widow 59
GRASS, Andrew 9
  Jacob 119
GRATE, John 75
  Nicholas 78
GRAY, Jacob 79
  James 66
  John 79
  Samuel 83
  Thomas 83
  William 83
GRAYBILL, John 9
  Michael 3
GREAMS, Hugh 87
  Malcolm 89
  William 87
GREAVER, Werner 55
GREBER, Henry 9

GREBER, Henry 9
  Philip 9
GREEN, George 79
  John 67
  Joseph 67
GREENEWALD, Stophel 9
GREFF, Patrick 82
GREGG, John 123
GREGORY, John 96
GREY, William 38
GRIBBLE, Widow 97
GRIER, David 2, 9, 59
  Patrick 48
GRIFFEY, Jacob 67(2)
  Widow 67
GRIFFIN, Stephen 89
GRIFFITH, Abraham 21
  David 33, 55
  Evan 34(2) 37
  John 27, 32, 34(2), 96
  Widow 51
  William 51
GRIFFY, John 35
GRIM, Balzer 9
  Charles 45
  John 2
GRIME, Daniel 21
GRISS, Stephen 79
GRIST, Daniel 97
  John 67(2)
  Thomas 100
  William 94
GROFF, Henry 9
  Jacob 2, 9
GROGG, Jacob 79
GROIL, John 9
GROSS, Dewald 9
  George 45
  Henry 90
  John 44
  Michael 44
  Samuel 9
  Wendel 45
GROSSCAST, Daniel 83
  John 83
GROSSMAN, Benjamin 103
GROVE, Christian 75(2)
  Francis 27, 71, 117
  Jacob 113
  Samuel 21
GROVES, Francis 114
  Thomas 113
GRUBB, Israel 21
  Michael 21

GRUBER, Godfrey 27
GRUDY, Elisha 51
GUALT, Thomas 48
GUCKES, Harmanus 9
  John 9
GUEST, Benjamin 103
  Robert 40
GUINN, Andrew 48
  Hugh 48
  Patrick 103
  William 48(2)
GUISS, John 79
GUIST, John 38
GUMP, George 2
GUN, John 90
GUNTY, Peter 15
GURLY, Thomas 119
GWINN, William 19
GYGER, Conrad 27
  Paul 27
  Widow 27

HACKMAN, Abram 109
  Henry 78
HADAN, Samuel 87
HAFFNER, Jacob 59
HAGAN --- 63
HAGEL, John 78
HAGEY, Jacob 77
HAGGY, George 63
  John 63
HAGON, Edward 65
  Henry 63
  Patrick 63
HAHN, Jacob 9
  John 79
  Michael 3, 9
HAIL, Hugh 94
HAILEY, Patrick 55
HAIR, Daniel 117
HAIRING, Philip 55
HAKE, Andrew 9
  Conrad 3
  Jacob 9
HALEBACH, Christoph 63
HALFPENNY, Patrick 71
HALL, Edward 119
  William 119
Haller, Christian 94
  John 13
HAM, Balzer 45
  Christian 48
  Daniel 59, 62
  John 59
HAMER, Frederick 28

INDEX

HAMERSLY, Robert 22
HAMILTON, Archibald 123
  Brethy 87
  Hugh 119
  James 52
  John 38, 87, 119
  Joseph 103
  Thomas 42
  William 52(2), 52, 97
HAMMER, Baltis 51
  Peter 13
  William 51
HAMMERS, John 32
HAMMON, James 32
HAMMOND, Nathan 54
HAMMONS, James 51
HAMPTON, Robert 52
HANCOCK, James 22
HANK, Philip 16
HANNA, Alexander 94
  James 94
HANNAH, William 90
HANOVER, Christopher 71
HANSEL, Casper 79
HANSS, Andrew 45
HARBISON, John 38
HARE, James 22
HARGER, Andrew 79
HARLON, Samuel 52
HARMAN, George 71
HARNISH, John 108
  Samuel 16
HARPER, James 35
  Samuel 36, 87
HARRIS, George 22
  Thomas 61, 73
HARRISON, John 94
HART, Jacob 21
  John 119
  Widow 37
HARTFORD, Mathew 38, 114
HARTLEY, Thomas 3, 111
HARTMAN, Henry 28
  Philip 83
HARTMAN, Tobias 72
HARTZEAL, Jacob 83(2)
HARVEY, Thomas 117
HASELET, Andrew 45
  Francis 16
HASTY, Able 54
HAUCK, Barnet 75
  David 75
  Jacob 75
  Michael 75
HAUGHEELIN, Ezechiel 63

HAUK, Jacob 16
HAUSER, Peter 59
HAVERSTOCK, Andrew 55
  Conrad 57
  Philip 55
  Tobias 55
HAWK, Peter 3
HAY, John 3, 109
Hay, John & Moul,
  George 3
HAYES, George 87
  John 89
  Samuel 87(2)
HAYNES, Nicholas 9
HAYS, Jesse 22
HAZELIT, Robert 90
HEAR, Christian 63
HEARHART, Thomas 72
HEART, Andrew 103
  David 103
  Martin 71
  Widow 103
  William 103
HEARTHART, William 72
HEATON, Jeremiah 38
HECHLER, George 9
HECK, Conrad 45
HECKENDORN, John 27
HECKENTORN, Christiann 3
  John 3
HECKERT, Jacob 3
  Philip 3
  Widow 3
HECKLER, Jacob 9
HEDERICH, Jacob 59
HEFFNER, William 55
HEGY, Adam 75
  Jacob 16
HEIBELY, Jacob 71
HEIDELBACH, Jacob 22
HEIDERICK, Jacob 71
HEIDLER, John 55
HEIM, Charles 56
  Christian 56
HEINER, Henry 55
  Ludwig 55
  Yost 55
HEINS, John 75
HEINSLER, Michael 72
HEISER, Tietrich 75
HEISS, Jacob 71
HEIST, Vinald 72
HELL, Jacob 109
HELLER, Martin 55

HELLMAN, Herman 45
  Sebastian 59
HELM, Daniel 79
HELMAN, Jacob 75
  Laurence 62
HELMS, Francis 48
HELSEL, Henry 28
  Jacob 28
HELTZEL, Philip 9
  Tobias 55
HEMPHILL, James 90
HEMPTON, John 90
HENDERSON, Alexander 28
  Andrew 119
  James 113
  John 83, 113
  Samuel 94
HENDRICKS, Nathan 52
  Samuel 52
HENDRIX, Isaac 71
HENDRIXON, Adam 71
HENEISY, Widow 3
HENGST, Michael 109
HENICH, Peter 59
HENIGO, Michael 109
  Widow 111
HENISEN, John 45
HENNEY, Patrick 103(2)
HENRY, Adam 73
  Conrad 55
  Frederick 16
  George 113(2), 114
  Jacob 57, 59
  Michael 28(2)
  Nicholas 16, 36, 59, 71
  Peter 67
  Robert 3
  William 113
HENS, Jacob 99
HERBACH, Casper 67
  John 109
  Yost 9
HERBISON, Francis 107
HERBOLT, George 45
  Michael 45
  William 45
HERING, James 113
HERKINS, Daniel 28
  Daniel 28
HERLEMAN, Sebastian 59
HERMAL, Craft 28

INDEX

HERMAN, Adam 90, 100
  Christian 3, 9
  Dewalt 28
  Emanuel 9
  Frederick 90
  George 70, 83
  Jacob 9
  John 9, 32, 100
  Michael 71
HERMS, Thomas 72
HERR, Eberhard 3
  John 42
  Michael 16
HERRETTER, John 16
HERRING, Henry 16
  John 35
HERROLD, Peter 22
HERSHY, Andrew 9, 55, 73
  Joseph 55
  Peter 55
HERSINGER, Widow 28(2)
HERTLEIN, George 109
HESLET, Samuel 36
HESS, Dewalt 67
  Felty 100
  Henry 74
  Isaac 99
  John 3
  Ulrich 72
  Valentine 99
HESSLET, James 106
HETIG, Ludwig 3, 9
HETMAN, Bastian 109
HETRICK, Jacob 16
HETZER, Adam 45
HEVISEY, John 90
  Philip 90
HEWET, George 52
  Jonathan 54
  Joseph 52
HEXT, Christian 98
HICKENLOOPER, Andrew 51(2)
HICKES, George 97
  Peter 99
HIDE, Christian 9
HILDENBRAND, Casper 74
  Felix 71
  Jacob 71
  John 71
HILES, Jacob 114
HILL, James 113
  John 113, 117
  Robert 117
  William 103

HILLMAN, John 59
  Philip 59
HIMBLE, Christian 79
HIME, Francis 16, 75
HINCHEL, Anthony 59
HINCKEL, Anthony 16
  John 16, 75
  William 16
HINDLE, Adam 28(2)
  Laurence 27
  Stophel 28
HINDS, Anthony 28
  James 28
  John 22
HINEMAN, John 90
  Philip 90
HINER, John 48
HINGARDNER, Charles 22
HIRE, Charles 22
  Frederick 22
HIRSHY, Andrew 59
  Christian 16(2), 57
  John 16, 59
  Peter 59
HIVEL, Jacob 42
  Stophel 42
HIVELY, Stophel 36
HOCK, Conrad 75
  Michael 22
HOCKELBERGER, Jacob 90
HOCKMAN, Peter 79
HODGE, Samuel 90
  William 90
HOFE, Andrew 59
  Francis 59
HOFF, Henry 16
  Henry, doctor 16
HOFFACHER, Michael 16
HOFFMAN, Adam 59
  Charles 45
  Henry 22
  Jacob 45
  John 22(2)
  Michael 78
  Nicholas 45(2)
  Philip 9, 13, 45
  Stophel 94
HOFMAN, Andrew 3
  Mathias 75
  Peter 16
HOGE, John 113
HOKE, Andrew 9
  Casper 16
  Henry 78
  John 9, 59
  Peter 9

HOLAPETER, Mathias 67
HOLDER, Michael 28
HOLLAND, Henry 67
HOLLES, William 45
HOLLINGSWORTH, Jehu 21
HOLLIS, Richard 3
HOLMES, Edward 22
HOLMS, Thomas 51
HOLP, Ernst 71
HOLTON, William 113
HOLTZAPFEL, Bernard 9
HOLTZAPFL, Erasmus 9
HOLTZAPFLE, Adam 9
HOLTZBAUM --- 3
  Conrad 111
  Widow 3
HOLTZINGER, Jacob 100
HOMSPOKER, George 71
  Valentine 71
HONER, Michael 16
HONNAN, John 103
HOOBER, John 70
  Ulrich 59
HOOBLEY --- 51
HOOBMAN, Jacob 75
HOOFMAN, Christian 75
HOOKER, John 100
HOOL, Jacob 67
  John 42
  Samuel 67
HOOPS, Daniel 21
HOOVER, John 79
  Martin 43
HOPE, Adam 119
  Augustus 49
HOPKIN, Levins 38
HOPPEL, George 94
HOPSON, Francis 52
  Joseph 52
HORN, Frederick 9
  Henry 75
HORNER, David 48
  Robert 48(2)
HORSEMAN, Ebenezer 67
HORSMAN, Abram 100
HOSACK, Henry 119
  John 119(2)
  Michael 119
HOSE, Philip 109
HOSELER, Michael 59
HOSHBURN, Alexander 71
HOSLER, Joseph 59
HOSS, John 45
HOSSLER, Christian 59

INDEX

HOSTETTER, Christian 100
  Francis 75
  Henry 75
HOUCK, George 79
HOUGHDELIN, Abraham 65
  William 49
HOULSWORTH, Joseph 89
  Samuel 87
HOUREY, Jacob 55
HOUSE, Benjamin 22
  Michael 77
HOUSEHOLDER, Henry 34
  Jacob 34
HOUSEMAN Frederick 3
  Christian 28
  Jacob 28
HOUSER, John 59
HOUSIL, Frederick 109
  Peter 83
HOUTS, John 63
  Stophel 83
HOVEIS, Frederick 71
HOVER, John 94
HOWE, John 100
  William 67
HOWEL, Jehemiah 100
HOWER, William 109
HOWLAY, William 107
HOY, Charles 33
HOYER, George 42
  Jacob 42
HUBBERT, Adam 16
HUBER, Conrad 45
  George 59
  John 70
  Martin 42
HUCKSTATER, Ulrich 79
HUDSON, Mathew 103
HUFF, Adam 21
  Daniel 22
  Peter 21
HUFT, Jacob 9
  Widow 9
HUGH'S, Matson 116
HUGHES, Barnabas 103
  Thomas 83
HUGHS, Barney 49
  Daniel 49
  David 119
  Francis 119
  John 49, 119
  Walter 21
  Widow 113
  William 3
HULAND, Marks 21

HULL, Abraham 83
  Andrew 19
  Henry 90
  Isaac 78
  John 83
  Philip 83
HUMBEL, Garret 22
HUMES, Solomon 75
HUMMEL, Frederick 21
HUMRICHHAUSER, John 9
HUMS, Charles 113
HUNSINGER, Simon 42
  William 42
HUNT, Edward 90, 99
  John 100
  Samuel 90
HUNTER, Alexander 49
  James 49
  John 63
  Joseph 21, 49
  Samuel 48
  William 22(2)
HUPPERT, Adam 19
  Catharine 63
HUSSEY, Christopher 52
HUTCHESON, James 35, 49, 87
  Robert 49
HUTCHINSON, John 107
  Joseph 119
HUTT, Nicholas 83
HUTTON, Elizabeth 100
  James 100
  John 32, 52
  Joseph 21
  Joshua 9
  Leonard 100
  Levy 51
  William 51
HUZZEY, George 21
  Jediah 93
HUZZY, Jediah 92
  Riccord 70
HYKESS, George 94(2)
HYMES John 78

ICKES, Henry 83
  John 16
  Nicholas 83
  Peter 83
ILGENFRITZ, Christian 3
IMMEL, John 109
IMSELLER, Jacob 30
IMSWELLER, Peter 30

INNERS, Jacob 109
IPE, Jacob 94
IRICH, Bastian 109
IRION, Jacob 2
IRONS, Thomas 3
IRWIN, Arthur 22
  George 3, 10
  John 90
  Widow 119
ISAAC, John 42
ISENHAUER, Leonard 42

JACK, Andrew 103
  James 103
  William 107
JACKSON, Joseph 113
JACOB, George 9, 14
  John 13
  Jonathan 9, 13
JACOBS, George 56
JAMES, Alexander 117
  John 87
JAMESON, David 3, 34, 109
  Enos 22
  Thomas 36
  Widow 90
  William 36
JEFFERIES, John 49
JEFFERYS, Joseph 109
JENKINS, David 22
  Moses 119
  Walter 119
JENNINGS, Thomas 22
JOB, John 32
JOHN, Abel 52
  Butch 52
  Ebenezer 22
  Evan 22
  Jacob 10
  John 30, 99
  Joseph 52
  Thomas 91
JOHNSON, Andrew 119
  Bernard 119
  Charles 38
  James 87, 119
  John 119
  Thomas 63, 103, 119
  Widow 111
  William 87, 90, 91
JOHNSTON, Ephraim 52
  Jacob 16, 40, 75(2)
  James 22, 49
  John 22, 52

INDEX

Stephen 22
Thomas 22, 94, 113
William 109, 113, 119
JOLLY, James 113
JONAS, Daniel 59
JONES, Amos 67
  Benjamin 41
  David 22
  Edward 22(2)
  Elijah 101
  Francis 10
  Henry 87
  Isaac 3, 38
  Jacob 100
  James 109
  John 3, 13, 16, 67
  Richard 30
  Robert 10
  Samuel 22
  Theophilus 38
JORDAN, David 67
  Jarman 67
  John 42, 43
  Lewis 67
JOSEPH, John 56
JULIUS, Jacob 45
  Philip 48

KABB, Martin 10
KALTRIDER, George 61
KAR, James 120
KARCH, Andrew 16
KARL, George 75
  Michael 17
KARR, Joshua 63(2)
KAUFELDER --- 16
KAUFFELT, Jacob 3
KAUFFMAN, Conrad 111
  Henry 109
  John 10
  Solomon 109
KAUFMAN, --- 112
  John 10
  Widow 111
KAURTS, Martin 38
KAYES, John 87
KAYLER, Daniel 109
KEAGY, Jacob 75
  John 75
KECHERIES, Christian 31
KEEFER, Frederick 80
  Henry 109
KEENER, Geo'r. 117
KEEPERS, Joseph 56
KEFFER, John 111

KEGEREIS, Christian 109
KEHLER, Michael 75
KEIFFER, Henry 10
  Widown 3
KEINER, George 109
KEISER, George 31
KEITH --- 114
  Ludwig 114
KELL, Christian 56
  John 56
KELLER, Abraham 62
  George 59(2)
  Jacob 10, 59, 62, 109
  John 75, 79
  Michael 3, 10
  Wendel 75
KELLEY, Francis 73
  James 94
  John 117
  Thomas 114
KELLOUGH, John 120
KELLY, James 38, 107
  Thomas 16
  William 67
KEMERLY, Christian 17
KEMP, Christopher 56
KENNEDY, David 34, 103
  Hugh 67
  James 67
  John 93
  William 67
KENNY, Christopher 107
KENWORTHY, Widow 100
KEPLER, Samuel 22
  Widow 86
KEPLEY, Tobias 84
KEPPELE, Henry 3
KEPPLER, Jacob 22
KERBOUGH, George 83(2)
  Jacob 80
  John 83
  Martin 79
  Nicholas 83
KERHARD, Yost 109
KERKER, Jacob 59
KERN, Jacob 3, 10
  Michael 22(2)
  Widow 109
KERR, Andrew 107
  George 103
  James 65
  John 17, 94(2), 103
  Thomas 103
  William 103(2)

KERSEY, William 4
KERVER, Casper 56
KESEY, John 34
KESHONER, David 119
  John 119
KESSLER, Henry 59
  Michael 59
KIBINGER, Peter 16
KIEF, David 83
KIEFABER, Conrad 16
  Nicholas 16
KIEGLER, Cornelius 65
KILL, Samuel 123
KILLCANON, John 59
KILLGROVE, Mathew 113
KILLPATRICK, William 114
KIMMEL --- 13
  Anthony 45
KINCADE, Samuel 38
KINCAID, Michael 103
  Robert 103
KINDICH, Henry 42
KINDLEIN, John 59
KINER, Adam 114
KINEY, Henry 80
  John 80
KING, Abraham 79
  Charles 42
  Christopher 94
  Elias 83
  Esaiah 91
  George 79
  Godfrey 10
  Henry 3
  Jane 119
  John 32
  Michael 67, 91
  Nicholas 91
  Patrick 114
  Philip Jacob 3, 10
  Thomas 91
  William 32, 87
KINKADE, Thomas 87
KINSOR, George 91
KINT, Christian 79
  Jacob 81
KIPP, John 63
KIRCHHARD John 112
  Widow 111
KIRK, David 96
  Ezechiel 22
  Jacob 22
  Jonathan 22
  Thomas 67
  Timothy 22(2)
  William 22

INDEX

KIRKPATRICK, Andrew 107
  William 103, 107
KIRKS, James 113
  John 113
KIRKWOOD, John 113
  Thomas 113
KIRSH, Jacob 59
KISSINGER, Conrad 109
KISTER, George 22
  Henry 22
KITCH, John 10
KITHCART, Joseph 38
KITZMILLER, George 17
  Jacob 79
  John 17, 77
KLAR, Simon 75
KLATFELTER, Felix 59
  Henry 61
  Michael 59
KLECKLER, John 14
KLEIN, Henry 19, 109
  Jacob 75
  John 19
  Michael 14
  William 75
KLEINDIENST, David 59
  Godfrey 59
KLEINPETER, Adam 57
  Rudolph 56, 57
KLEMMER, George 79
  Laurence 80
  Valentine 79
KLIN, John 62
KLINE, Frederick 80
  Gerlach 84
  Henry 16, 80
  Ludwig 80(2)
KLINGMAN, Frederick 14
  George 10
  Jacob 10
  Stophell 10
KLOY, Jacob 75
KLUNK, Martin 83
  Peter 83
KNAB, Casper 10, 13
  Jacob 13
KNERTZER, Balzer 22
KNEYER, Leonard 59
KNOP, Valentine 91
KNOUS, John 79
KNOUSE, Francis 52
KNOX, James 32
  Samuel 103
KOBB, Widow 10
KOBER, Andrew 45

KOCH, Andrew 16
  George 16
  Jacob 109, 112
KOCHENAUER, Jacob 16
KOCHENOUR, Jacob 48
KOCHINOWER, Joseph 45
KOCK, George 16
  Peter 16
KOHLER, Andrew 10
  Balser 10
  Joseph 13
  Valentine 13
KOLMAN, Valentine 10
KONN, George 45
KONRAD, George 56
KOOCH, George 45
  John 48
KOOLER, Michael 79
KOONTZ, George 79
KOPPENHAVER, Simon 10, 13
KOPPENHEFER, Michael 75
KORELL, Jacob 109
KORPMAN--Schill, John 3
KOUNTZ, Michael 80
KOUSLER, Bernhart 109
  John 109
KRABILL, John 84
KRAFT, Jacob 16
  John 75
  Joseph 3
  Ludwig 3
KRANTZ, George 10
  Valentine 3, 10, 109
KRAYBILL, Joseph 10
KREBER, Adam 3, 16
  Gabriel 16
  Gerhard 16
  Henry 3
  John 7
  Martin 4
  Philip 3
KREBS, George 112
  Peter 79
KREENEWALT, Henry 4
KREISS, Jacob 59
KREMER, Helfrich 16
KREPS, George 61
  Ludwig 59
KREPS, Peter 59
KRIFFEY, Patrick 80

KRIM, John 83
  Peter 109
  Philip 109(2)
KROH, John 16
KROLL, John 59
KRON, Philip 45
KRONBACH, Jacob 45
KRONE, Laurence 56
KRUGENER, John 19
KRUM, Peter 16
  George 83
KUHN, Henry 59
  Peter 13
  Widow 86
KULP, Valentine 56
KUNCKEL, Adam 91
  Balzer 42
  Christian 42
  Godlieb 42
  John 3
  John 3
KUNTZ, Abraham 59
  Francis 3, 109
  Michael 80
  Peter 59
  Philip 81
  Samuel 4
  William 109
KURTZ, Conrad 71
  Frederick 75
  John 13
  Michael 109
  Nicholas 107
  Peter 3
KYSER, Jacob 59
  Teeter 94

LACHY, George 64
LACKY, Alexander 65
  George 63
LAIRD, Hannah 120
  Hugh 22
  James 114
  John 34
  William 120
LAMBERD, Michael 28
LAMBERT, Casper 45
  Jacob 45
LAMPERT, Frederick 28
LAMUTH, Daniel 76
  Francis 57
  John 56, 78
LANDIS, Christian 28(2)
  John 28
  Samuel 28(2)
  Stephen 109

INDEX

LANDMESSER, Jacob 72
LANE, John 56, 84
  Peter 84
LANGWORTHY, Mr. 4
LANIUS, Henry 42
  Jacob 42
  William 4
LANTZ, Andrew 28
  John 74
  Philip 28
LAREW, Francis 92
LARIMOR, Hugh 32
LARIMORE, John 84
LARKIN, George 67
LARMOR, John 49(2)
  Thomas 49
LASH, Henry 80
LATHAN, David 33
LATIMORE, George 38
  James 40
LATSH, Martin 80
LATSHAR, John 4
LATSHAW, Isaac 91
  Joseph 52
  Peter 67
LATTA, Thomas 103, 120(2)
LAU, Michael 10
  Philip 10
LAUCH, Philip 72
LAUDEBACH, Henry 63
LAUER, Mathias 17
LAUGHLIN, William 97
LAUMAN, Christopher 4
  Widow 4
LAUMASTER, Frederick 4
LAURENCE, Detter 90
LAUTEMAN, Peter 76
LAW, Andrew 60
  George 60
  Michael 60
  Peter 60
  Philip 60
  Thomas 104
LAWRENCE, Ephraim 52
  Joseph 52
LAWSON, David 49
  Isaac 49
  John 72
  Robert 49
  Widow 60
LAZIER, Nicholas 104
LEAKNER, John 80
LEAMAN, Christian 42

LEAMER, John 67, 95
  William 95
LEAPER, Alexander 114
  James 34, 114
  Samuel 114
LEAPHARD, John 28
LEAR, Conrad 28
  Valentine 60
LEARD, James 41
LEAS, Alexander 56
  Daniel 91
  John 91(2)
  Leonard 91(2)
  Samuel 91
  Stephen 91
LEATHER, Frederick 45(2)
  Jacob 4
LEATHERMAN, Conrad 4, 111
  Widow 4
LEBOW, Abraham 80
LECHNER, Michael 60
LECHRON, Leonard 10, 14
LEECH, Henry 32, 95
  James 32
  Robert 32
  Thomas 67
LEEDY, Jacob 42
  Samuel 4
LEEPER, Samuel 116
LEFEVER, George 28
  Jacob 109
LEFLER, George Lewis 4, 10
LEH, George 109
LEHMAN, Jacob 109
  Joachim 109
  Peter 112
  William 114
LEIB, Ulry 73
LEIDIG, Michael 45
LEINBACH, Christian 56
LEINBAUCH, Conrad 45
  Felix 45
LEIP, Christian 10
LEISNER, Conrad 109
LEISSER, John 4
LEITNER, Adam 4
  George 80
  Naatz 10
  Nathaniel 4
  William 80
LEMMON, John 38

LENEY, Joseph 52
LENHARD, Frederick 10
  George 22
  Godfrey 4
LEONARD, Charles 60
  John 84
LEONHART, Stophel 45
  William 45
LEREW, George 101
  Jacob 101
LERU, Francis 93
LESHEY, Jacob 56
LESHY, Jacob 60
LESSLY, Hannah 120
  John 120
  Samuel 120
LEVER, Conrad 28
  Jacob 28
  John 28
  Nicholas 28
LEVERKNIGHT, Frederick 28
LEVINSTON, John 38
LEWDIN, John 35
LEWIS, David 95
  Ellis 23
  Ely 23
  John 26, 84
  Lewis 26, 97
  Robert 13, 26
  Samuel, renter 22
  William 23
LEYER, Martin 17
LEYSER, George 45
LICE, Peter 72
LICHEY, John 91
LICHTENBERGER, Casper 10
  George Adam 13
  George 10
  Killian 10
LIEBHART, Henry 42
  Valentine 42
LIFE, Christian 112
  Martin 10
LIGGET, James 59
  William 37(2)
LIGGETT, James 59
LIGGIT, Alexander 33
  George 28
  Widow 28
  William 28
LIGGITT, Joseph 28
LIGHT, Jacob 52
LIGHTNER, James 97
  William 101

INDEX

LILLEY, John 63
  Joseph 77, 84
  Thomas 84
LILLY, Thomas 63
LINCEY, James 52
LIND, Peter 13
LINDSAY, James 63
  John 64
  Joseph 64
  William 120
LINDY, John 4
LINEFELTER, Jacob 84
LINER, Henry 17(2)
LINGHEART, Bernhard 104
LINGLE, Nicholas 17
LININGER, George 17, 45
LINN, Adam 120
  Andrew 120
  David 120
  John 120
  Samuel 49
  William 49
LINTILL, William 107
LISCHY, Henry 17
LIST, George 114
LITTEN, Thomas 36
LITTLE, Andrew 49
  Casper 49
  David 49, 104
  George 49
  Henry 49(2)
  Jacob 49
  John 63
  Widow 114
LIVINGSTON, Adam 87
  George 10
  James 95
  John 87(2)
  Michael 10
LOAG, Hugh 104
LOBACH, Abraham 95
  Daniel 95
LOBACK, Andrew 101
LOCKART, Moses 63
LOCKHEAD, John 38
LOG, James 114
LOGAN, Hugh 76
  James 22
  John 23, 95
LOGE, Adam 88
LOHMAN, Atony 60
LOMASK, Conrad 52

LONG, Adam 84
  Conrad 17
  Frederick 17
  George 109
  Henry 38, 56, 72
  Jacob 17, 57
  John 17, 19, 52, 109
  Jonathan 120
  Martin 17
  Michael 109
  Peter 10
  Philip 80
  Robert 120
  Widow 10
  William 4, 114
LOOKUP, Conrad 28, 114
LORE, Andrew 80
LORICK, Jacob 60
LOSTETTER, Jacob 77
LOTTMAN, George 4
LOVE, James 22, 104
  John 4
  Samuel 22
  William 4, 23
LOWBRIDGE, Joseph 72
LOWE, David 80
  John 72
  Joshua 72
LOWER, Jacob 45
LOWERY, William 88
LOWICK, Philip 91
LOWREY, Conrad 33
LUCKY, James 107
LUDWIG, Charles 7
LUKENBACH, Henry 81
LUKENS, Heres 97
  Jesse 101
LUSK, John 114
LUTZ, Christian 28
  Widow 28, 76
LYON, Hugh 120
  James 88

MACHLIN, Alexander 52
MACKEY, James 84
MACKLIN, Widow 68
  William 68
MAGINTY, Patrick 84
MAHOLD, George 84
MAHOLLEN, William 123
MAILS, George 101
  Samuel 101
MAJOR, John 39
MALAUN, Mathias 91
MANCOM, Patrick 88

MANDLE, William 39
MANDORF, John 101
MANESS, Charles 29
MANFORD, Francis 49
  Peter 49
MANIFOLD, Benjamin 33
  Edward 39
  Joseph 35, 39
MANSBERGER, George 23
  John 23
MANSON, David 28
MANTEETH, Daniel 88
  John 84
  John 84
MANTLE, George 42
MARCH, George 46
  Jacob 45
MARCHEL, Henry 60
MARICKEL, Henry 72
MARKS, Gastner 31
  Jacob 110
  Joseph 42
MARLAIN, John 115
  William 115
MARROW, Samuel 88
MARSDEN, James 65
  Mathew 65
MARSDILL, Edward 63
MARSHAL, James 104, 107
MARSHALL, Francis 84(2)
  Isaac 35
  James 72, 104, 123
  John 123
  Paul 107
  Peter 84
  Samuel 121
  William 120, 123
MARTIN, Andrew 23, 76
  Daniel 89
  David 46
  Henry 17
  Robert 104(3), 114
  Samuel 36, 114
  Thomas 121(2)
  William 4
MARTORF, Conrad 45
MARX, Jacob 56
MASH, Gravener 68
  John 67
  Jonathan 67
MASK, Jonathan 68
  Peter 68
MASTERS, George 121

INDEX

MATE, Casper 42
  George 32
  John 42(2)
  William 32
MATHEW, George 17
MATHEWS, Samuel 97
  Thomas 43
  William 23, 114
MATHIAS, Henry 23
  Widow 17
MATSON, Richard 68
  Thomas 39
MATTER, George 19
MATZ, Jacob 60
MAUGHLIN, Hugh 68
  Samuel 67
  William 67
MAUL, George 4
  Philip 17
MAULSBACK, Peter 57
MAULSBY, David 4
  Rosannah 23
  William 23
MAURER, Herman 46
MAXFIELD, George 28
MAXWEL, Henry 32
  James 32(2)
  John 32(2)
MAXWELL, Alexander 121
  Conrad 23
  John 23, 63
  Patrick 115
  William 115
MAY, Daniel 46
  Jacob 101
  John 45, 68
MAYER, Frederick 46
  Jacob 46
  Peter 45
MAYRICE, George 80
MAYS, Charles 52, 104
  Samuel 52
  William 53
McADAM, David 107
McADAMS, Gilbert 104
  Thomas 23
McAFFET, John 121
McALLISTER, Abdil 63, 78
  James 49, 104
  John 64
McALLISTERS, James 34
  John 46
McANULTY, Charles 49

McBRIDE, Daniel 49
  John 4, 120(2)
  William 52, 107
McBRIER, James 107
McBROOM, William 121
McCALL, John 104, 114
  Mathew 115
  Robert 4
  Thomas 32
  William 115
McCALLEY, Andrew 91
  John 91
McCALLISTER, John 4
  Richard 76
McCALLS, John 114
McCALMAND, Jane 4
McCANCE, Benjamin 88
  David 88(2)
McCANDLESS, James 39
  John 117
  William 39
McCANS, George 88, 89
  John 89
  William 89
McCARLEY, John 121
McCARROL, Thomas 41
McCARTER, Alexander 63
McCASKEY, William 39
McCASLIN, Thomas 52
McCAY, William 104
McCHERRY, Barnabas 104
  Edward 80
  John 89
  Patrick 63, 76, 80
McCLARY, John 35
McCLEAN, Alexander 104
  Archibald 4, 77
  James 76
  John 52
  Moses 121
  William 104
McCLEARY, George 53
  James 52
  Michael 120
  Thomas 120
  William 39
McCLEAVE, Robert 53
McCLELLAN, David 104
  Jacob 120
  John 120
  Thomas 104
  William 67, 120, 121
McCLENAN, Dav'd. 84
McCLINTACK, Daniel 107

McCLORGE, Hugh 34
  Mark 35, 37
  Widow 114
  William 37, 114
McCLURE, Andrew 117
  James 121
  John 63, 88, 89, 123
McCLURE, Martin 121
  Samuel 95
  Thomas 84
  William 121
McCOLLOUGH, Alexander 114
  James 39
  John 35
  Peter 39
  Robert 65
  William 115
McCOLOUGH, Widow 104
McCOMB, George 29
McCOMBS, George 88
McCOMMICK, John 121
McCONAUGHY, John 120
McCONKEY, Alexander 4
McCONNELL, James 23
  Robert 23
McCONOUGHY, David 52
  Robert 52
  Samuel 52
McCORCKEL, James 91
  Robert 91
McCORD, James 39
McCORMICK, John 120
McCOY, John 29
  Nathaniel 117
  Robert 121
McCRACKEN, James 65
McCREA, David 39
McCREADY, John 26
McCREARY, John 53, 65
  Jonathan 23
  Thomas 64
  William 120
McCREE, Widow 107
McCREERY, Amos 64
  John 64
  Widow 49
McCRERY, William 88
McCRUE, Nathan 32
McCULLOUGH, George 117
  William 88
McCUNE, Thomas 49(2)

INDEX

McCURDY, Daniel 95
  Hugh 121
  John 91
  Robert 84, 92, 93, 121
  Samuel 63
McCURLEY, Patrick 39
McCURLY, Robert 4
McCUSH, James 88
  Samuel 49, 121
  Widow 88
McCUTCHEN, James 63
McDEARMOND, William 23
McDONNALD, John 72
McDONNEL, James 34
McDONNELL, Richard 36
McDOWEL, William 120(2)
McDOWL, John 115
McELHANNON, John 115
McELHENNY, James 49
  Robert 80, 88
  Samuel 49
  William 49, 53
McELROY, James 29, 104
  Samuel 68
McELVAIN, Andrew 63
  John 63
  Moses 63
  William 64
McELVAY, William 114
McELWAIN, Andrew 84
McELWAY, Charles 67
  James 68
  Samuel 67
McENTIRE, Robert 53
McFADEN, Hugh 39
  Samuel 41
McFARLAND, James 91
  Thomas 91
  William 91
McFARLEN, Thomas 120
McFARLIN, John 88
  Thomas 88
McFEE, Michael 114
McFERRIN, John 120(2)
  William 120
McFERRON, Andrew 52
McGARROUGH, Henry 29
McGAUGHEY, Alex'r. 104
  James 104, 120
  Thomas 104
McGAVOCK, James 29
McGAW, John 33
McGEE, Barnet 88
  James 117
  Patrick 115
  Robert 117

McGIHAN, Daniel 84
McGIMSY, Robert 104
McGINLEY, John 104
  Widow 104
McGINNES, Patrick 89
McGINNIS, Samuel 23
McGLAUGHLEN, Owens 28
McGLAUGHLIN, James 35
  John 120
McGOMERY, Thomas 96
McGONE, William 121
McGOWAN, Rob't 49
McGowan, Samuel 117
  Thomas 114
  Widow 49
  William 49
McGOWN, Isaac 117
McGRAIL, James 52
  Owen 52
  William 52
McGRAW, William 89
McGREW, Alexander 32
  Archbald 101
  Finley 32
  James 52, 101
McGrew, James 52, 101
  John 97
  Peter 32
  Robert 88
McGUFFEN, James 80
McGUFFY, Joseph 64
  William 115
McGURHAN, John 107
McHARTER, Moses 115
McHENRY, Daniel 23
McHOLLAND, John 29
McINTIRE, Alexander 84
McISAAC, Isaac 35
McKAIN, Hugh 121
  Robert 121
McKATRICK, John 35
McKEE, Joseph 104
  Thomas 107
McKELLIP, John 49
McKENNEY, Andrew 49
  John 49
  Robert 49
McKIESH, George 23
McKINDLEY, Benjamin 104
McKINDLY, James 107
  William 104
McKINLEY, Benjamin 120
  Isaac 52
  John 120
  Stephen 115

McKINNEY, William 120
McKINSTRY, James 120
McKISSION, Alexander 104
McKISSOCK, John 117
  Widow 115
McKISSON, James 104(2)
  John 28
  William 104
McKITRICK, Alexander 4
McKNIGHT, John 32
McLAUGHLIN, James 4
  William 114
McMACHAN, James 104
McMACING, Patrick 64
McMAHONEY, John 72
McMASTER, Gilbert 84
  James 84(2)
  John 23
McMAUGHAN, James 49
McMICHAEL, Samuel 115
McMILLIAN, William 104
McMORRISON, Hans 88
McMULLEN, George 39, 95
  Hugh 95
  James 39
  John 4, 39, 67, 123, 124
  Mathew 68
  Michael 40
  Samuel 68, 121
  Thomas 67, 124
  William 67
McMULLIN, George 67
  James 36, 39
McMUN, William 120
McMUNN, William 4
McNARE, Alexander 104
  Samuel 104
McNAUGHT, James 52
  Joseph 52
  William 52
McNAY, Thomas 115
McNEA, John 104(2)
McNEALY, William 23
McNEARY, David 115
  James 29
McNEARY, John 115
McNEES, Isaiah 23
McNICHOL, James 95
  Rebecca 84
McNIGHT, James 121
  Thomas 32, 65
McNULLEN, Robert 117

INDEX

McNUTT, Francis 52
  Mathew 120
  Robert 120
  Thomas 121
  Widow 52
McORR, John 107
McPEAK, Daniel 120(2)
  James 121
  John 120
  William 120
McPHERSON, Frederick 39, 115
  John 4
  Robert 121(2)
  William 121
McQUAY, Thomas 115
McQUIRE, Nathan 23
McQUOWN, David 54, 68
  John 52
  Lawrence 53
  Thomas 53
  William 53
McSWINE, James 35, 72
McTAGGART, James 84
  John 84
McTINEY, Thomas 104
McVAY, William 104
McWILLIAMS, Alexander 115
  James 88
  John 89, 120
MEADS, John 35
MEALS, Jacob 52
MEASE, John 56
MEASEBOUGH, George 68
MEEM, John 4
MEENICH, Jacob 32(2)
MEFFORD, John 80
MEHL, Frederick 4
MELAUN, John 91
MELHORN, Andrew 46
  James 114
  Michael 10
  Simon 76(2)
MELLINGER, David 42
MENEIGH, Philip 101
MENGES, George 13
  Peter 10
MERCER, Peregin 88
MEREDITH, Francis 104
  Rees 15
MESSEMER, Yoder 17
MESSENKOP, Jacob 45
MESSERLY, Abraham 48
  Daniel 45

MESSERSMITH, George 95
  Widow 111
METZGER, George 10
  Paul 76
METZLER, Thomas 46
MEYER, Adolph 80
  Andrew 72
  Christian 72
  David 91
  Frederick 17, 60
  George 17, 23, 72
  Henry 110
  Jacob 72, 109
  John 56, 60, 72, 80, 112
  Martin 72
  Nicholas 45
  Philip 56, 76
  Simon 45
MEYERS, Catharine 23
MEYREISS, John 74
MICHAEL, Adam 46
  Jacob 4, 49, 110(2), 112
  Nicholas 46
  Wendel 111
  Wilhelm 26
  William 17, 23
MICHLEY, Christian 72
MICKEL, John 35
  Thomas 36
MICKLE, Elijah 53
  John 52
  Samuel 32
MIDDLEHAUF, Leonard 76
MILEY, Jacob 91
  John 91
MILHIME, Christian 76
MILHOFF, Philip 29
MILLEKAN, Mark 121
MILLER, Abraham 4, 68
  Adam 14, 23
  Andrew 23, 45, 60, 72
  Barnet 46
  Casper 4
  Conrad 80
  Daniel 33, 84
  Edward 17
  Francis Jacob 4, 110
  Frederick 72(2)
  George 10, 23, 28, 48, 60, 62, 84, 95
  Henry 4, 19, 23, 29, 48, 68, 73, 74, 80

  Herman 72
  Jacob 4, 46, 48, 62, 80, 84, 110
  James 17, 49, 63, 107
  John 10, 35, 45, 72(2), 76, 104, 111, 112
  Ludwig 49, 80
  Martin 72
  Mathias 10
  Michael 28, 42, 48, 97
  Nicholas 49, 80(2)
  Paul 76
  Peter 32, 60
  Philip 10, 17, 95
  Richard 107
  Robert 23(2), 39
  Rudy 29
  Samuel 10, 23, 67
  Tobias 72
  Widow 60
  William 4, 36, 107, 109
MILLHIME, Christian 77
MILLHOUSE, Peter 68
MILLICHAN, William 41
MILLIGAN, James 39
  Mark 121
MILLS, James 23, 89
  John 23
  William 95
MINCH, Daniel 95
MINEHART, Peter 67, 91
  Philip 67
MING, Ulrich 4
MITCHEL, Andrew 99
  George 39(2)
  John 35
  William 95
MITCHELL, John 101
MITTMAN, Charles 45
MIXEL, Peter 65
MOCK, George 4
MODAN, John 91
MODARE, George 80
MODDY, Samuel 67
MOHLER, Henry 84
MOHR, Nicholas 10
MOLL, Henry 97
MOLLISON, Samuel 42
MONEY, John 53
MONFORD, John 88
MONFORT, James 63
  Laurence 88

INDEX

MONTGOMERY, David 107
  John 35, 53
  Nathan 104
  Robert 101
MOOBERRY, Robert 39
MOODY, John 68
  Samuel 88
MOOR, John 104
MOORE, Alexander 33
  Anthony 23
  David 120
  Henry 80
  Hugh 95
  James 52, 72, 95, 124
  John 104
  Peter 56
  Robert 53
  Samuel 36, 104(2)
  Widow 4, 46, 53
  William 53, 97, 120
MOOREHEAD, James 97
MORDACH, Mathew 32
  Robert 32
MORGAN, Isaac 95
  John 42
  Thomas 23
MORNINGSTAR, John 63
  Philip 17
MORRIS, --- 39
  Israel 35
  John 4
  Joseph 46
  Thomas 39
MORRISON, Hugh 52, 89
  James 91
  John 99, 115
  Joseph 121
  Michael 36
  Robert 121
  William 68, 114(2)
MORROW, George 28
  James 97
  Joseph 29
  William 36, 120
MORTON, John 52, 63
MOSE, Jacob 42
MOSER, Abraham 29
MOSSELBACH, John 42
MOSSER, Christian 42
  Daniel 112
  Jacob 110
  Michael 42, 110(2)
  Samuel 36, 110(2)
MOTTS, Henry 74
MOUDY, Balzer 95

MOURER, John 60
MOUSE, George 63
  Ludwig 63
MOWER, Andrew 84
MOYER, Frederick 84
  John 56
  Michael 74
MUGGROVE, Edward 109
MUHLHEIM, George 17
MULL, Henry 101
MULLEN, John 84
  Patrick 23
MUMMERT, John 56
  Matthias 56
  Richard 56, 58
  William 56
MUMPER, Michael. 95
MUNDLE, John 67
MUNDORF, Peter 5
MUPHET, James 35
MURDY, Rev'd. 124
MURPHY, Hugh 120, 121
  Isaac 23
  James 29
  John 115, 120, 123
MURRAY, Duncan 104
  James 110
  John 104(2)
  Robert 120
MUSHRUSH, Jacob 17
MYAR, Peter 26
MYER, Jacob 23
  John 4, 13, 17, 28, 80, 91
  Joseph 4
  Martin 111
  Michael 74
  Peter 23
  Widow 4
MYERS, Christian 91
  Frederick 48, 97
  George 67
  Henry 28, 49, 99
  Jacob 29(2), 99
  John 67, 68, 91, 123
  Ludwig 91, 99
  Martin 63
  Michael 63
  Nicholas 91(3), 101
  Peter 67

NAAS, Michael 17
NAGLE, John 56
NAILER, Elizabeth 23

NEAF, Abraham 46
  Jacob 29
  John 110
  Ulrich 110
NEAL, John 39
NEALE, Thomas 39
NEBBINGER, George 110
  Widow 5
NEBENGER, John 10
NEBINGER, George 5
NEBITT, John 68(2)
NEEL, Samuel 32
NEELY, John 91, 97
  Jonathan 32, 91
  Samuel 32
  Thomas 64, 65, 91, 97
  Widow 32
  William 32
NEFF, Daniel 43
  George 112
  Henry 60
  Michael 32
NEISS, Michael 74
NELL, Henry 91
NELLY, Joseph 107
NELSON, James 68
  John 34, 56
  Lazarus 68
  Robert 68
  Samuel 68, 95, 115
  Thomas 68
  William 46
NERBASS, Francis 46
NESBITT, Alexander 68
NESS, George 76
  Henry 10
  Jacob 10, 72
  Mathias 76
NESSLEY, Samuel 95
NESSLY, John 95
NEUCOMER, Christian 68
  George 68
NEUMAN, David 76
NEVETT, William 68
NEWCOMER, Abraham 114
  Christopher 43(2)
  Jacob 17
  Ulrich 43(2)
NEWEL, Andrew 53, 122
  John 122
NEWLAND, Elijah 53
  William 53
NEWMAN, Michael 17
  Nicholas 17
NEYCOMER, Henry 60

INDEX

NEYMAN, George 60
  Jacob 5
NIBBLE, John 5
NICHMAN, John 91
NICHOL, George 39
  Joseph 122
NICHOLS, John 23
NICHOLSON, James 29
NICKLE, James 101
NISLEY, Anthony 68(2)
  John 68
NOASER, Jacob 76
NOBLET and ARMOR 23
NOBLET, Agnes 23
NOEL, Jacob 84
  Widow 84
NOIL, Daniel 122
NOLAND, Joseph 34
NOLL, George 84(3)
  Jacob 60
  Yost 84
NORBURY, Jacob 23
NORRIS, William 5
NORTHEN, Isaac 46
NOSSETT, Peter 23
NUNEMACHER, Godlieb 19
NUNEMAKER, Solomon 72
NUNNEMACHER, Jacob 17
NUNNEMAKER, Abraham 5
  Andrew 5
NUSS, Jacob 17, 72

OAR, Alexander 122
  Charles, Ju'r 65
  Patrick 123
  Robert 122
OASON, George 115
OBERDIER, John 46
  Ludwig 17
OBERDLER, Philip 110
OBERDORF, George 29
OBLENUS, John 91
OBOLD, Bastion 76
  Joseph 76
OCKER, Henry 101
ODERMAN, George 11
ODEWALT, Jacob 115
OHAIL, Edward 96
  John 96
OHARA, John 39
OHIMBOUGH, Antony 91
  John 91(2)
OLDHAM, Thomas 13
OLDSHOE, John 101
OLLINGER, Peter 60

OLP, John 74
OLSHOSE, John 95
OLVERT, Andrew 95
OPP, Jacob 46
  Peter 46
ORBAN, John 46
ORBISON, Thomas 49
ORENDORF, Henry 95
ORNT, Jacob 123
ORR, Arthur 97
  Author 32
  James 104
  John 35, 107
  Robert 64
  William 64, 105(2)
ORSAN, George 91
  William 91
ORT, Henry 10
ORTMAN, John 60
OSBURN, Alexander 33
OTS, Laurence 95
OTT, John 60
OTTINGER, Henry 10
  Jacob 11(2)
  Peter 11
OTZ, Daniel 80
OULWILER, Jacob 29
OVERHULSER, John 91
OVERMILLER, Martin 36
OWENS, John 76
  Roberts 76
  Thomas 5, 76
  William 76, 84, 115
OWINGS, Joshua 78
OYLER, Felty 53(2)
  Jacob 122
OYSTER, George 53
  Jacob 84

PAGE, Nathaniel 29
PAIN, Elizabeth 34
PAINTER, Peter 92
PALLEY, Andrew 56
PANTON, David 65
PARK, William 95
PARKER, James 115
  John 39
  Moses 68
PARKHILL, David 122
PARKINSON, James 68
PARKS, James 115
  John 39, 64
  Robert 68
PARR, John 80

PARSIL, Peter 85
  Richard 85(2)
  Rudolph 85
PARSILL, Isaac 85
PATTERSON, David 117
  Garrett 64
  Hugh 122
  James 35, 85
  Nathaniel 105
  Robert 101
  Samuel 36
  Thomas 64, 105
  Widow 115
  William 53(2), 72
PATTON, Alexander 107
  David 54
  James 64
  John 105(2), 117
  Robert 105
PAULUS, Adam 29
  Laurence 29
PAXTON, Andrew 115
  George 123
  John 49, 122(2)
  Joseph 105(2), 122
  Nathaniel 122
  Samuel 122
PAY, Philip 19
PEAFFER, John 72
PEARSON, Mary 24
  Vintz 96
PEARY, Abraham 72
  George 72
  Nicholas 74
PEATER, Andrew 95
PECKER, John 91
PECKLEY, Christian 72
PEDEN, Benjamin 115
  James 115
  Samuel 95, 105(2)
PEDEY, William 117
PEIFER, Adam 56
PENCE, John 68
  Joseph 68
  Nicholas 29
PENCELY, Felix 68
PENDRY, Robert 115
PENNINGTON, Moses 35
PENROSE, Thomas 68
PENSIL, Casper 56
PENTZ, Nicholas 56
  Philip 23
PERSILL, John 84

INDEX

PERSON, Elias 101
  Henry 95
  Isaac 99
PETER, Michael 60
  Michael Geoge 110
  Peter 110
  Stephen 60
PETERMAN, Daniel 29, 72
  John 29
  Michael 29
  Widow 29
PETERS, Christopher 29
  Richard 62, 95
PETERSON, Andrew 88
  John 88
PETTY, John 32, 99
PEW, Joseph 48
PFANNEBECKER, William 19
PFLEIGER, George 112
  Jacob 112
PFLIEGER, Frederick 110
  Jacob 110
  Jacob 61
PHILIP, Jacob 56
PHILIPS, George 24
  Joseph 96
  Nathan 68
PHILLIPS, John 68
PICK, Jacob 72
PICKEN, Henry 93
  John 91
PIKE, Isaac 23
  John 24
PILE, Peter 43
PILKETON, Vinson 101
PILLOW, Henry 53
PIN --- 36
PINCHIN, John 105
PIPER, Peter 122
PISLE, Joseph 68
  Peter 68
  Philip 68
PISLER, Daniel 68
PLEASER, Herman 68
PLONK, Michael 56
PLOW, John 23
PLUCKET, William 24
POE, Alexander 122
POFF, George 29
POLK, Joseph 85
POLKE, David 92
  James 92(2)
  John 92(2)
  Joseph 92
  Robert 92

POLLINGER, Michael 24
  Peter 23
POLLOCK, John 53
  Joseph 53
  Richard 53
  William 37, 53
POPE, Bernard 72
  John 32, 53
  Ludwig 72
PORTER, Alexander 122
  Andrew 122
  George 117
  James 107, 115
  John 122
  Samuel 32, 105, 122
  Thomas 32
  William 32, 39, 95,
    105, 122
PORTMESSER, Philip 68
POSTERMAN, Michael 92
POTTER, David 88
  John 64, 96
  William 95
POTTS, David 53
PREAM, Jacob 68(2)
PRIAN, Philip 84
PRIGONER, Godlieb 122
PRINCE, John 95
PRIOR, Thomas 32
PRISILL, David 84
  Michael 84
  Valentine 84
  Widow 84
PROUDFOOT, Andrew 33
  David 33
  Robert 36
PRUBACHER, Teeterich
  84
PRUNCH, John 23
PRYFOGLE, Peter 36
PRYON, Augusta 86
PUE, David 68
PUFF, Christopher 41
PUGH, Elisha 34
PUPP, George 92
  Peter 92
PURDEY, Arch'd. 115
PURDY, James 34
PUSE, John 57
  Peter 56
PUSSEL, Thomas 56

QUARTERMAN, John 72
QUICKEL, Adam 48
  George 46
  Michael 46
  Philip 46
QUIGGEL, Hannichel 117
QUIGGLE, Hanichel 115
QUIGLEY, James 95

RABENSTINE, Widow 17
RACK, Christian 80(2)
RAFFSNEIDER, Ernst 29
RAGHY, Henry 17
  Stophel 17
  Wendel 17
RAHAUSER, Daniel 46
  Jacob 46
RAIMER, Francis 56
RALSON, Widow 105
RALSTON, John 39
RAMBOW, Andrew 46
  William 26
RAMSAY, Alexander 46
  James 39
  William 36
RAMSEY, Alexander 33,
  39, 46(2)
  David 121
  John 117
  Oliver 48
  Reynold 105
  Robert 88
  Thomas 115
RANDALLS, William 24(2)
RANEY, Alexander 88
RANG, Philip 110
RANGER, John 64
RANKIN, John 24
  William 24
RATHFANG, Christian 29
RAUDBUCH, Henry 85
RAUDEBUSH, Henry, Jun'r.
  85
RAUP, Peter 29
RAUS, Lucas, Parson 110
RAY, Robert 32
  Thomas 36
RAYMER, Frederick 11, 13
REA, Samuel 105(2)
READYER, Augustus 29
REAMAN, Jacob 73
REAMER, Henry 97
REANEY, John 35
REAVER, Abraham 72
REBLOGEL, Balzer 80

INDEX

REDY, Peter 105
REED, Adam 33
  David 68
  Emanuel 35
  James 32, 41, 95
  John 32, 68, 88, 115, 117
  Joseph 115, 117
  Michael 80
  Robert 5, 68
  Thomas 88, 92
  William 39, 115, 117
REEL, Peter 5, 11
  William 5
REES, George 95
REGAN, Daniel 46
REHM, Godfrey 5
  Widow 5
REIBOLD, Michael 62
REID, Benjamin 105
  Daniel 121
  Hugh 117
  James 105
  John 105, 115(2), 121
  Joseph 115
  Samuel 105
  Thomas 105
  William 105, 115, 116, 121
REIDINGER, Henry 19
  Stephen 11
REIFF, Jacob 24(2)
  John 11
REIGERT, John 110
  William 110
REIGHLE, Henry 18
REINECKER, Casper 17, 76
REINGEY, Antony 31
REINHARD, Conrad 18
REINYMAN, William 17
REIP, Nicholas 73
REISINGER, Conrad 46
  John 11, 76
  Martin 46
  Peter 29
REIST, Christian 13
  John 43
RENBERGER, Henry 29
RENECKER, George 78
RENFREW, John 121
RENOLLY, Peter 61
RENOLY, Daniel 60(2)
RENTZLER, Widow 56
REVER, John 60
REY, Joseph 29

REYMER, Frederick 53
  John 53
REYNOLDS, William 64
RICE, John 50
  William 11
RICHARD, Godlieb 13
RICHARDS, Peter 84
  Samuel 26
RICHARDSON, -- 26
  Jacob 95
RICHESON, Edward 99
  Hannah 101
RICHEY, Alexander 88
  Andrew 39, 98
  David 97
  Elijah 34
  John 33, 35(3)
  Mathew 32
  Robert 36
RICHMOND, John 24
  William 5
RICHOSON, James 49
RICHTER, George 46
  Paul 46
RIDDLE, David 121
  James 121
  John 105
  Widow 75
RIDER, Daniel 29
  Frederick 69
  John 105
  Lawrence 29
RIDINGER, Stephen 46
RIED, Patrick 107
RIESS, John 5
RIFFET, Jonathan 5
RIGEL, Ludwig 60
RIGG, Clement 24
  John 69
RIGHTSELL, George 121
RIGINGER, Stephen 46
RIGLE, John 80(2)
RILEY, Barnet 93
  John 85
RINEBERGER, William 105
RINEHARD, George 17
RINEHART, George 29
RING, Stephel 80
RINGER, George 11
  Michael 13
RINGLAND, John 50
RINGLER, Jacob 101

RIPOLD, Adam 60
  Andrew 60
  George 60
RIPOLT, Nicholas 61
RIPPEY, John 115, 117
RISH, William 53
RISINGER, Nicholas 13
RISK, Robert 105
RITCHEY, Samuel 39
RITTENHOUSE, Gerard 99
RITTER, Andrew 11
RITZ, Anthony 5
  Antony 110
  John 110
ROADS, Abraham 56
  Christian 56
  George 56
  Jacob 56
  Peter 26
ROASER, Adam 72
  John 72
  Laurence 72
ROBB, James 5
  John 115
  Joseph 115
ROBERSON, John 29
  Thomas 29
ROBERT, Jacob 24
  John 11
ROBERTS, George 105(2)
  John 40, 99
  Peter 36
ROBESON, Thomas 101
ROBINET, Allen 99
  George 97
  James 99, 101
ROBINSON, George 24
  John 98, 105
  Walter 114
ROBISON, Henry 117
  Isaac 50, 105
  James 39, 115
  John 96, 115
  Samuel 95
  Thomas 95, 105
  William 39
ROBUCK, Michael 80
ROCKWELL, Joseph 5
RODE, Herman 85
  John 80
ROFFELSBERGER, Martin 56
ROFFELSPERGER, Christian 85
ROFFERSBERGER, Christian 56

150

INDEX

ROGERS, Ellis 24
  Laban 24
  Linens 29
ROHRBACH, John 61
  Lawrence 60
ROHRBOUGH, Christian 60
ROMIG, George 46
ROMING, Michael 11
ROOP, Christian 43
ROOPER, Martin 69
ROSE, George 110
  John 121
ROSEBOROUGH, Samuel 36
ROSEMILLER, Ludwig 101(2)
ROSENBAUM, John 11
ROSS, Alexander 69
  David 89
  George 95
  James 96
  John 24, 121
  Joseph 39, 107
  Michael 60
  Robert 96
  William 64, 88, 115
ROTH, Anthony 11
  Henry 11
  John 11, 110
ROTHENHEISER, John 24
  Peter 98
ROTHIHERSE, Nicholas 73
ROTHROCK, George 13
  Jacob 5
  John 5
  Joseph 5
  Philip 13
ROTS, Peter 56
ROUDEBUSH, Jacob 85
  Michael 85
ROUSH, Anthony 13
ROUTBOUGH, John 50
  Zacharias 50
ROWAN, Andrew 39
  Henry 105
  James 107
  William 13, 39
ROWANZANER, Christian 80
ROWENZAHAN, John 17
ROWENZANER, Adam 80
ROWLANDS, Margaret 39
RUBBERT, John 97
RUBEL, Christian 62
RUBY, Henry 29
  Jacob 29
  Widow 29(2)

RUCE, Andrew 69
  Frederick 69(2)
RUDEY, George 56
RUDISIEL, Widow 5
RUDISIL, Jacob 76
RUDISILL, Andrew 18
  Balzer 11
  Jacob 11, 60
  John 5, 46, 48
  Jonas 11
  Ludwig 17
RUDOLFH, Stephen 64
RUDOLPH, Peter 81
RUDRAUF, Jonas 110
RUDRAUFF, John 46
RUDY, George 46(2)
  Henry 46
  Jacob 13
  Michael 43
RUHL, John 60(2)
  William 60
RULE, Frederick 72
  George 76
RULEMAN, Christian 17
  George 17
RUMBLE, George 92
  Jacob 92
RUMBO, Moses 24
RUMMEL, Frederick 5
RUMP, George 112
RUNCKEL, Jacob 17
  Ludwig 17
RUNK, Valentine 62
  Yost 60
RUP, Stephen 43
  Yost 43
RUPPERT, Deetrich 11
RUSH, Christian 72
  Jane 35
RUSSEL, Alexander 107
  Andrew 105
  James 121
  John 29, 39, 107
  Joshua 121
  Robert 121
  Samuel 121
  Thomas 123
  William 53, 105
RYAN, Thomas 5
  William 121
RYLEY, Barney 93
RYNOLDS, Anthony 53
  John 53
  William 65

SAAK, Widow 37
SABLE, Leonard 18
  Peter 18
SABOUGH, Jacob 60
SADLER, Frederick 34
  Isaac 101
  Jacob 35
SAILER, Christian 31
SALGROVE, James 24
SANDERSON, Alexander 98
SANTZ, Andrew 95
SARBACH, Jacob 57, 85
SARBACK, Jacob 58
SAVAGE, Henry 40
  Hill 18
SAY, John 33
SAYLER, Henry 30
  Ulry 30
SAYLOR, Christian 30
SAYRES, James 24
SCANTLIN, Adam 29
SCARLET, William 24
SCHANCK Joseph 6
SCHEFFER, Henry 24
  Peter 11
SCHELLY, Abraham 24
SCHENCK, Jacob 6
SCHENK, Adam 11
SCHETTRONE, Casper 24
SCHINCK, John 18
SCHINDEL, Frederick 11
SCHLEMER, Peter 30
SCHLEMMER, Peter 6
SCHLESSMAN, George 61
SCHLOSSER, Ernst 6
SCHLOTTHAUER, Nicholas 18
SCHLOTTHAUR, Michael 19
SCHMALL, Laurence 5
SCHMELTZER, Adam 57
SCHMUCK, John 6, 30(2)
SCHNEERINGER, Laurence 81
SCHNEIDER, Dewalt 17
  Jacob 6
  John 18, 46
  Stophel 18
SCHNELL, John 95
SCHNELLBECHER, George 47
SCHNIERER, Jacob 5
SCHRACK, Henry 5
SCHRAM, Jacob 6
  John 13
  Widow 11
SCHRECK, John 6

INDEX

SCHREIBER, Jacob 5
  John 11
  Michael 11
  Peter 11
SCHREINER, William 24
SCHREIVER, Conrad 81
SCHRREYER, John 81
SCHULER, Christian 24
SCHULTZ, Michael 61
  Peter 11
  Thomas 24
  Valentine 24
SCHWARTZ, Mathias 47
  Peter 7
SCHWARTZBACH, John 18
SCOTT, Allen 116
  Archibald 30
  David 88, 122
  Gain 116
  Gavin 117
  Semple 117
  John 39, 105, 122
  Joseph 107
  Moses 30
  Patrick 40
  Robert 107, 122
  Samuel 105
  Thomas 116
  William 6, 105
SEALER, Casper 116
  Peter 81
SEALIS, John 30
SEAR, Halbert 26
SEBALD, Jacob 110
SECATZ, Peter 24
SECH, Henry 110
SEELEY, Henry 85
SEFFERENTZ, George 6
SEHLERS, Peter 24
SEICKLY, Jacob 73
SEIDEL, George 97
  Godfrey 96
SELICKS, Thomas 53(2)
SELL, Abraham 81
  Adam 81
  Isaac 81
  Jacob 81(2)
SEMPLE, Cunningham 40
  John 40, 88
SENCE, Peter 112
SENFT, Philip 60(2)
SENGURY, Peter 115
SENSE, Nicholas 110
SENSENICH, Peter 5
SEVER, Henry 96

SHAACK, John 18
SHAAD, David 11
SHADE, John 69
SHADLER, Andrew 61
SHAFER, Catharine 73
  David 73
  Frederick 53
  Henry 30, 78
  Jacob 61
  Paul 30
  Philip 57
  Samuel 29
  Stophel 30
SHAKELY, John 122
SHALL, John 6
SHALLER, George 43(2)
SHANBERGER, Balzer 30
  John 29
SHANK, Henry 61
  Joseph 110
  Michael 61
SHANKS, Thomas 69
SHANNON, James 24
  John 97(2)
  Joseph 105
  Patrick 95, 96
  Thomas 105
SHAPMAN, William 57
SHARP, James 24
  John 88
SHATOE, Nicholas 69
SHATRON, Jacob 46
SHAVOUR, Jacob 35
SHAW, Archibald 114, 116
  Daniel 117
  James 6
  Robert 116
  Widow 116
SHAY, Edward 98
SHEAKLEY, George 64
SHEARER, Jacob 35
  John 35
  Philip 69
SHEELY, Jacob 50
  Nicholas 50
SHEET, John 85
SHEFER, Henry 74
SHEFFER, Henry 31, 77
  Jacob 6, 7, 48
  John 46, 110
  Philip 73
SHEIRER, John 18, 73
SHELDON, James 34

SHELLEBERGER, Henry 122
SHELLY, Daniel 21
  Jacob 64
  John 74
  Widow 64
SHENCK, Christian 24
SHEPHERD, George 122
  Henry 96
SHERB, John 11
SHERER, Jacob 61, 110
  John 61
SHERMAN, Conrad 18
  Jacob 18, 81, 82
SHERRETZ, Arnold 18
  Conrad 18
  Daniel 18
  Ludwig 18
SHETLER, Mary 111
SHETRON, John 46
SHETTER, Jacob 24
  John 24
  Martin 24
SHETTLEY, Frederick 6
  George 47
SHEW, William 30
SHEYRER, John 74
SHIELY, Christopher 6
SHIERY, Jacob 73
SHIFFLER, Casper 77
SHIKEMER, Ebenezer 98
SHILLING, Bastian 73
  John 19
SHILT, Henry 80
SHINARD, Abraham 33
  John 35
  Thomas 36
  Widow 37
SHINDLER, Christopher 73
  Conrad 110
SHINNERMAN, David 73
SHIPTON, Thomas 101
SHIRK, John 57
SHITZ, Anthony 101
  Peter 5
SHNIDER, Henry 81
  Martin 61
SHOE, Henry 85
  Zachariah 61
SHOEMAKER, John 110
  Peter 74
SHOEMAN, John 24
SHOLL, Jacob's widow 61
  Philip 76
  Widow 18
SHOMAN, David 96

INDEX

SHORE, John 81
SHORP, John 76
SHOWN, John 46
  Nicholas 50
SHREIBER, Andrew 76
  Conrad 76
  Jacob 76
  Ludwig 76
  Peter 76
SHREIPER, Philip 97
SHRETE, Martin 5
SHREYER, George 76
SHRIBER, Philip 92
SHRIVER, John 64
SHROLL, Christian 43
  John 43(2)
SHROTH, John 98
SHRYACK, John 13
SHRYER, John 81
SHUCK, George 5
  Jacob 5, 12
SHULTZ & KOPPENHAFER 11
SHULTZ, Ferdinand 85
  Frederick 76
  Henry 11, 76
  Jacob 43(2)
  John 3, 6(2), 111
  Joseph 81
  Lawrence 60
  Michael 61
  Peter 11, 76
SHUPE, Jacob 64
  Martin 64
SHUSS, George 18
SHUY, Daniel 110
  Peter 76, 85
SHWING, Dennis 61
  Michael 6
SHYRER, Martin 61
  Michael 61
SICHRIST, George 81
SICRIST, Francis 34
SIDES, John 73
  Joseph 73
SIDLER, Jacob 5
SIEGRIST, Jacob 5
SIER, Albright 24
SIFFERT, Adam 46
  Michael 47
SIGLER, John Michael 30
  Michael 30
SIHILL, John 6
SILER, Bartley 30
SIMERMAN, Michael 50

SIMMERMAN, Ludwig 96
  Michael 29
SIMMONS, Adams 101
SIMON, Casper 60
  John 60
SIMONS, Jacob 85
  James 98
SIMOTTEN, John 33
SIMPSON, James 53, 122
  John 53
SIMS, Jacob 54
  John 106
SIMSON, David 88
  John 30
SINGHORSE, Abraham 101
SINKEY, Ezeckiel 30
SINN, Christian 5, 6
  George 7
SIPE, Andrew 47
  Emanuel 47
  Philip 47
  Tobias 48
SIPES, George 122
SITES, Aron 78
  Benjamin 76
  Michael 112
SITESINGER, Leonard 33
SKAKELEY, William 64
SKEAR, John 30
SKIDMORE, John 85
SKILLS, Henry 60
SLAGEL, Daniel 85(2)
  Henry 85
  Jacob 85(2)
  Stophel 85
SLANE, Daniel 24
SLANKER, Andrew 30
SLEGEL, Daniel 92
  Jacob 77, 92
SLEGLE, Stophel 11
SLEMONDS, James 105
SLEMONS, John 105
SLEMONS, Robert 122
SLENCH, Philip 64
SLENTZ, Philip 76
SLIFER, Peter 30
  Stophen 30
SLIT, James 88
SLONE, Andrew 33
SLONICHER, Christian 57
SMALL, Killian 6
  William 111
SMATZ, John 101
SMELSER, Philip 30

SMELTZER, John 76
  Michael 43
SMELZER, Widow 61
SMILER, William 40
SMITH, Abraham 106
  Alexander 33
  Andrew 11(2), 50, 73, 78, 122
  Balzer 69
  Barney 39
  Charles 5, 65, 77
  Ebenezer 40
  Gabriel 69
  George 30, 61
  Godlieb 85
  Henry 69
  Jacob 47, 95(2), 110
  James, English 11
  James, German 11
  James, lawyer 11
  James 6, 11, 24, 33, 34(2), 40, 50, 88, 98, 111
  John 6, 29, 34(3), 37, 69, 73(2), 81, 85, 95, 98(2), 105, 110, 123
  Joseph 5, 34, 40, 116
  Ludwig 30
  Mathias 61
  Patrick 116
  Peter 47, 69, 73
  Robert 105, 116
  Samuel 36, 50, 69, 112
  Stophel 80
  Widow 111, 116
  William 33, 37, 40, 85(3), 98
SMOCK, Barney 64
  John 64
  Mathias 64
SMYSER, Jacob 12
  Mathias 11
  Michael 11
SNEIDER, Anthony 57
  Jacob 57
SNIDEMAN, Daniel 43
SNIDER, Abraham 53
  Andrew 13
  Dewald 61
  Henry 60
  John 53(2), 86
  Michael 61, 86
  Peter 101, 116
SNODGRESS, William 39

INDEX

SNYDER, Conrad 11(2)
  George 24
  Jacob 11, 24
  John 33
  Martin 5
  Michael 92(2)
  Peter 11
  Philip, Ju'r 11
SORBOUGH, David 92
SOUER, Leonard 60
SOWER, Adam 18
  Andrew 24
  John 19
  William 80
SOWERS, Adam, Ju'r. 85(2)
  Daniel 85
  David 85(2)
  Jacob 85
SPADE, John 24
SPAHR, Adam 46
  Casper 47
  Frederick 46
  George 47
  Michael 48
  Philip 48(2)
SPANGLER, Andy 85
  Balzer 6, 111(2)
  Bernard 56, 111
  Charles 112
  George Michael 6
  George 110
  Henry 112
  John 6, 111
  Jonas 111
  Joseph 46
  Michael 112
  Peter 33
  Rudolph 5, 56, 111(2)
  Widow 111
SPARE, John 33
SPARKS, Thomas 73
SPARROW, Henry 81
  Valentine 81
SPEAR, Robert 105
SPECK, Martin 110
  Michael 11
SPEECE, Christopher 57
SPEER, Alexander 123
  James 116, 123(2)
  John 123
SPENCE, George 24
SPENCER, Isaac 53
  Widow 53
SPENCKEL, Peter 61

SPENGLER, Balzer 61
  Bernard 57
  George 110
  Henry 56, 57
  Philip Casper 110
SPICKER, Widow 5
SPICKERT, Philip 11
SPIES, Peter 47(2)
SPIKEMAN, Joshua 101
SPITLER, Jacob 64, 73, 110
  John 76
  William 37
SPONSYLER, Andrew 81
  George 81
  Jacob 81
  Widow 81
SPOSSART, Michael 60
SPOTS, Jacob 116
  Joseph 117
SPRENCHEL, Henry 81
SPRENCKEL, Daniel 5
  George 11
  Michael 14
  Peter 12, 14, 110
SPRING, Laurence 92
SPROGELL, Widow 5
SPROUT, Hugh 116, 117
  Samuel 117
SPURR, Leonard 24
SQUIBB, William 96
St. CLAIR, Daniel 116
  James 34, 122
  John 117
St. MIRE, Barnabas 123
St. MYER, Bernard 122
  Christopher 122
STAGG, James 92
STAGNER, Jacob 30
STAHL, Peter 5
STAIR, Henry 34
  John 24
  Mathias 5
  Peter 36
STAKE, Christian 6, 13
  George 5, 12
STALEY, Malachia 24
STALL, Jesse 24
STAMBACH, Jacob 18, 19, 61
  Peter 61
  Philip 61
STAMBACK, John 18
STANLEY, John 122
  William 122

STANOVER, Frederick 53
STANTON, Daniel 95
STAUB, Adam 76
  Jacob 77
  Philip 76
STAUCH, Andrew 48
STAUFFER, Daniel 110
  Henry 81(2), 110
STAULFER, Jacob 43
STAUTER, George 76
STEAS, Philip 30
STEBLER, Henry 110
STEBLEY, John 74
STEEL, George 96(2)
  Godfrey 95
  Isaac 96
  James 34, 69
  John 106
  Mr. 89
  Rachel 40
  Samuel 65
  Thomas 40, 89
  William 123
STEEPLE, Nicholas 36
STEES, Rudy 95
STEFFLER, John 85
STEHR, Christopher 5
STEINBRECHER, Sebastian 18
STELEY, Joseph 81
  Stophel 81
STELIG, John 81
STEMY, Christian 76
STENTZ, Jacob 43
  Philip 5
STEP, Peter 29
STEPHEN, Widow 18
STEPHENS, Thomas 98
STERGEON, William 65
STERLING, James 88
STERNER, Bernard 18
STETLER, Jacob 112
STEVENSON, Charles 33
  George 98
  James 106, 122
  John 105
  Joseph 69
  Widow 69
  William 105, 106
STEWARD, Joseph 89
  Widow 116
  William 101
STEWART, Alexander 123
  Andrew 117
  David 53

INDEX

James 50, 54, 106, 116
John 53, 116
Robert 26, 50, 101, 122(2)
William 50, 98, 122
STIBLER, Christian 73
STICKEL, Christopher 69
  George 69
  Jacob 69
  Peter 69
STIESS, Zachariah 18
STIFLER, Jacob 57
STILEY, Andrew 117
STILLEY, Andrew 115, 116
  Jacob 115
  Stephen 115
STILLINGER, Michael 122
  Richard 5
STIRLING, Joseph 98
STITT, David 107
  Isaac 107
STIVERS, Lewis 106
STOCKSLAGEY, John 122
  Widow 122
STOCKTON, David 53
  John 53
  Joseph 53
  Robert 105
  Thomas 88
STOFER, John 56, 69
STOLL, George 6
  Godfrey 76
  Widow 5
STONE, David 34
  Jacob 73
STONEBACH, Adam 80
STONEBRAKER, Bastian 81
STONER --- 114
  Christian 24, 43
  Frederick 11, 24, 50
  George 76
  Isaac 11
  John 43
STONG, John 81
STOOBS, Robert 53
STORM, Paul 11
STORMER, Rosanna 73
STOUCH, Frederick 46
  George 46
STOUFER, Daniel 61
STOUFFER, Abram 96
STOUSENBERG, Conrad 6
STOUVER, John 81

STOVER, Frederick 57
  Jacob 56
  Nicholas 57
STRACK, Yost 11
STRAIR, Nicholas 36, 116
STRASBACK, Michael 57
STRATTON, Abraham 122
STRAUCH, William 18
STRAWFORD, Robert 36
STRAWMONGER, Jacob 30
STREBER, Peter 6
STREBIG, Jacob 6
STREHER, Peter 47
STREHR, Jacob 47
STREIN, Adam 24
  George 24
STRELEY, Stephen 47
STRICKHOUSER, Widow 61
STRICKLER, Conrad 43
  Henry 43(3)
  Jacob 43(2)
  John 28, 43
STRIEBIG, Jacob 110
STRINE, Peter 47
STRITE, David 30
STROHMAN, Jacob 7
  John 6
STRONG, James 30
  John 81
STROUCE, Michael 30
STUART, James 64
  John 69, 110, 112, 116
  Joseph 106
  Mathias 112
  Robert 30, 116(2)
  Rowland 36
  Samuel 105, 117
  Thomas 107
  William 30, 53
STUCK, Jacob 5
  Martin 111
  Peter 61
STUDDEN, Joseph 73
STUDEBAKER, Clementz 58
STUDENBAKER, David 85
  Peter 85
STUMPF, Peter 18
STURGEON, Henry 64, 85
  Jeremiah 65
  Robert 89
  Samuel 88
  William 85

SULTZBACK, Philip 43
SULTZBERGER 6
  George 111
SUMBERLAND, James 85
  John 85
  William 85
SUMMER, John 18
SUMWALD, Balzer 110
  Godfrey 112
SUNDAY, Jacob 57
  John 57
  Joseph 58
SURGERT, Abraham 85
SUTER, George 39
SUTTER, John 122
SWAN, Robert 36
SWANE, Benjamin 76
SWANEY, Alexander 122
  James 122
  John 122
  Miles 122
  Thomas 122
SWARTZ, Andrew 73
  Conrad 73
  Frederick 34
  George 112
  Henry 73, 110
  Herman 94
  Jacob 73
SWEIGERT, Jacob 57
SWEISGUTH, Laurence 57
SWIGERT, John 64
SWISHER, Laurence 96
  Peter 122
SWITZER, Anthony 33
  Jacob 69
SWOOPE, Conrad 76
  Michael 5, 110
SWOPE, Adam 43
  John 43
SWORD, George 73
SYFORT, John 77

TACHENBACH, Mathias 101
TAGGART, John 40
TAKERY, Thomas 25
TARBERT, James 40
  Robert 40
TARR, Peter 54
TATE, Isaac 25
  Jacob 25
  Solomon 25
  William 123
TATER, Archibald 123

155

INDEX

TAYLOR, Abraham 73
  Benjamin 54
  George 73
  John 40, 73(2), 106
  Joseph 25, 54, 69
  Philip 36, 73
  Robert 123
TEETER, Joseph 64
TEIGEL, John 73
TENTLINGER, Anthony 81
TENTZEL, Daniel 25
  John 25
TERR, John 25
TEST, George 6
THAESER, Henry 96
THEOBAT, Shollas 64
THOMAS, Francis 6
  George 6
  James 69
  Jehu 69
  John 69, 77
  Mary 69
  Nathan 25
  Peter 92
  Philip 43
THOMPSON, Andrew 33
  William 43
THOMSON, Andrew, Esq'r. 98
  George 116
  James 106, 107
  John 92, 96, 98(2), 106, 116, 123(3)
  Joseph 50
  Robert 85
  Samuel 41, 88
  William 54, 50, 88(2), 98
THORELEY, Abraham 25
  George 25(2)
THORELY, William 25
THORNBROUGH, Robert 25
THRON, Abraham 18
  John 18
TICE, George 30
TICKERHUFF, Frederick 64
TICKERT, Henry 30
TICKS, Todley 85
TICKSON, James 85
TIMMONS, Charles 50
  Paul 50
  Philip 77
  Thomas 85
TINKEY, John 73
TITRICH, Baltzer 33

TITRICH, Baltzer 33
  Nicholas 33
TODD, Andrew 107
  James 25
  Joseph 7, 26
  William 2
TOFFEY, Thomas 85
TOLAND, James 25
TOMEY, Thomas 47
TOMMACK, John 73
TORBERT, Allen 96
TORBETT, John 88
TORBIT, David 96
  Robert 96
TORRENS, William 64
TOWNSEND, Benjamin 54
TOWNSLEY, George 50
  John 50
TRAVILLEA, James 25
TRAVIS, John 34
TREIBER, Michael 12
TREICHLER, John 111
TRESSLER, George 57
TRIMMER, Andrew 57, 92(2)
  John 57
TRINE, Jacob 77
TRIPLET, Francis 96
TRIPPET, Joseph 77
TRITT, Jacob 30
  Peter 30
TRORBACH, Mathias 73
TROSBOUGH, Peter 54
TROUB, Henry 92
  Paul 92
  Peter 92
TROUP, John 96
TROXEL, Daniel 81
  David 81
  Jacob 81
TRUCK, George 43
TRUEL, Anthony 77
TRUMP, Casper 30
  Peter 57
TRUSSEL, John 77
TRYNE, Peter 47
TUCKER, Tempest 57
TUDRO, Michael 69
TUMPF, Mathas 57
TURNER, Peter 57
TUSH, George 31
  Michael 30
TWIGGS, John 40
TWINAM, James 92
  William 92

TYSON, Benjamin 30
  Henry 30

UHLER --- 6
ULAND, Michael 18
UNDERWOOD, Benjamin 69
  Elihu 69(2)
  Jacob 70
  Mary 69
  Nehemiah 69
  William 69
  Zephaniah 25
UNRUE, John 81
UPDEGRAFF, Ambrose 6
  Derick 25
  Herman 6, 25
  Jacob 6(2), 111
  Joseph 6(3), 12
  Nathan 6
  Samuel 6, 12
  William 69
UPP, Jacob 6
UPPA, Teeter 69
URBAN, John 48
URT, Melchior 30

VAMBACH, George 30
  Michael 30
  Peter 30
  Philip 30
VANASDELIN, Abraham 86(2)
VANCE, John 92
  Nicholas 92
  Urban 50
VANDERBILT, David 89
VANDERPELT, James 88
VANDIKE, John 86
  Peter 65, 86
VANDINE, Charles 65
  David 88
VANE, Frederick 81
VANSCOFE, Aron 101
  Moses 101
VANTINE, Charles 64
  Javish 64
VANTZ, George 123
VARNON, Aaron 25
VARTIN, Richard 47
VEAL, Robert 69(2)
  William 69
VEAR, Christopher 69
VERNER, Jacob 81
VESTERVELT, Abraham 64
VINTNER, Savage 65

156

INDEX

VOAR, Isaac 69
  Jacob 69
  Jesse 69
VONADEL, Garret, Ju'r. 89
VONASDAL, Cornelius 89
  Garret 88
  John 89
  Simon 88, 89
VORE, Peter 25

WABLER, Ludwig 89
WACHTEL, George 31
WADE, Ebenezer 123
WAGGONER, Casper 98
  John 112
  Michael 112
  William 86
WAGNER, Conrad 18
  Frederick 7
  Henry 73
  Jacob 7, 12, 25
  Ludwig 18
  Melchior 74
  Peter 18
  Philip 7, 12
  Yost 18, 57
WAGONER, Jacob 96
WAHL, Yost 12
WAILER, Henry 57
WALDER, Adam 57
  Henry 57
WALKER, Able 69
  Benjamin 70
  Ezael 92
  Gabriel 123
  James 33, 123
  John 106, 123
  Joseph 33, 123
  Samuel 33
  William 33
WALKMAN, Henry 77
WALL, Absolom 25
  John 7
  William 12
WALLACE, Aron 117
  John 116(3)
  Mary 35
  Mathew 116
  Moses 116
  William 40, 117
WALTEMEYER, Henry 73
WALTEMYER, Ludwig 7
  Philip 7

WALTER, George 61
  Henry 7, 111
  Jacob 61
  John 61
  Ludwig 18
  Nicholas 77, 81
  Peter 77
WALTIMYER, David 98
WALTMAN, Henry 112
  John 77
  Ludwig 111
WAMPLER, George 7
  John 18
  Widow 7
WANDER, Stephen 98
WARAM, Abraham 40
WARM, Michael 116
WARON, David 25
WARREN, Thomas 25
WARRINGTON, Frederick 54
WARTON, Thomas 26
WASON, James 116
WATKINS, Thomas 25
WATSON, Andrew 123
  James 54
  John 101
  Samuel 36
  William 64
WATT, George 123
WATTSON, John 65
  William 19
WAUGH, David 106
  Widow 106
  William 106
WEAKLEY, William 92
WEAR, James 89
WEAST, Henry 34
WEASTER, Jacob 86
WEATHERSPOON, John 86
WEAVER, Adam 26, 54
  Boston 64
  Conrad 96
  David 92
  Frederick 112
  Henry 70
  Jacob 13, 101
  John 61, 77, 81
  Leonhard 86
  Martin 47
  Nicholas 101
  Reinhard 86
WEBB, James 40
  John 25, 40
  Richard 40
  William 69

WEBER, Philip 6
  Ulrick 31
WEBSTER, Richard 92
WEEMS, John 50
  Thomas 50
WEER, Andrew 89
WEHR, Frederick 7
  George 7
WEIGEL, Leonard 12, 13
  Martin 12
  Peter 13
  Sabastian 12
WEINAND, Philip 57
WEINBRECHT, Michael 18
WEISANG, Ludwig 7
WEISHANTZ, William 112
WEISS, John 19
WEISTER, Jacob 117
WELCH, George 12
WELDON, Jacob 34
WELLER, George 6
  Martin 111
WELLER, George, & ROTHROCK 112
WELSCH, John 73
WELSH, Andrew 25
  Erasmus 7
  Gerrard 25
  Henry 6, 77
  James 25
  John 7(2), 106
  Joseph 26
  Margaret 25
  Michael 6, 7, 12(2)
  Peter 77
  Widow 7
  William 7
WELSHANTZ, Abram 111(2)
  David 7
  Jacob 7(2), 111
  Joseph 7, 111
WELSHN, Andrew 7
WELSHOVER, Jacob 43
WELTNER, John 31
WELTY, George 47
  Henry 19
  Jacob 12, 48, 77
  John 18
  Michael 48
  Peter 19
  Philip 47
WELTZHEIMER, Philip 7
WENDLE, Wolf 43

INDEX

WENTZ, Frederick 19
  Michael 81
  Philip 47
  Valentine 19
WERCKING, Nicholas 18
  Philip 18
  Philip, Vance 18
  Valentine 18
WERKING, Philip 19
WERLEY, George 61
  Henry 61
  Michael 77
WERNER, Balzer 77
  Daniel 92
  George 18, 81
  John 61
  Melchior 18
WERT, John 19
WERTS, Peter 92
WERTZ, Daniel 62
  John 61
WESSLER, Henry 98, 101
  John 99
  William 96
WEST, Charles 25
  George 40
  Isaac 40
  James 50
  Samuel 40
  Thomas 25
WESTLER, Joseph 70
WESTON, Joseph 43
WETHERSPOON, James 92
WETHROW, John 47
WETSHOFER, Henry 13
WEYANT, Peter 13
WEYER, Andrew 13
  John 25
  Ludwig 25
WHEELER, John 86
WHINNERY, Robert 25
  Thomas 25
  William 25
WHITE, Andrew 40, 92
  Bastian 86
  Casper, Ju'r. 86
  George 57
  James 92(3)
  John 33, 123(3)
  Joseph 40
  Joshua 92
  Peter 92
  Robert 77
  Thomas 57
  William 57, 96, 106

WHITEFORD, Hugh,
  Mary'l 40
WHITEMAN, Samuel 123
WHITLEY, Benjamin 64
WIANT, David 31
  Nicholas 61
WICKERSHAM, Isaac 69
  James 25
  Jesse 25
WIDEMAN, Henry 61
  Sebastian 61
WIDENER, Michael 6
WIERMAN, Benjamin 101
  Henry, Ju'r. 101(2)
  Jacob 111
  John 101
  Nicholas 101(2)
  William 101
WIEST, Christian 57
  John 57
WIGEL, Jacob 47
WIKER, George 77
WIKERSAM, Widow 69
WIKESON, John 89
WILAND, John 43
WILDGOOSE, James 73
WILEY, David 34
  Joseph 40(2)
  Mathew 41
  Nathaniel 40
WILFORD, Peter 64
WILHELM, Henry 61, 73
  Michael 96
WILKISON, Jacob 18
  Samuel 18
WILL, George 81
  Jacob 77
  John 31, 77
  Martin 77
  Michael 78
  Nicholas 77
  Peter 77
WILLET, Stophel 18
WILLEY, Adam 69
  Aquilla 73
  John 116
  William 73
WILLIAM, George 111
  Hezekiah 25
  John 111
  Mordicai 70
WILLIAMS, Abraham 70, 96
  Abram 70
  Amos 96

  Andrew 96
  Benjamin 31, 70
  Daniel 96
  Isaac 116
  Jacob 69, 77
  James 89
  John 96(2), 123
  Jonathan 97
  Joseph 30
  Joshua 86
  Lewis 96
  Solomon 43
  Thomas 54
  William 54
WILLIAMSON, George 89
  John 98
WILLIS, John 12
  Richard 25
  William 7, 12, 25, 43, 48
WILLS, John 48
WILLSON, Robert 50
WILSON, Alexander 25, 96
  Andrew 96(2)
  Benjamin 40, 117
  Charles 50(2)
  Daniel 96
  Daron 50
  David 106
  Elizabeth 40
  Hugh 106, 123
  James 35, 40, 89, 96, 99, 106
  John 25, 33, 35, 40(2), 50, 96(4), 123(2)
  Joseph 50, 57, 123
  Marmaduke 92
  Robert 89, 123
  Samuel 41, 50, 98
  Thomas 40, 116
  Widow 106(2)
  William 25(2), 36, 96, 106, 116, 117
WILT, Adam 12
  Nicholas 12
  Peter 25, 77
  Samuel 47
  Sebastian 25
  Valentine 12
WILTE, John 47
  Paul 47
WIMLEY, John 77
WINDER, Jacob 86
WINDERODE, Jacob 81

INDEX

WINDEROTH, Adam 82
WINE, Adam 78
  George 77
  Henry 78
WINEBRECHT, Martin 77
  Michael 77
WINEBRENNER, George 77
  Peter 77
WINEHOLT, George 31
WINEMILLER, Christian 64
  Francis 61
  Stophel 58
WINKLER, Francis 57
WINTER, Eberhard 77
  Jacob 61
  John 18
  Peter 31
  Philip 116
WINTERMEYER, Anthony 47
WINTERMYER, Philip 12
WINTERSMSITH Ch's. 112
WIRKING, Philip 77, 78
WISDEL, Widow 50
WISELEY, William 98
WISELY, John 101
WISENDAHL, Henry 111
WISHARD, Nicholas 86
WISHART, Christopher 33
WISLER, John 77
WISLEY, Edward 98
WISMAN, Godlieb 31
WISON, Valentine 77
WITCOCK, Ambrose 47
WITERRECHT, George 12
  Michal 12
  Peter 12
WITHERO, John 70(2)
  William 69
WITHEROW, William 106
WITSEL, Peter 106
WITTMEYER, Simon 12
WOGAN, Jacob 12
WOHLFART, Philip 18
  Stophel 111
WOHLGEMUTH, Henry 25
WOLF, Adam 6, 12
  Andrew 86
  Conrad 47
  Frederick 86
  George 7, 12
  Henry 6, 7, 12, 30, 98
  Jacob 77
  John 7(2)
  Jonas 86

Peter 7, 12, 57, 58, 111
  Philip 12
WOLFGANG, Nicholas 18
WOLK, John 47
  Philip 47
WOLLET, George 57
WOLPACK, George 30
WOLST, Philip 57
WOODS, Elias 62
  James 107
  Samuel 40
WORK, Robert 123
WORLEY, Daniel 12
  Francis 7, 12(2)
  Jacob 12
  James 12
  Nathan 7, 12
  Samuel 47
WORST, Jacob 57
WRESSLER, Mathias 25
WRIGHT, Aaron 25
  Aron 70
  Benjamin 54
  Henry 54
  James 54
  John 43, 54(2), 70
  Jonathan 54
  Samuel 43
  Widow 54
  William 54
WULDRICH, Michael 86
WULRICH, John 116
WUNDER, Christian 19
WYLEY, Robert 98
WYLICH, John 98

YAGER, John 54
  Simon 3
YANTIS, Daniel 81
YARNELL, Jesse 25
YEGER, Henry 16
YEKE, Adam 47
  Peter 47
YENEWEIN, Leonard 16
YENGLING, Abraham 81
YESSLER, Henry 111
YESSLEY, Michael 43
YODER, Daniel 92
YONER, Jacob 47
  John 47
  Nicholas 47
YONT, Jacob 35
YOST, Nicholas 109(2)
  Rudy 36

YOUCE, Frederick 7, 111
YOUNG, Abraham 31
  Adam 16
  Charles 16
  Christian 57
  Edward 43
  Francis 54
  Frederick 64, 111
  James 34, 106
  Mathew 96
  Nicholas 31(2)
  Peter 47, 64
  Robert 50
  Samuel 54
  William 31, 54
YOUNGBLOOD, Daniel 16

ZACHARIAS, George 19
ZANGER, George 81
ZAUCKEN, Widow 81
ZECH, George 112
  Jacob 111
ZEICH, Michael 73
ZEIGLER, Killian 12
ZENLOP, George 81
ZIEGEL, Godlieb 7
  Widow 7, 111
ZIEGLER, Andrew 14
  Barnet 61
  George 77, 98
  Henry 98
  Jacob 12, 61
  John 98
  Nicholas 61
  Philip 12(2), 98
ZIGLER, Jacob 101
ZIMERMAN, Bernard 12
ZIMMER, Mathias 7, 77
  Michael 77
ZIMMERMAN, Christian 19
  Henry 7
  John 19
  Michael 82
  Stophel 19
ZINN, Nicholas 47
  Philip Jacob 47
ZOLLINGER, Peter 57, 58
ZORGER, Frederick 26

Other books by F. Edward Wright:

Abstracts of Bucks County, Pennsylvania Wills, 1685-1785
Abstracts of Cumberland County, Pennsylvania Wills, 1750-1785
Abstracts of Cumberland County, Pennsylvania Wills, 1785-1825
Abstracts of Philadelphia County Wills, 1726-1747
Abstracts of Philadelphia County Wills, 1748-1763
Abstracts of Philadelphia County Wills, 1763-1784
Abstracts of Philadelphia County Wills, 1777-1790
Abstracts of Philadelphia County Wills, 1790-1802
Abstracts of Philadelphia County Wills, 1802-1809
Abstracts of Philadelphia County Wills, 1810-1815
Abstracts of Philadelphia County Wills, 1815-1819
Abstracts of Philadelphia County Wills, 1820-1825
Abstracts of Philadelphia County, Pennsylvania Wills, 1682-1726
Abstracts of South Central Pennsylvania Newspapers, Volume 1, 1785-1790
Abstracts of South Central Pennsylvania Newspapers, Volume 3, 1796-1800
Abstracts of the Newspapers of Georgetown and the Federal City, 1789-99
Abstracts of York County, Pennsylvania Wills, 1749-1819
Bucks County, Pennsylvania Church Records of the 17th and 18th Centuries Volume 2: Quaker Records: Falls and Middletown Monthly Meetings
Anna Miller Watring and F. Edward Wright
Caroline County, Maryland Marriages, Births and Deaths, 1850-1880
Citizens of the Eastern Shore of Maryland, 1659-1750
Cumberland County, Pennsylvania Church Records of the 18th Century
Delaware Newspaper Abstracts, Volume 1: 1786-1795
Early Charles County, Maryland Settlers, 1658-1745
Marlene Strawser Bates and F. Edward Wright
Early Church Records of Alexandria City and Fairfax County, Virginia
F. Edward Wright and Wesley E. Pippenger
Early Church Records of New Castle County, Delaware, Volume 1, 1701-1800
Frederick County Militia in the War of 1812
Sallie A. Mallick and F. Edward Wright
Inhabitants of Baltimore County, 1692-1763
Land Records of Sussex County, Delaware, 1769-1782
Land Records of Sussex County, Delaware, 1782-1789
Elaine Hastings Mason and F. Edward Wright
Marriage Licenses of Washington, District of Columbia, 1811-1830
Marriages and Deaths from the Newspapers of Allegany and Washington Counties, Maryland, 1820-1830
Marriages and Deaths from The York Recorder, 1821-1830
Marriages and Deaths in the Newspapers of Frederick and Montgomery Counties, Maryland, 1820-1830

Marriages and Deaths in the Newspapers of Lancaster County, Pennsylvania, 1821-1830
Marriages and Deaths in the Newspapers of Lancaster County, Pennsylvania, 1831-1840
Marriages and Deaths of Cumberland County, [Pennsylvania], 1821-1830
Maryland Calendar of Wills Volume 9: 1744-1749
Maryland Calendar of Wills Volume 10: 1748-1753
Maryland Calendar of Wills Volume 11: 1753-1760
Maryland Calendar of Wills Volume 12: 1759-1764
Maryland Calendar of Wills Volume 13: 1764-1767
Maryland Calendar of Wills Volume 14: 1767-1772
Maryland Calendar of Wills Volume 15: 1772-1774
Maryland Calendar of Wills Volume 16: 1774-1777
Maryland Eastern Shore Newspaper Abstracts, Volume 1: 1790-1805
Maryland Eastern Shore Newspaper Abstracts, Volume 2: 1806-1812
Maryland Eastern Shore Newspaper Abstracts, Volume 3: 1813-1818
Maryland Eastern Shore Newspaper Abstracts, Volume 4: 1819-1824
Maryland Eastern Shore Newspaper Abstracts, Volume 5: Northern Counties, 1825-1829
F. Edward Wright and Irma Harper
Maryland Eastern Shore Newspaper Abstracts, Volume 6: Southern Counties, 1825-1829
Maryland Eastern Shore Newspaper Abstracts, Volume 7: Northern Counties, 1830-1834
Irma Harper and F. Edward Wright
Maryland Eastern Shore Newspaper Abstracts, Volume 8: Southern Counties, 1830-1834
Maryland Militia in the Revolutionary War
S. Eugene Clements and F. Edward Wright
Newspaper Abstracts of Allegany and Washington Counties, Maryland, 1811-1815
Newspaper Abstracts of Cecil and Harford Counties, Maryland, 1822-1830
Newspaper Abstracts of Frederick County, Maryland, 1816-1819
Newspaper Abstracts of Frederick County, Maryland, 1811-1815
Sketches of Maryland Eastern Shoremen
Tax List of Chester County, Pennsylvania 1768
Tax List of York County, Pennsylvania 1779
Washington County Church Records of the 18th Century, 1768-1800
Western Maryland Newspaper Abstracts, Volume 1: 1786-1798
Western Maryland Newspaper Abstracts, Volume 2: 1799-1805
Western Maryland Newspaper Abstracts, Volume 3: 1806-1810
Wills of Chester County, Pennsylvania, 1766-1778

www.ingramcontent.com/pod-product-compliance
Lightning Source LLC
Chambersburg PA
CBHW062224080426
42734CB00010B/2019